The Closed Commercial State

The Closed Commercial State

Perpetual Peace and Commercial Society from Rousseau to Fichte

ISAAC NAKHIMOVSKY

PRINCETON UNIVERSITY PRESS
Princeton and Oxford

Published by Princeton University Press, 41 William Street, Princeton, New Jersey 08540
In the United Kingdom: Princeton University Press, 6 Oxford Street, Woodstock, Oxfordshire OX20 1TW
press.princeton.edu

Library of Congress Cataloging-in-Publication Data
Nakhimovsky, Isaac, 1979-
The closed commercial state : perpetual peace and commercial society from Rousseau to Fichte / Isaac Nakhimovsky.
p. cm.
Includes bibliographical references and index.
ISBN 978-0-691-14894-6 (hardback : alk. paper) 1. Fichte, Johann Gottlieb, 1762–1814. Geschlossene Handelsstaat. 2. Rousseau, Jean-Jacques, 1712–1778—Political and social views. 3. Kant, Immanuel, 1724–1804—Political and social views. 4. State, The—History—18th century. 5. Commercial policy—History—18th century. 6. Social contract—History—18th century. 7. Republicanism—History—18th century. I. Title.
JC181.F615 2011
320.101—dc22 2010046860

British Library Cataloging-in-Publication Data is available

This book has been composed in Minion Pro
Printed on acid-free paper. ∞
Printed in the United States of America
10 9 8 7 6 5 4 3 2 1

To my parents

Contents

Acknowledgments

The terms used in the title of this book belong to a language of political reflection that is at once familiar and remote. They evoke concerns that we consider our own—capitalism, the welfare state, democracy, globalization—in the foreign voice of a past age imagining its future. For introducing me to this language, teaching me to appreciate it, and encouraging me to persevere in studying it, I am deeply grateful to Istvan Hont, Michael Sonenscher, and Richard Tuck.

This book began as a dissertation in the Department of Government at Harvard University, where I was lucky to have the guidance and support of many other teachers, colleagues, and friends, especially Noah Dauber, Ioannis Evrigenis, Stanley Hoffmann, Daniel Hopkins, Yevgeniy Kirpichevsky, Joseph Kochanek, Phillip Lipscy, Karuna Mantena, Colin Moore, Glyn Morgan, Russell Muirhead, Eric Nelson, Aziz Rana, Nancy Rosenblum, Verity Smith, Mark Somos, and Annie Stilz. It was completed during what was meant to be only a yearlong stay in England but very fortunately became a Junior Research Fellowship at Emmanuel College, University of Cambridge. During this time, I learned a great deal from collaborations, discussions, and exchanges with Duncan Bell, Richard Bourke, Christopher Brooke, Raymond Geuss, Shruti and Vijay Jayaraman, Béla Kapossy, Duncan Kelly, Avi Lifschitz, Reidar Maliks, Almut Moeller, Douglas Moggach, Sarah Mortimer, the late Emile Perreau-Saussine, Sophus Reinert, Alexander Schmidt, and Koen Stapelbroek, among many others.

Ian Malcolm has been an expert editor, and I am grateful to two anonymous readers for Princeton University Press for their incisive comments. I am also grateful for all the valuable feedback I received on presentations I made at the following workshops, seminars, and conferences: the Harvard Political Theory Workshop; the Center for Early Modern Studies at Erasmus University, Rotterdam; the Harvard Graduate Seminar on Ethics; the Seminar in the History of Ideas at the University of Lausanne; the New England Political Science Association annual meeting; the workshop "Trade and War: The Neutrality of Commerce in the Interstate System" at the Helsinki Collegium for Advanced Studies; the Cambridge Seminar in the History of Political Thought; the conference

"Civic Virtue and Modernity: Debates on Rousseau in German-Speaking Europe and in Britain" at the German Historical Institute, London; the workshop "Commerce and Perpetual Peace in the Eighteenth Century" at King's College, Cambridge; the Northeastern Political Science Association annual meeting; the American Political Science Association annual meeting; the UK Association for Political Thought annual conference; the "State of the State" workshop at the University of Bremen; and the "Antimachiavellian Machiavellism" conference at the University of Sussex. For financial support and for a succession of congenial working environments, I would like to thank the Department of Government, the Committee on Social Studies, Mather House, the Center for European Studies, the Center for Ethics, and the Program on Constitutional Government, all at Harvard; the Centre for the History of Economics, at Cambridge; the American Council of Learned Societies and the Mellon Foundation; and Emmanuel College, Cambridge. An early version of part of chapter 2 appeared in *Collegium: Studies across Disciplines in the Humanities and Social Sciences* 10 (2011), an issue titled "Trade and War: The Neutrality of Commerce in the Interstate System," edited by Koen Stapelbroek.

My family and friends deserve more thanks than I can convey here. My parents and my sister have given me more than I could ever say. And finally, though she disapproves of this particular literary convention, I do in fact owe the ultimate in everything to my partner in everything, Chitra Ramalingam.

The Closed Commercial State

Introduction

The idea of a peaceful community of nations, sustained by democratic institutions and joined by trade, occupies a prominent place in our political imagination. This vision is generally traced back to a celebrated essay on "perpetual peace," *Zum ewigen Frieden*, written in 1795 by the philosopher Immanuel Kant (1724–1804).[1] In the twentieth century, Kant's essay became an important reference point for discussions of how to apply liberal ideals to international relations.[2] This book returns to the late-eighteenth-century instance of these debates, to which Kant's essay was seen as a contentious contribution. The focus of this book is on the most sympathetic, insightful, and farsighted contemporary reader of Kant's essay, Johann Gottlieb Fichte (1762–1814), whose own investigation of the idea of perpetual peace culminated in his *Der geschlossene Handelsstaat*, or *The Closed Commercial State* (1800).[3] Fichte was a sometime disciple and self-appointed successor of Kant, and is widely regarded as a major philosopher in his own right, but much of his political thought has yet to receive the sustained attention it deserves. Fichte's *Closed Commercial State* was a

[1] I have generally cited the translation by H. B. Nisbet, *Perpetual Peace: A Philosophical Sketch*, in Immanuel Kant, *Political Writings*, ed. Hans Reiss, 2nd ed. (Cambridge: Cambridge University Press, 1991), 93–130. "Perpetual peace" became an important part of the eighteenth-century political lexicon following the War of the Spanish Succession, the publication of the abbé de Saint-Pierre's *Projet pour rendre la paix perpétuelle en Europe* (1713–17), its many subsequent restatements, and their influential reworking during the Seven Years' War by Jean-Jacques Rousseau in his *Extrait du projet de paix perpétuelle de Monsieur l'abbé de Saint-Pierre* (1761).

[2] For a partial survey of the text's reception in the Anglophone world, see Eric S. Easley, *The War over Perpetual Peace: An Exploration into the History of a Foundational International Relations Text* (New York: Palgrave Macmillan, 2004).

[3] Johann Gottlieb Fichte, *Der geschlossene Handelsstaat: Ein philosophischer Entwurf als Anhang zur Rechtslehre und Probe einer künftig zu liefernden Politik* (Tübingen: Cotta, 1800). I have cited the critical edition in Fichte, *Gesamtausgabe der Bayerischen Akademie der Wissenschaften*, part 1, vol. 7, ed. R. Lauth and H. Gliwitzky (Stuttgart–Bad Cannstatt: Frommann, 1988). All translations are my own. Some excerpts are available in English in Hans Reiss, ed., *The Political Thought of the German Romantics, 1793–1815* (Oxford: Blackwell, 1955). A full English translation by Anthony Adler is currently under preparation. There are two French translations: *L'état commercial fermé*, ed. J. Gibelin (Paris: Librairie generale de droit et de jurisprudence, 1940); and *L'état commercial fermé*, ed. Daniel Schulthess (Lausanne: L'Age d'homme, 1980).

pivotal development of Kant's model of perpetual peace. This book shows how Fichte redefined the political economy of the Kantian ideal and extended it into a strategic analysis of the prospects for pacifying modern Europe.

Fichte was a theorist of the social contract who radicalized that tradition by demanding that the state secure the citizen's right to work. This demand was part of an argument about the economic conditions for effective political citizenship, largely conducted in terms set by the Genevan philosopher Jean-Jacques Rousseau (1712–78). *The Closed Commercial State* was part of Fichte's attempt to reformulate Rousseau's theory of popular sovereignty and constitutional government in order to accommodate the changing nature of economic activity in a "commercial society," or an increasingly postagrarian society marked by an extensive and expanding division of labor.[4] Fichte's demand was also a response to a problem that had preoccupied both Rousseau and Kant: how to neutralize an unstable system of international relations whose escalating violence threatened to undermine the logic of the social contract and make it impossible to create and maintain a government of laws. *The Closed Commercial State* was Fichte's sequel to Rousseau and Kant's writings on perpetual peace. Fichte claimed that Europe could not transform itself into a peaceful federation of constitutional republics unless economic life could be disentangled from the competitive dynamics of relations between states. He further claimed that this transformation could be achieved through a transition to a planned and largely self-sufficient national economy, made possible by a radical monetary policy.

The Closed Commercial State was a proposal for how to implement such a transition in a German state at the turn of the nineteenth century; its audacity inspired some and terrified most. But it also could be read in a rather different spirit, as it was by some important figures at the time: as a provocative, exaggerated, but nonetheless unusually philosophically rigorous restatement of Rousseau and Kant's prognosis for the creation of a republican peace in modern Europe. This characteristic ambiguity, which pervades Fichte's response to Rousseau and Kant, also carries a wider significance. More than two centuries of debate have not resolved the problems that Fichte took up in his investigation of perpetual peace. Nor have they extinguished the persistently recurring

[4] This is Adam Smith's classic definition in *An Inquiry into the Nature and Causes of the Wealth of Nations* [1776], ed. R. H. Campbell, A. S. Skinner, and W. B. Todd (Oxford: Clarendon Press, 1979; repr., Indianapolis, Ind.: Liberty Classics, 1981), bk. 1, ch. 4, para. 1. For a genealogy of the concept's origins in seventeenth-century natural jurisprudence, see Istvan Hont, *Jealousy of Trade: International Competition and the Nation-State in Historical Perspective* (Cambridge, Mass.: Harvard University Press, 2005), 159–84, originally published as "The Language of Sociability and Commerce: Samuel Pufendorf and the Theoretical Foundations of the 'Four-Stages' Theory," in *The Languages of Political Theory in Early-Modern Europe*, ed. Anthony Pagden, 253–76 (Cambridge: Cambridge University Press, 1987).

appeal of economic independence as a potential solution to those problems. Among those who have given serious consideration to this approach to international relations, one of the most noteworthy was the twentieth-century economist John Maynard Keynes (1883–1946). In a remarkable article entitled "National Self-Sufficiency," Keynes described his growing sense that the "fundamental truths" of nineteenth-century English liberalism were no longer adequate "as a working political theory" for a rapidly changing world.[5] Both experience and foresight, Keynes wrote in 1933, suggested that maximizing economic interdependence was "likely or certain in the long run to set up strains and enmities which will bring to nought the financial calculation." Keynes's article proceeded to deliver a delicately poised defense of his judgment that "a gradual trend in the direction of economic self-sufficiency may be more conducive to peace than economic internationalism."[6] Comparisons to Fichte's *Closed Commercial State* have often served a merely pejorative function.[7] Yet *The Closed Commercial State* remains a uniquely systematic and complete discussion of the political theory of national self-sufficiency, undertaken in the classic and familiar idiom of the social contract. Fichte's book has resurfaced, in various guises, with nearly every crisis of globalization since the Napoleonic wars. So long as eighteenth-century visions of perpetual peace retain a hold on our political imagination, it is worth taking a close look at Fichte's provocative contribution to the genre.

Beyond a growing but highly specialized circle of philosophers, the English-speaking world still encounters Fichte primarily as an apostle of German nationalism—the unfortunate result of late-nineteenth-century mythmaking efforts and the fallout from two twentieth-century world wars.[8] For some readers, the monstrous character of Fichte's political thought still asserts itself, even when some of the myths surrounding his famous *Addresses to the German Nation* (1807–8)—"oft quoted, seldom read, and at the time hardly heard by anyone"—are set aside.[9] In this view, *The Closed Commercial State*

[5] John Maynard Keynes, "National Self-Sufficiency," *Yale Review* 22, no. 4 (June 1933): 755, 757.

[6] Ibid., 758.

[7] See, e.g., Michael Heilperin, *Studies in Economic Nationalism* (Geneva: Droz, 1960).

[8] For a sketch of Fichte's reception in the nineteenth and early twentieth centuries, see Helmuth C. Engelbrecht, *Johann Gottlieb Fichte: A Study of his Political Writings with Special Reference to his Nationalism* (New York: Columbia University Press, 1933), 160–90. According to Engelbrecht, the centenary of Fichte's birth in 1862 became a focal point for debates about German unification and Prussian constitutional reform, and the historian Heinrich von Treitschke was a key figure in transforming Fichte into what Treitschke called "the first prominent herald of the ideas that motivate Germany's national party today" (Treitschke, "Fichte und die nationale Idee" [1862], in *Deutsche Lebensbilder* [Leipzig: Fikentscher, 1927], 62). Fichte's reception in Wilhelmine Germany is also surveyed in Michael Burtscher, "Die Fichte-Rezeption im Kaiserreich: Ideenpolitische Aspekte" (master's thesis, Ludwig-Maximilians-Universität München, 1991).

[9] Helmut Walser Smith, *The Continuities of German History: Nation, Religion, and Race across the Long Nineteenth Century* (Cambridge: Cambridge University Press, 2008), 59.

seems to describe a horrific effort to remake the entire social world: it describes an intellectual elite imposing almost total control over everyday life in order to "impose morality by force."[10] As one early reader put it, it was a work written by a "philosophical Attila" that called to mind "Robespierre's System of Terror."[11] Of course, similar accusations have been directed at Kant (most famously by Heinrich Heine) as well as other important thinkers associated with the French Revolution, like Rousseau.[12] But it was Fichte's explicit ambition to develop Rousseau's and Kant's insights to their logical conclusions—and he also possessed what Anthony La Vopa has aptly called a "penchant for verbal brutality."[13] It is no accident, in this view, that aspects of Fichte's politics—including the regimented and largely autarkic economy described in *The Closed Commercial State*—were easily adapted to serve the militarism of later generations.[14]

[10] Ibid., 61–62. See also J. L. Talmon, *Political Messianism: The Romantic Phase* (New York: Praeger, 1960), 186–95; Susan Shell, "What Kant and Fichte Can Teach Us about Human Rights," in *The Philosophy of Immanuel Kant*, ed. Richard Kennington, 143–160 (Washington, D.C.: Catholic University of America Press, 1985); and Bernard Willms, *Die totale Freiheit: Fichtes politische Philosophie* (Cologne: Westdeutscher Verlag, 1967).

[11] Christian Gottfried Körner to Friedrich Schiller, 29 December 1800, in Erich Fuchs, Reinhard Lauth, and Walter Schieche, eds., *J. G. Fichte im Gespräch: Berichte der Zeitgenossen* (Stuttgart–Bad Cannstatt: Frommann-Holzboog, 1978), 2:423–24. A similar assessment was made by Samuel Taylor Coleridge, who had a long-standing interest in Fichte's philosophy, but wrote on the back cover of his copy of *The Closed Commercial State* that "Fichte would have made a more pernicious & despicable Tyrant than Caligula or Eliogabalus" (*Marginalia*, ed. George Whalley, vol. 12, pt. 2 of *The Collected Works of Samuel Taylor Coleridge*, ed. Kathleen Coburn and Bart Winer [Princeton, N.J.: Princeton University Press, 1984], 2:622).

[12] Heinrich Heine, "Einleitung zu 'Kahldorf über den Adel' (1831)," in *Historisch-kritische Gesamtausgabe*, ed. Manfred Windfuhr (Hamburg: Hoffmann und Campe, 1978), 11:134. After labeling Kant "our Robespierre," Heine went on to describe Fichte as the "Napoleon of philosophy."

[13] Anthony J. La Vopa, *Fichte: The Self and the Calling of Philosophy, 1762–1799* (Cambridge: Cambridge University Press, 2001), 132. In 1793, Fichte notoriously wrote that the only way to enlighten the Jews was to "cut off all their heads in one night and replace them with others in which there is not a single Jewish idea" (ibid; however, it is also worth noting that Fichte later resigned his position as rector of the University of Berlin over his colleagues' reluctance to punish the harassment of a Jewish student). On another occasion, he concluded one of his many polemical exchanges by "annihilating" his colleague: "I hereby declare that everything that Professor Schmid henceforth has to say concerning any of my philosophical assertions . . . *to be something which does not exist at all as far as I am concerned.* And I declare Professor Schmid himself to be *nonexistent as a philosopher* so far as I am concerned" (*Early Philosophical Writings*, ed. Daniel Breazeale [Ithaca, N.Y.: Cornell University Press, 1988], 335).

[14] On this adaptation, see Nelson Edmondson, "The Fichte Society: A Chapter in Germany's Conservative Revolution," *Journal of Modern History* 38, no. 2 (June 1966): 161–80; Reiner Pesch, "Die Politische Philosophie Fichtes und ihre Rezeption im Nationalsozialismus" (PhD diss., Phillips-Universität Marburg, 1982); and Raymond Geuss, "Kultur, Bildung, Geist," *History and Theory* 35, no. 2 (1996): 162–63. Comparisons between *The Closed Commercial State* and the German war economy were made during both world wars. For a sadly inopportune attempt to push back against some of these comparisons, see F. W. Kaufmann, "Fichte and National Socialism," *American Political Science Review* 36, no. 3 (June 1942): 460–70.

In 1822, long before Fichte became associated with modern German nationalism, the Prussian censor still considered Fichte a republican propagandist too subversive to allow into print; in the years leading up to the revolutions of 1848, "going back" to Fichte's philosophy seemed the way forward for some.[15] Beginning in the second half of the nineteenth century, a large literature developed that described Fichte's reworking of Rousseau's *Social Contract* as the intellectual birth of German socialism. Fichte gave the state a pivotal role in reorganizing society so that it could afford all its members the opportunity to cultivate their individuality to the fullest and richest possible extent. He was celebrated by Ferdinand Lassalle as the philosophical forerunner of a future German republic, and *The Closed Commercial State* was cited by writers including John Dewey, Jean Jaurès, Gustav von Schmoller, and Marianne Weber as an early proposal for a modern welfare state.[16] Of course, some have claimed that Kant belongs in a similar historical context, and many others have sought to show that his political philosophy provides a suitable framework for arguments for greater distributive justice.[17] But here again, Fichte drew much more explicit and radical conclusions than Kant: he loudly and clearly proclaimed that the state could not fulfill its limited duty to protect individual liberty and property rights without guaranteeing a right to work. Recently, this perspective on Fichte has begun to attract renewed attention. Samuel Fleischacker's *Short History of Distributive Justice* acknowledges Fichte as perhaps the true

[15] For Fichte and the Prussian censor, see Engelbrecht, *Johann Gottlieb Fichte*, 161. On "going back" to Fichte in the context of the revolutions of 1848, see Wilhelm Busse, *J. G. Fichte und seine Beziehung zur Gegenwart des deutschen Volkes* (Halle: Heynemann, 1848), 1:1. As a slogan for the barricades, it must be admitted, Busse's "*es muss auf Fichte zurückgegangen werden*" ("Back to Fichte!") compares rather poorly to the *Communist Manifesto*'s contemporaneous "*Arbeiter aller Länder, vereinigt euch*" ("Workers of all countries, unite!"). On the revival of interest in Fichte within Left Hegelian circles, see also Tom Rockmore, *Fichte, Marx, and the German Philosophical Tradition* (Carbondale: Southern Illinois University Press, 1980), 121–26.

[16] See, e.g., John Dewey, *German Philosophy and Politics* (New York: Holt, 1915), 74–76; Auguste-Marie-Joseph-Jean Jaurès, *Les Origines du Socialisme Allemande*, trans. Adrien Veber (Paris, 1927); Gustav von Schmoller, "J. G. Fichte: Eine Studie aus dem Gebiete der Ethik und der Nationalökonomie," in *Zur Litteraturgeschichte der Staats- und Sozialwissenschaften* (1888; repr., New York: Franklin, 1968), 50–51; Marianne Weber, *Fichte's Sozialismus und sein Verhältnis zur Marx'schen Doktrin* (Tübingen: Mohr, 1900), reprinted in Hans Lindau and Marianne Weber, *Schriften zu J. G. Fichtes Sozialphilosophie*, ed. Hans Baumgartner (Hildesheim: Olms, 1987), 1–122; and Henri Denis, *Histoire de la Pensée Économique* (Paris: Presses universitaires de France, 1966), 254–86. For a survey of both "socialist" and "totalitarian" readings of Fichte, see Andreas Verzar, *Das autonome Subjekt und der Vernunftstaat: Eine systematisch-historische Untersuchung zu Fichtes "Geschlossenem Handelsstaat" von 1800* (Bonn: Bouvier, 1979). On Lassalle and Fichte, see, e.g. J. B. Meyer, *Fichte, Lassalle und der Socialismus* (Berlin, 1879); and Edward Bernstein, *Ferdinand Lassalle as a Social Reformer*, trans. Eleanor Marx Aveling (London: Swan Sonnenschein, 1893), 108–9.

[17] Harry van der Linden, *Kantian Ethics and Socialism* (Indianapolis, Ind.: Hackett, 1988); Alexander Kaufman, *Welfare in the Kantian State* (Oxford: Oxford University Press, 1999).

"inventor/discoverer of modern distributive justice," and several others have approached his political thought from similar standpoints.[18]

These recent efforts to reenlist Fichte as a theorist of distributive justice have focused their attention on a rather narrowly circumscribed selection from his political thought. Fichte described *The Closed Commercial State* as an integral part of his overall philosophy; its subtitle bills it "A Philosophical Sketch as an Appendix to the Doctrine of Right and an Example of a Future Politics." The book comprises not only a "philosophical" statement of his property theory, but also a "historical" analysis of modern European economic relations and a "political" strategy for reforming them.[19] The second and third parts of this scheme have been left unexamined. In some cases, the selection from Fichte's ethical system deemed salvageable excludes not only the entire *Closed Commercial State* but most of Fichte's rights theory as well.[20]

According to his son, Fichte himself used to call *The Closed Commercial State* his "best, most thought-through [*durchdachtestes*] work."[21] It was not an awkward appendage to a philosophical "system of freedom." Rather, it was a profound and systematic discussion of the obstacles posed to the ideals of the social contract by two of the most dominant features of modern social life: the division of labor and the international states system. Fichte's intensive engagement with Rousseau and Kant can help illuminate these critical aspects of the social-contract tradition. Rousseau's ingenious analysis of the pathological origins and apocalyptic future of commercial society posed a tremendous challenge for those who wished to entertain a morally attractive vision of its poli-

[18] Fleischacker, *Distributive Justice*, 160–61. See also Alan Wood, "Kant and Fichte on Right, Welfare and Economic Redistribution," *Jahrbuch des deutschen Idealismus* 2 (2004): 77–101; and Nedim Nomer, "Fichte and the Idea of Liberal Socialism," *Journal of Political Philosophy* 13, no. 1 (2005): 53–73.

[19] As Fichte's table of contents spells out, "Philosophy" is "what is rightful in the rational state with regard to commercial relations"; "History" (*Zeitgeschichte*) is "of the condition of commercial relations in real states at present"; and "Politics" is "how the commercial relations of an existing state may be brought to the constitution demanded by reason, or, of the closing of the commercial state."

[20] Stephen Darwall, "Fichte and the Second-Person Standpoint," *International Yearbook of German Idealism* 3 (2005): 91–113; and Ulrich Thiele, *Distributive Gerechtigkeit und demokratischer Staat: Fichtes Rechtslehre von 1796 zwischen vorkantischem und kantischem Naturrecht* (Berlin: Duncker und Humblot, 2002), 7–8. These developments imply a partial retracing of long-running French debates about whether or when Fichte abandoned his commitment to the ideals of 1789 (or, alternatively, to those of 1793). For a survey, see Michel Espagne, "Die Rezeption der Philosophie Fichtes in Frankreich," *Fichte-Studien* 2 (1990): 193–222. The relative breadth of French, Italian, and Iberian scholarship on Fichte's political thought is on display in a recent volume of conference proceedings: Jean-Christophe Goddard and Jacinto Rivera de Rosales, eds., *Fichte et la politique* (Milan: Polimetrica, 2008), http://www.polimetrica.com/.

[21] Johann Gottlieb Fichte, *Sämmtliche Werke* (1845–46), ed. Immanuel Hermann Fichte (Berlin: de Gruyter, 1965), 3:xxxviii.

tics.[22] Rousseau himself was highly skeptical that his vision of a government of laws could be reconciled with forms of economic life dominated by the development of modern trade and finance.[23] Likewise, Rousseau's close study of the abbé de Saint-Pierre's writings on perpetual peace ultimately left him unconvinced that the logic of the social contract could be applied to relations between peoples.[24] Kant had gone considerably further than Rousseau in imagining the emergence of a pacified Europe, but not in specifying what kind of economic relations were presupposed by this vision.[25] Fichte's *Closed Commercial State* was an innovative attempt to elaborate on Kant's model of perpetual peace, without—as Fichte saw it—reproducing Rousseau's exclusion of the virtues as well as the vices of modern economic life. *The Closed Commercial State* was a distinctive post-Kantian reformulation of widespread eighteenth-century arguments about how it might be possible to tame intensifying interstate competition, relieve mounting class conflict, and bring about the moral transformation of modern political and economic relations.

Fichte's engagement with Rousseau and Kant is easily misjudged and remains unedifying without a more historically informed account of the full scope of his political thought. Fichte was a major participant in the formation and institutionalization of a German philosophical idiom that continues to be the object of specialized study. However, his political thought, like his intellectual biography, was never confined to this context. All three components of *The Closed Commercial State*—the historical analysis and political strategy as well as the property theory—represent important interventions in a broader set of contemporary debates about how to pacify modern Europe. These were not isolated German debates. On the contrary, they involved some of the most prominent political actors of the French Revolution as well as German phi-

[22] On the importance of this aspect of Rousseau's thought for his contemporary readers, particularly in German-speaking Europe, see Béla Kapossy, *Iselin contra Rousseau: Sociable Patriotism and the History of Mankind* (Basel: Schwabe, 2006). On its centrality for Rousseau's political thought, see also John Charvet, *The Social Problem in the Philosophy of Rousseau* (Cambridge: Cambridge University Press, 1974); and Nannerl O. Keohane, "'Masterpiece of Policy in Our Century': Rousseau on the Morality of the Enlightenment," *Political Theory* 6, no. 4 (1978): 457–84.

[23] See, e.g., Jean-Jacques Rousseau, "Government of Poland," in *The Social Contract, and Other Later Political Writings*, ed. Victor Gourevitch (Cambridge: Cambridge University Press, 1997), 224–26. Rousseau's proposed constitution was written in 1772, but became widely available only in the posthumous 1782 edition of his works. On its popularity with an ally of Fichte's in the 1790s, see note 67 to chapter 1, below.

[24] For a thorough study of Rousseau's failure to arrive at a solution to the problem of the international order in relation to his intensive engagement with Saint-Pierre in the late 1750s, see Céline Spector, "Le Projet de paix perpétuelle: De Saint-Pierre à Rousseau," in *Principes du droit de la guerre: Ecrits sur le Projet de Paix Perpétuelle de l'Abbé de Saint-Pierre*, ed. B. Bachofen and C. Spector, 229–94 (Paris: Vrin, 2008).

[25] For a concise overview of the debates among twentieth-century interpreters of Kant's political economy, see Alan Wood, "Kant and Fichte on Right," 79–88.

losophy professors. They were closely connected—not just in their content, but explicitly linked by Fichte and the other protagonists in the story told in this book—to long-running pan-European debates about the moral and political implications of the rise of modern commerce and finance.[26]

A crucial part of this story is the long-forgotten affinity between Fichte and Emmanuel-Joseph Sieyès (1748–1836), a leading figure in the constitutional debates of the French Revolution, who sought to show how a public debt could be combined with representative government.[27] Sieyès and Kant were considered kindred spirits by many contemporary observers. As recent scholarship has again emphasized, each read Rousseau's nuanced critique of Hobbesian moral and political philosophy in ways that set him apart from many other contemporary admirers of Rousseau.[28] Both Fichte's stature as a reader of Rousseau and the intensity of his interest in Sieyès as well as Kant were evident to contemporaries and long remained a fairly common feature of German-language histories of natural law and treatises in political science (*Staatswissenschaft*).[29] This book argues that Fichte sought a potentially much more radical reconfiguration of the compromises Sieyès and Kant had projected between what the

[26] On these debates, see, above all, the groundbreaking studies by Istvan Hont collected in his *Jealousy of Trade*.

[27] See three works by Michael Sonenscher: "The Nation's Debt and the Birth of the Modern Republic: The French Fiscal Deficit and the Politics of the Revolution of 1789," *History of Political Thought* 18, no. 1 (1997): 64–103, and no. 2 (1997) 267–325; introduction to Emmanuel Joseph Sieyès, *Political Writings: Including the Debate between Sieyès and Tom Paine in 1791*, ed. Michael Sonenscher (Indianapolis, Ind.: Hackett, 2003); and *Before the Deluge: Public Debt, Inequality, and the Intellectual Origins of the French Revolution* (Princeton, N.J.: Princeton University Press, 2007).

[28] Richard Tuck, *The Rights of War and Peace: Political Thought and the International Order from Grotius to Kant* (Oxford: Oxford University Press, 1999), 197–225; Hont, *Jealousy of Trade*, 474–508. On the revision of the standard post-Kantian history of moral philosophy, which this perspective builds upon, see Tuck, "The 'Modern' Theory of Natural Law," in *The Languages of Political Theory in Early-Modern Europe*, ed. Anthony Pagden, 99–119 (Cambridge: Cambridge University Press, 1987).

[29] See Otto Friedrich von Gierke, *Natural Law and the Theory of Society, 1500 to 1800* [1913], trans. Ernest Barker (Cambridge: Cambridge University Press, 1934), 131–35, 151–52. One twentieth-century Fichte scholar repeatedly emphasized Fichte's attention to the Hobbesian aspects of Rousseau after 1795 and the consequences for Fichte's post-1795 theory of the state: Richard Schottky; see his "Untersuchungen zur Geschichte der staatsphilosophischen Vertragstheorie im 17. und 18. Jahrhundert (Hobbes—Locke—Rousseau—Fichte)" (PhD diss., Munich, 1962), published posthumously in *Fichte-Studien-Supplementa* 6 (1995): 1–319; "Das Problem der Gewaltenteilung bei Rousseau und Fichte," *Fichte-Studien-Supplementa* 6 (1995): 343–68; "Staatliche Souveränität und individuelle Freiheit bei Rousseau, Kant und Fichte," *Fichte-Studien* 7 (1995): 119–42. Schottky also recognized that Fichte's *Closed Commercial State* reflected the continuation of his thinking about the problem of perpetual peace; see his "Internationale Beziehungen als ethisches und juridisches Problem bei Fichte," in *Der Transzendentale Gedanke: Die gegenwärtige Darstellung der Philosophie Fichtes*, ed. Klaus Hammacher, 254–55 (Hamburg: Meiner, 1981). This last connection was also made in Domenico Losurdo, "Fichte, die Französische Revolution und das Ideal vom ewigen Frieden," in *Fichte—die Französische Revolution und das Ideal vom ewigen Frieden*, ed. Manfred Buhr and Domenico Losurdo, 74–136 (Berlin: Akademie Verlag, 1991).

revolutionary conspirator Philippe Buonarroti called the "order of egoism" and the "order of equality": between, on the one hand, the vast inequalities of modern commercial society, grounded in property rights secured by state power, and, on the other, the ancient ideal of a political community whose citizens were equally empowered and collectively in command of their destiny.[30] Much of the world has come to inhabit some shifting version of this kind of compromise. This book reveals a new dimension of a formative and exceptionally incisive moment in its intellectual history by showing how *The Closed Commercial State* emerged out of Fichte's encounter with Rousseau, Kant, and Sieyès in the middle of the 1790s.

The moral outrage animating Fichte's *Closed Commercial State* was profoundly shaped by this encounter, but hardly originated with it. Fichte's first literary venture—conceived "in a sleepless night" during the summer of 1788, but never executed—was to have been a satirical critique of luxury, an attempt to reveal the decadence and moral deformity of commercial society, loosely inspired by Montesquieu's *Persian Letters*.[31] The difficulties Fichte himself encountered in overcoming his plebeian origins lent a great deal of intensity to his condemnations.[32] Born in 1762, Fichte was the son of a Saxon weaver. Sent off to be educated for the pulpit when his precocious intelligence was spotted by a traveling nobleman in 1770, Fichte strained to make the accommodations that would secure him a clerical career, and his isolating experiences during several stints as a household tutor only deepened his frustrations. The search for tutoring appointments took Fichte to the far corners of the German-speaking world, from Zürich to Königsberg. In Zürich, Fichte met his future wife, Johanna Rahn; in Königsberg, Fichte met Kant. In a desperate bid to impress his intellectual hero, Fichte dashed off an "Attempt at a Critique of all Revelation" in the Kantian mode. Though Kant denied the penniless young man's request

[30] Philippe Buonarroti, *Conspiration pour l'égalité dite de Babeuf* (1828; repr., Paris: Éditions sociales, 1957), 26–38. Rousseau, of course, was the standard bearer for the "party of equality." The interpretation of Buonarroti's distinction mentioned here is a leitmotif in John Dunn's investigations of democracy and capitalism; see Dunn, "The Identity of the Bourgeois Liberal Republic," in *The Invention of the Modern Republic*, ed. Biancamaria Fontana, 206–25 (Cambridge: Cambridge University Press, 1994); *Setting the People Free: The Story of Democracy* (London: Atlantic, 2005); *Democracy: A History* (New York: Atlantic Monthly Press, 2005); and "Capitalist Democracy: Elective Affinity or Beguiling Illusion?" *Daedalus* 136, no. 3 (Summer 2007): 5–13.

[31] The work was to be called "Briefe des Marquis von St . . . an seinen Freund, den Vikomte X . . . in Paris, aus den neuentdekten südlichen Polarländern" (Fichte, "Zufällige Gedanken in einer schlaflosen Nacht," *Gesamtausgabe*, pt. 2, 1:104–9).

[32] There is an excellent biography of Fichte up to 1799 by Anthony La Vopa, which I am following here; see also La Vopa, "The Revelatory Moment: Fichte and the French Revolution," *Central European History* 22 (1989): 130–59. Fichte's years at Jena and the evolution of his relationship with Kant are also illuminated by Daniel Breazeale in his introduction to Fichte, *Early Philosophical Writings*. The most complete account of Fichte's life remains Xavier Léon, *Fichte et son temps*, 2 vols. (Paris: Colin, 1922).

for a personal loan, he was sufficiently impressed to recommend the work to his publisher. The enthusiastic reception it received (it was published in 1792 without attribution, and was initially mistaken for a work by the great master himself) instantly transformed Fichte into a celebrity.

Despite the reputation as a dangerous republican propagandist that Fichte was also earning—he was the presumed author of an anonymous *Contribution to correct the judgment of the public about the French Revolution* (1793)—he was appointed professor of philosophy at the University of Jena in 1794. It was at Jena ("the Athens of Germany," as Madame de Staël later called it) that Fichte published his first account of the foundations of the *Wissenschaftslehre*, his philosophical system.[33] In a letter written in the spring of 1795, Fichte asserted that his philosophical achievement was intimately linked to his support for the French Revolution:

> My system is the first system of freedom. Just as [the French] nation frees man from his external chains, my system frees him from the shackles of things in themselves, from the external influences which have afflicted him more or less in all previous systems—even the Kantian. In its first principle, my system establishes man as an independent being. It was during the years when the French nation was fighting with external force for its political freedom [that I was fighting] an inner struggle with myself against all ingrained prejudices . . . It was their valor [*valeur*] that spurred me even higher and gave me the energy to grasp my system. As I was writing about their revolution, I was rewarded, so to speak, by the first hints and intimations of this system. Therefore—in a certain sense the system already belongs to the nation.[34]

In his work as well as in his own life, Fichte linked the unchaining of the human mind to the creation of a republic. At around the same moment, in mid-1795, however, Fichte was starting to rethink his views on what a republic was and how to proceed toward creating one. As we shall see, this significant rethinking

[33] Fichte's "theory of scientific knowledge," which he continued to revise and extend throughout his life, is often confused with his first attempt to present the first principles of that doctrine (the only such attempt he published in his lifetime); see Fichte, *Introductions to the Wissenschaftslehre, and Other Writings, 1797–1800*, ed. Daniel Breazeale (Indianapolis, Ind.: Hackett, 1994), x–xi. On Staël's visit to Jena, see Anne-Louise-Germaine de Staël, *De l'Allemagne*, ed. Simone Balayé (1810; repr., Paris: Garnier-Flammarion, 1967), 1:125, cited in La Vopa, *Fichte*, 234. Stäel's famous travels through Germany included a memorable meeting with Fichte in Berlin in 1804; see Fichte, *Lettres et Témoinages sur la Révolution française*, ed. Ives Radrizzani (Paris: Vrin, 2002), 110–16.

[34] Fichte to Jens Baggesen, April/May 1795, *Gesamtausgabe*, pt. 3, 2:298. The letter was written, it should be noted, in pursuit of a pension (in exchange, Fichte promised to acknowledge the French nation in his book and specified, echoing Rousseau, that he would consider no title other than "Citizen").

coincided with Fichte's encounter with Sieyès's political writings as well as with Kant's essay *Perpetual Peace*.

Fichte lost his professorship at Jena in 1799, nearly as abruptly as he had acquired it: he was felled by a scandal that began with charges of atheism but was greatly magnified by the reckless self-righteousness of Fichte's response. As a result, Fichte was compelled to seek refuge in Prussia, and it was in Berlin, a year later, that he dedicated *The Closed Commercial State* to a senior Prussian official, the finance minister Carl August von Struensee (1735–1804). Yet it would be a grave error to suppose that this book reflects Fichte's efforts to adapt his Athenian philosophizing to the Spartan climate he encountered in Prussia. On the contrary, Fichte's *Closed Commercial State* was the continuation of the encounter with Rousseau, Sieyès, and Kant that had begun while Fichte was still at Jena. As its subtitle announced, it was indeed an extension of the treatise on natural rights that he had published in 1796–97.[35]

Fichte saw himself as surpassing the letter of Kant's philosophical system in order to perfect its spirit, and he described his relation to Sieyès's political thought in similar terms.[36] The fundamental question that must be asked of both Fichte's defense of a right to work and his analysis of what it would take for modern European societies to secure it is whether they do indeed represent a powerfully farsighted projection of Kant's and Sieyès's constitutionalism, or whether, in changing the letter, Fichte ultimately abandoned the spirit. Within Fichte's encounter with Rousseau, Sieyès, and Kant—and within the reactions of contemporaries to the tensions and ambiguities it contains—we already find the outlines of recurring debates over the political and economic identity of the modern representative republic. Moreover, we find them in relatively transparent form, lacking many layers of polemical ideology that (as Albert Hirschman once observed) are the legacy of successive centuries of conflict.[37]

Chapter 1 recounts how Fichte's theory of the state was profoundly shaped by his encounter with Rousseau, Sieyès, and Kant. Fichte developed a more radical version of the constitutional theory that had been advanced by Sieyès and Kant during the French Revolution, one that sought to improve upon Rousseau's description of constitutional government and to institutionalize his account of popular sovereignty. According to his many German admirers, it was

[35] Fichte, *Foundations of Natural Right: According to the Principles of the Wissenschaftslehre*, ed. Frederick Neuhouser (Cambridge: Cambridge University Press, 2000). This is a translation by Michael Baur of Fichte's *Grundlage des Naturrechts nach der Principien der Wissenschaftslehre* (1796–97).

[36] Fichte's draft of a letter to Karl Leonhard Reinhold, 20 February 1793, in *Early Philosophical Writings*, 363; for Fichte's relation to Sieyès's political thought, see Johann Rudolf Steck to Johannes Samuel Ith, ca. fall 1796, in Fuchs, Lauth, and Schieche, *Fichte im Gespräch*, 6.1:228.

[37] Albert Hirschman, "Rival Views of Market Society," in *Rival Views of Market Society, and Other Recent Essays* (New York: Viking, 1986), 105–41.

Sieyès, and not his Jacobin opponents, who was the real inheritor of Rousseau, because the kind of egalitarian democracy demanded by Robespierre and others was unable to function as a government of laws in a modern European state. Fichte declared that he had produced the definitive statement of this Sieyèsian constitutionalism and claimed he had captured its true spirit by showing how it did not permanently exclude the possibility of far more egalitarian systems than those proposed by either Sieyès or Kant.

Chapter 2 shows how Fichte's response to Kant's essay *Perpetual Peace* culminated in *The Closed Commercial State.* Kant's essay defined the legal character of a peaceful international community. It also identified the historical processes favoring the emergence of an increasingly legalized and demilitarized European states system. *The Closed Commercial State* elaborated Kant's historical model into an account of the rise of global trade and its impact on state formation. Fichte concluded that the pacification of Europe envisioned by Kant was predicated on a resolution to the conflicts unleashed by heightened economic competition, both between and within states. In making this argument, Fichte developed an account of commerce and international relations that was closely aligned with contemporary pro-French and anti-English views of global trade and the European states system. Like Kant's *Perpetual Peace*, Fichte's *Closed Commercial State* was a highly abstracted theoretical investigation occasioned by a French diplomatic initiative championed by Sieyès. However, Fichte was much more willing than Kant to work out the details of a reform strategy predicated on Sieyès's efforts to engineer a French-led restructuring of the European balance of power.

Chapter 3 reveals that Fichte's proposal for a planned economy was an application of widespread eighteenth-century thinking about the positive possibilities created by modern finance: in this view, the state's ability to control the monetary system created an unprecedented opportunity to bring about a moral transformation of economic relations. It held out the promise of restoring a greater measure of equality to the modern division of labor without requiring massive expropriations or reversing the centuries of growth and development that had been fueled by the expansion of trade. For many other eighteenth-century minds, however, giving a government control over the money supply was a recipe for a new form of complete despotism. In the context of the French Revolution, Sieyès had advanced the position that a carefully designed government could safely manage a limited public debt so long as it was subordinated to the sovereign authority of the nation. Fichte again took a big step beyond Sieyès and Kant in suggesting that this kind of constitutionalism could restrain an administration with a vastly greater responsibility: it would have to control the monetary system and regulate the entire economy in order to realize a significantly more expansive conception of justice.

In making this kind of proposal, as contemporaries realized, *The Closed Commercial State* extended Fichte's rights theory into a critique of political economy.

Chapter 4 describes how Fichte's book was perceived as an important challenge by admirers of Adam Smith because its normative evaluation of market society was grounded in a theory of property rights whose foundational principle was the natural liberty of the individual. Fichte denied that the inequalities produced by the expanding division of labor could be justified by appealing to this principle. However, he was also highly critical of those who prioritized equality over autonomy by discerning inherent moral limits on the nature and scope of individual activity. To claim that property relations had to keep pace with the changing nature of this activity in an industrializing society, Fichte extended his mission to eliminate "the last vestiges of hypostasis still clinging to the Kantian system" into an effort to excise any semblance of natural rights from property theory.[38] From this perspective, as Chapter 4 shows, Fichte's *Closed Commercial State* emerges as an important contribution to the nineteenth-century critique of the discipline of political economy. It was a pivotal attempt to reclaim the emancipatory spirit of seventeenth-century natural jurisprudence from its eighteenth-century interpreters and make it available to emerging postrevolutionary discussions of a world of competitively industrializing nation-states.

Fichte's defense of a right to work, as well as his analysis of the economy and the states system, must be understood as a response to the political problems of that world.[39] *The Closed Commercial State* told would-be reformers of European monarchies that the legitimacy of the state ultimately depended on its capacity to rein in the insecurities attending modern economic life and prevent them from inhibiting individual flourishing. *The Closed Commercial State* further maintained that only a monetary policy as radical as the one it proposed could head off growing class conflict and bring the European balance of power under control before it was too late. The immodesty of Fichte's ambition should certainly give us pause, but so should the acuity of his imagination. *The Closed Commercial State* claimed that realizing the ideal of a peaceful community of nations entailed not the withering away of the state but the taming of its economic interventions. It claimed that a more peaceful global order could not be established unless the West was exclusively made up of states capable of securing the economic welfare of their own citizens, and of doing so without undermining the economic welfare of the rest of the world. Viewed from this perspective, the world of the closed commercial state appears rather less distant than hindsight might otherwise suggest.

Fichte's vision of perpetual peace was a profound prognosis of the obstacles confronting the pacification of Europe, as well as a radical strategy for over-

[38] Frederick C. Beiser, *Enlightenment, Revolution, and Romanticism: The Genesis of Modern German Political Thought, 1790–1800* (Cambridge, Mass.: Harvard University Press, 1992), 57.

[39] See Deborah Baumgold, "Hobbes's and Locke's Contract Theories: Political not Metaphysical," *Critical Review of International Social and Political Philosophy* 8, no. 3 (2005): 289–308.

coming them. *The Closed Commercial State* makes for disconcerting reading because it rendered both elements of this vision in the familiar idiom of the social contract. Fichte claimed that bringing *closure* to the theory of the social contract meant securing every citizen's right to work—not only to secure the economic conditions for political citizenship, but also to address the economic causes of international conflicts that posed a manifest contradiction to the internal logic of the social contract. Fichte's further claim was that a strategy for addressing these problems presupposed the *closure* of the economy, or the elimination of most forms of international interdependence. However remote this prospect may often seem, we would do well to recall how vivid it has sometimes become.

Chapter 1

Perpetual Peace and Fichte's Theory of the State

Herder's Letter

In the summer of 1792, the German writer Johann Gottfried Herder (1744–1803) traveled to Aachen on the French border and began what became his *Letters for the Advancement of Humanity*, a work that appeared serially through 1797. The original draft of his eighteenth letter asked a series of penetrating questions about the political implications of the revolution unfolding in France.[1] We shall have to see, Herder began, whether France will manage to create a republic, as it should. If France were to demonstrate that a republic could successfully be established in such a large country, this would truly represent a revolution in political theory. Herder's next set of questions was about the international environment. How would France cope with the external pressures generated by the European states system? Unfortunately, France was not an island, like Britain, or an ocean away, like America, and so could certainly expect military intervention by other European states. The success of the republican experiment would depend very much on whether France managed to meet this grave threat without allowing its new republican ideals and institutions to be deformed. Next, Herder asked, how would France fare as a "commercial state" (*Handelsstaat*) in the competition for international markets, and what were the implications for the success of its republican experiment, for the future of economic reform?[2] Fortunately, Germans like himself could sit back and address this last question

[1] Johann Gottfried Herder, *Briefe zu Beförderung der Humanität* (1793–97), ed. Hans Dietrich Irmscher, vol. 7 of *Werke*, ed. Martin Bollacher (Frankfurt am Main: Deutscher Klassiker Verlag, 1991), 785–89; trans. Michael N. Forster in Herder, *Philosophical Writings* (Cambridge: Cambridge University Press, 2002), 361–69.

[2] Herder's questions about commerce are skipped over in Beiser's account (*Enlightenment, Revolution, and Romanticism*, 218). Irmscher's note in the Deutscher Klassiker edition, repeated in the Cambridge edition, suggests that Herder's question about the "Ökonomistische System" ("Will the economistic system, against which many doubts have been raised with the greatest plausibility, persist? Or will it suffer change even in France?") is a question about the future of "mercantilism," which is inaccurate. In eighteenth-century terms, the "economists" were the Physiocrats—François Quesnay and his many followers. They developed a comprehensive and elaborate reform program and advocated free markets in subsistance goods. On the German reception of Physiocracy, and

as a matter of pure theory, Herder wrote, because they themselves did not yet live in true commercial states. In other words, their livelihood did not depend on success in international markets.

Herder's letter indicates the problem that Fichte went on to address in *The Closed Commercial State*. Fichte's book represents a significant development of the insight that Kant presented in his "Idea for a Universal History with a Cosmopolitan Purpose" (1784): "The problem of establishing a perfect civil constitution is subordinate to the problem of a law-governed external relationship with other states, and cannot be solved unless the latter is also solved."[3] The challenge posed by international relations to an ideal view of politics—a preoccupation of many eighteenth-century writers—was famously and vividly described by Rousseau in his reworking of the abbé de Saint-Pierre's writings on perpetual peace:

> It is not necessary to have meditated for very long on the means of perfecting any Government whatsoever to notice the perplexities and obstacles that are born less from its constitution than from its external relations; so that one is constrained to give to its security the majority of the efforts that ought to be devoted to its public order, and to consider putting it in a condition to resist others more than to make it perfect in itself. If the social order were, as is claimed, the work of reason rather than the passions, would it have taken so long to see that either too much or too little has been done for our happiness in it; that since each of us is in the civil state with his fellow citizens and in the state of nature with all the rest of the world, we have forestalled private wars only to ignite general ones, which are a thousand times more terrible; and that by uniting ourselves to several men, we really become the enemies of the human race?[4]

This chapter shows how Fichte arrived at his approach to this problem in the context of the French Revolution, as viewed from Germany.

---

the attempt to put it into practice in Baden, see Keith Tribe, *Governing Economy: The Reformation of German Economic Discourse, 1750–1840* (Cambridge: Cambridge University Press, 1988), 119–31.

[3] Kant, *Political Writings*, 47.

[4] Jean-Jacques Rousseau, "Abstract of Monsieur the Abbé de Saint-Pierre's Plan for Perpetual Peace" (1761), in *The Collected Writings of Rousseau*, ed. Christopher Kelly (Hanover, N.H.: University Press of New England, 2005), 2:28. Rousseau also wrote a "Judgment" of Saint-Pierre's plan, which was published posthumously in 1782. Unlike the "Constitution of Poland," it seems not to have been known to Kant or Fichte or many of their contemporaries; see Spector, "Le Projet de paix perpétuelle," 4–5.

Perpetual Peace and Power Politics

Much eighteenth-century analysis of the relationship between political communities was shaped by moral condemnation of European power politics and the regimes that conducted it. Herder's questions about the French Revolution were embedded in this kind of criticism. The European states system, the manuscript to his eighteenth letter to humanity explained, had originated in the conquest of Rome by barbaric Germanic tribes. Only "a prophet of doom" would construe this "miserable system of war and conquest" as "the sole, immovable basis" of those societies. Just as the medieval church had successfully been reformed, so too would the remnants of an outdated feudal military order. "We live at the end of the eighteenth, no longer in the eleventh, century," Herder wrote.

> The stupidity of wars, both wars of religion and succession and wars of trade and ministers, will become obvious, and already is so now; innocent, industrious peoples will politely decline the duty and honor of strangling other innocent, peaceful, industrious peoples because the regent or his minister is tempted to receive a new title, a further piece of land in addition to those lands which he already cannot govern.[5]

Herder's letter expressed the hope that an alternative to this corrupt system was ultimately possible. "So let me believe, my friend, that the mad, raging system of conquest is not the basic constitution of Europe, or at least need not be so, and also will not be so for ever. Speremus atque amemus [Let us hope and love]."[6] In his *Another Philosophy of History for the Education of Mankind* (1774), Herder had mocked Voltaire and the other eighteenth-century historians who celebrated the balance of power as the fundamental institution of the European republic of states and the great achievement of an enlightened age.[7] Herder's ideal was a fraternal community of peoples, and he wanted nothing to do with supposedly "enlightened" notions of reason of state. The contrast is especially clear in a famous passage from the appendix to his fifty-seventh letter to humanity, dating from 1795:

> Cabinets may deceive each other; political machines may be moved against each other until one blows the other to pieces. But *fatherlands* do not move against each other like this; they lie quietly side by side

[5] Herder, *Philosophical Writings*, 365.

[6] Ibid.

[7] Johann Gottfried Herder, *Another Philosophy of History, and Selected Political Writings*, ed. Ioannis Evrigenis and Daniel Pellerin (Indianapolis, Ind.: Hackett, 2004), 60. This is a translation of *Auch eine Philosophie der Geschichte zur Bildung der Menschheit* (1774).

> and assist each other as families do. *Fatherlands against fatherlands* in a bloody struggle—that is the worst barbarism of the human language.[8]

Fichte himself developed a radical version of this moral critique of European power politics in his early writings on politics of 1793–94. The first part of his *Contribution to correct the judgment of the public about the French Revolution* (1793) culminated in a ferocious condemnation of the European states system. Modern states were mere accidents of history. They were not genuine political communities, Fichte wrote, but resembled gatherings of various species of carnivorous animals that lived by the principle that the strong eat the weak and the weak eat the weaker.[9] The gears of this "artificial European machine" were powered by "the miraculous trick of the subordination of ranks [*Stände*]." From the sovereign on down, each class oppressed its subordinates; variations in local circumstances determined whether the end result of this perverse machine was a kind of federative republic, like the German Empire, or a centralized monarchy, like France.[10] Externally, the same heartless machinery grasped blindly at hegemony, perversely exploiting the patriotic sentiments of its citizens in the process. Such a world of rapacious states could hope to hold itself together only through a balance of power, but the problems of a world of despotic states were not the problems of society in the abstract. Fichte had no patience with those who claimed that, unfortunately, sovereign states were a necessary condition of social life and, therefore, that a certain degree of violence and domination could not be avoided. In Fichte's eyes, this was to justify the existence of states by pointing to the problems that states themselves were causing. As a result, Fichte was especially outraged by those who defended intervention in France in the name of the balance of power. Instead, he looked to the emancipated French people as the agent that might be able to overthrow the European states system and replace the power politics of the old regime with a perpetual peace.[11]

Fichte's condemnation of the European states system in 1793–94 was rooted in a humanitarian vision of a cosmopolitan moral community. Ultimately, one way or another, the gears of the European machine state would grind to a halt. Individuals would be free to act as independent rational beings and reunite themselves by participating in "the sweetest commerce of humanity" (*das*

[8] Ibid., 116–17. For a full discussion of Herder's critique, see Sankar Muthu, *Enlightenment against Empire* (Princeton, N.J: Princeton University Press, 2003), 210–58. Compare Carl von Clausewitz's observation in 1812 that the clash of political machines had come to encompass entire populations: "It is not [now] the king who wages war on the king, not an army against another army, but a people against another people" (quoted in David A. Bell, *The First Total War: Napoleon's Europe and the Birth of Modern Warfare* [London: Bloomsbury, 2007], 10).

[9] Fichte, *Gesamtausgabe*, pt. 1, 1:224.

[10] Ibid., 1:249.

[11] Ibid., 1:248.

süßeste Commerzium der Menschheit).[12] In his wildly popular public lecture series "Morality for Scholars," which he delivered as a newly appointed professor at the University of Jena in the spring and summer of 1794, Fichte developed a vivid account of this kind of community. In place of the state as a soulless machine of class conflict, Fichte depicted humanity as a vast machine of mutual aid. Fichte closed his second lecture, "Concerning Man's Vocation within Society," with a description of this humanitarian ideal:

> I am acquainted with few ideas, gentlemen, more sublime than this idea of the way the entire human race generally works upon itself—this ceaseless living and striving, this lively competition to give and take which is the most honorable thing in which men can participate, this universal intermeshing of countless gears, whose common mainspring is freedom, and the beautiful harmony that grows from this. Everyone can say: "Whoever you may be, because you bear a human face, you are still a member of this great community. No matter how countlessly many intermediaries may be involved in the transmission—I nevertheless have an effect upon you, and you have an effect upon me. No one whose face bears the stamp of reason, no matter how roughly, exists in vain for me." "But I am unacquainted with you, as you are with me!" "Still, just as it is certain that we share a common calling—to be good and to become better and better—it is equally certain that there will come a time (it may take millions or trillions of years—what is time!) when I will draw you into my sphere of influence, a time when I will benefit you too and receive benefit from you, a time when my heart will be joined with yours by the loveliest bond of all—the bond of free, mutual give and take."[13]

The basis of society, Fichte explained in the same lecture, was the human capacity to cooperate in the mutual satisfaction of human needs. "The social drive [*der gesellschaftliche Trieb*]," Fichte proclaimed, "is one of man's fundamental drives."[14] Society was no more than a contractual arrangement among autonomous individuals to assist one another in fulfilling their moral duty to cultivate their moral personalities. Throughout his early works of 1793–94, Fichte argued that it was therefore an inalienable human right to participate freely in society, but that nobody could be compelled to do so.[15] In his lecture "Concerning Man's

[12] Ibid., 1:253; and Fichte, "Zurückforderung der Denkfreiheit," in ibid., 177.

[13] Fichte, *Early Philosophical Writings*, 160–61. I have modified the translation.

[14] Ibid., 156.

[15] See Frederick Neuhouser, "Fichte and the Relationship between Right and Morality," in *Fichte: Historical Contexts/Contemporary Controversies*, ed. Daniel Breazeale and Tom Rockmore, 158–80 (Atlantic Highlands, N.J: Humanities Press, 1994); Luc Ferry, "The Distinction between Law and Ethics in the Early Philosophy of Fichte," *Philosophical Forum* 19, nos. 2–3 (1987-8): 182–96; and

Vocation within Society," Fichte spelled out the implications of this position for his theory of the state:

> You see how important it is not to confuse society as such with that particular, empirically conditioned type of society which we call "the state." Despite what a very great man has said, life in the state is not one of man's absolute aims. The state is, instead, only a *means for establishing a perfect society*, a means which exists only under specific circumstances. Like all those human institutions which are mere means, the state aims at abolishing itself. *The goal of all government is to make government superfluous*. Though the time has certainly not yet come, nor do I know how many myriads or myriads of myriads of years it may take (here we are not at all concerned with applicability in life, but only with justifying a speculative proposition), there will certainly be a point in the a priori foreordained career of the human species when all civic bonds will become superfluous. This is that point when reason, rather than strength or cunning, will be universally recognized as the highest court of appeal. I say "be recognized" because even then men will still make mistakes and injure their fellowmen thereby. All they will then require is the goodwill to allow themselves to be convinced that they have erred and, when they are convinced of this, to recant their errors and make amends for the damages. Until we have reached this point we are, speaking quite generally, not even true men.[16]

This passage was cited in the contemporary German press as evidence of Fichte's Jacobinism, and caused him a great deal of trouble. Fichte's caveat about the indefinite timescale in which states would wither away was easily swept aside. The abbé Barruel's *Memoirs Illustrating the History of Jacobinism* (1797) complained that a professor at Jena was corrupting the youth by "telling them that governments are contrary to the laws of Reason and Humanity" and promising them "that therefore in twenty, in fifteen, perhaps even in ten years there will be no further government in the world."[17]

Fichte's condemnation of European power politics in 1793–94 does share some fundamental premises with arguments advanced by radical revolutionaries like Saint-Just and Robespierre. Like them, Fichte insisted on a strong opposition between society, which was rooted in the mutual satisfaction of human

---

Alexis Philonenko, *Théorie et praxis dans la pensée morale et politique de Kant et de Fichte en 1793* (Paris: Vrin, 1968).

[16] Fichte, *Early Philosophical Writings*, 156–57.

[17] Cited in Engelbrecht, *Johann Gottlieb Fichte*, 195. See also Léon, *Fichte et son temps*, 2:20. Fichte's concern to contain this story (which also appeared in the literary press in Germany) is the reason the lectures were published at all at this point. See Fichte, *Early Philosophical Writings*, 139–40.

needs, and the political state, which had distorted society by turning it into a war machine. They also shared the view that eliminating the external pressures generated by European power politics would create the conditions for genuine community. As Saint-Just claimed in a 1793 speech to the National Convention, "The enslavement of peoples originates in the complex force of governments; they made use of the same power against peoples that they had used against their enemies."[18] Another important point of congruence was their evocation of Rousseau when making these arguments against absolute monarchy and in favor of popular sovereignty.

This vision of an escape from the states system to a fraternity of nations, from reason of state to philanthropic patriotism, was not exclusive to Fichte or the Jacobins. The eighteenth century produced many versions of this humanitarian vision, in opposition to seventeenth-century theories of natural jurisprudence that were perceived as being all too accommodating to the absolute sovereignty of European states. As the Archbishop Fénelon demanded in his immensely popular epic *Telemachus* (1699), Europe had to dismantle its war machines and recognize the bonds of shared humanity:

> Your several nations for the future will be but one, under different names and governors. Thus it is, that the just gods, who formed and love the human race, would have them united in an everlasting bond of perfect amity and concord. All mankind are but one family dispersed over the face of the whole earth. All nations are brethren, and ought to love one another as such. May shame and infamy overtake those impious wretches who seek a cruel unnatural glory, by shedding the blood of their brethren, which they ought to regard as their own.[19]

Herder also belonged to this broadly humanitarian discourse.[20] He defined nations as natural societies, akin to extended families, whereas machine states were monstrous "instruments of human pride."[21] What distinguished Herder from others like Fichte and Saint-Just was his insistence that the transformation of states into nations take place on a local scale, within local cultures. Herder considered enlightened cosmopolitanism to be a facade for the worst kind of

[18] Louis-Antoine-Léon-Flozelle de Saint-Just, "Discours sur la constitution de la France, prononcé à la Convention nationale dans la séance du 24 avril 1793," in *Oeuvres complètes*, ed. Michèle Duval (Paris: Lebovici, 1984), 417.

[19] François de Salignac de La Mothe-Fénelon, *Telemachus, son of Ulysses* (1699), ed. and trans. Patrick Riley (Cambridge: Cambridge University Press, 1994), 147.

[20] Herder praised Fénelon in the 115th of his *Briefe zu Beförderung der Humanität*; see Herder, *Philosophical Writings*, 386–89.

[21] Johann Gottlieb Herder, *Ideen zur Philosophie der Geschichte der Menschheit* (1785), bk. 9, chap. 4, trans. Evrigenis and Pellerin in Herder, *Another Philosophy of History*, 128.

reason of state—a rather astute observation, given the disastrous results of the French attempt to realize that humanitarian vision by overturning the European states system through military force.[22]

The Citizen of Fréjus and the Philosopher of Königsberg

Immanuel Kant's 1795 essay *Perpetual Peace* now holds an iconic status for many as a statement of cosmopolitan ideals.[23] But many of its initial readers did not consider it to belong to the humanitarian discourse exemplified by Herder and the early Fichte. Kant's essay stipulated that all states had to have republican constitutions. But this demand was preceded by a blunt denial of natural sociability:

> A state of peace among men living together is not the same as the state of nature, which is rather a state of war. For even if it does not involve active hostilities, it involves a constant threat of their breaking out. Thus the state of peace must be formally instituted, for a suspension of hostilities is not in itself a guarantee of peace. And unless one neighbour gives a guarantee to the other at his request (which can happen only in a *lawful* state), the latter may treat him as an enemy.[24]

In his *Idea for a Universal History with a Cosmopolitan Purpose* (1784), Kant had famously claimed that "man is *an animal who needs a master*," a claim that Herder, who had studied under Kant in Königsberg, angrily denounced as a "wicked" proposition.[25] Instead, Herder suggested that "a man who needs a master is an animal." There were many natural human relations based on needs, Herder replied to his former teacher, but "the notion of needing a despot who is also a man does not lie within the concept of the human being."[26] The machinery of the state, in this view, was a highly contingent and late-developing phe-

[22] See Hont, *Jealousy of Trade*, 504.

[23] See, e.g., J. Bohman and M. Lutz-Bachmann, eds., *Perpetual Peace: Essays on Kant's Cosmopolitan Ideal* (Cambridge, Mass.: MIT Press, 1997).

[24] Kant, *Political Writings*, 98.

[25] Ibid., 46.

[26] Herder, *Another Philosophy of History*, 127. Kant issued a scornful reply in his review of the first two parts of Herder's *Ideen zur Philosophie der Geschichte* in the *Allgemeine Literaturzeitung*. Herder was an excellent poet but a miserable philosopher, Kant wrote, and the principle in question was "not as *evil* as the author believes—although it may well have been stated by an *evil man*" (Kant, *Political Writings*, 220). Contrast Kant's remark with Thomas Paine's claim that he first began to think about "systems of government" around 1773 after hearing a "mere John Bull in England" describe Frederick the Great as "the right sort of man for a king for he has a deal of the devil in him." "This set me to think if a system of government could not exist that did not require the devil," Paine wrote. The result was Paine's *Common Sense* (quoted in David Wootton, ed., *Republicanism, Liberty, and Commercial Society, 1649–1776* [Stanford, Calif.: Stanford University Press, 1994], 4).

nomenon. Unlike Herder and the early Fichte, both of whom defended models of natural sociability, Kant had developed a theory of what he called "unsocial sociability" (*ungesellige Geselligkeit*). Human beings were both united and divided by their needs. They did have the tendency to cooperate in developing their natural capacities, Kant explained, but each also possessed "the unsocial characteristic of wanting to direct everything in accordance with his own ideas." It was, in fact, the ceaseless antagonism between these two characteristics that had propelled humanity out of its stultifying "Arcadian, pastoral existence of perfect concord, self-sufficiency and mutual love" and set it on a path towards freedom.[27] This historical process, driven by the expansion of commerce as well as the intensification of war, required human beings to create an increasingly legalized order for themselves. States, in short, were a foundational feature of social life. The pressing question was how their destructive powers could be reigned in and subjected to the rule of law.

Many of the earliest readers of *Perpetual Peace* linked Kant's approach to this problem to the work of Emmanuel-Joseph Sieyès, a prominent participant in the constitutional debates of the French Revolution. Sieyès had just reemerged into active political life after the Terror, and was taking a leading role in the diplomacy that led to the signing of a separate peace treaty between France and Prussia at Basel in 1795. Kant's essay was widely seen as an endorsement of Sieyès's agenda. The affinity between Kant and Sieyès was especially apparent to the circle of German émigrés who lived in Paris and became close associates of Sieyès during the revolution.[28] A concerted and unprecedented effort to popularize Kant's essay in France was undertaken by these German followers of Sieyès—one of whom, Charles-Guillaume Théremin, attempted to establish a correspondence between Kant and Sieyès.[29] A series of reviews of Kant's essay immediately appeared in the French press, including the *Journal d'Economie*

[27] Kant, "Idea for a Universal History with a Cosmopolitan Purpose" (1784), in *Political Writings*, 44–45. On some of the important background to this position in the German reception of Rousseau and Scottish moral philosophy, see Kapossy, *Iselin contra Rousseau.*

[28] F. Azouvi and D. Bourel, *De Königsberg à Paris: La réception de Kant en France, 1788–1804* (Paris: Vrin, 1991); Alain Ruiz, "A l'aube du kantisme en France": Sieyès, Karl Friedrich Reinhard et le traité 'Vers la paix perpétuelle' (hiver 1795–1796)," *Cahiers d'études germaniques* 4 (1980): 147–93; and Jean Ferrari and Simone Goyard-Fabre, eds., *L'année 1796: Sur la paix perpétuelle de Leibniz aux héritiers de Kant* (Paris: J. Vrin, 1998). Kant and Fichte were also mentioned in the *Moniteur* in the spring of 1795 as voices encouraging the French effort to liberate Germany from its princes. See also Jacques Droz, *L'Allemagne et la Révolution française* (Paris: Presses universitaires de France, 1949), 63–88. For an overview of German intellectual life during the French Revolution, see Thomas Saine, *Black Bread–White Bread: German Intellectuals and the French Revolution* (Columbia, S.C.: Camden House, 1988).

[29] The episode did produce a single (and long-forgotten) letter from Kant to Sieyès, carefully limited to an ostensibly "purely literary" discussion whether his philosophical works might be translated into French; see Alain Ruiz, "Neues über Kant und Sieyès: Ein unbekannter Brief des Philosophen an Anton Ludwig Théremin (März 1796)," *Kant-Studien* 68, no. 4 (1977): 446–53.

Politique, which was run by Pierre-Louis Roederer, a close ally of Sieyès. A French translation by Karl Friedrich Reinhard also appeared with uncommon alacrity in the summer of 1796.[30] According to one account, Sieyès himself was even presented with a personal copy of Kant's essay, bound up in a tricolor ribbon.[31] Sieyès was described by one admirer as the French Kant, but the affinity between the two figures was evoked most grandly by Konrad Engelbert Oelsner (1764–1828), a radical German publicist and an adventurous, battle-chasing war journalist. "The citizen of Fréjus and the philosopher of Königsberg," Oelsner proclaimed, "are creating a continuous chain of thought from the shores of the Mediterranean to the Baltic. Calvin and Luther, a Frenchman and a German, reform the world."[32] Oelsner, an intimate associate of Sieyès, lived in Paris until he escaped the Terror by fleeing to Switzerland with the notes for Sieyès's autobiographical essay in his head. In his 1796 German edition of Sieyès's works, Oelsner celebrated the philosophical as well as the political convergence between Sieyès and Kant:

> The two most outstanding thinkers now living, Sieyès and Kant, setting out from opposite points, met at the same goal. Sieyès through a posteriori synthesis, and Kant through a priori analysis, unite in a stirring and inestimable practical result that destroys despotism forever and founds an eternally perfectible freedom. Man, they say, is never a mere means of society, still less of princes; he is an end to himself.[33]

The constitutional arrangements Sieyès sought seemed eminently compatible with a Kantian insistence upon autonomy—and the metaphysical views Sieyès expressed in conversation struck many of his German interlocutors as rather Kantian in spirit.[34] Likewise, Kant's account of a republican constitution, and particularly his insistence on a strong distinction between sovereignty and government, made his politics look quite Sieyèsian.

Kant's account of a republican constitution in *Perpetual Peace* reflects Sieyès's contributions to contemporary French debates about popular sovereignty

[30] Normally, Oelsner remarked in his introduction to Sieyès's autobiographical sketch, it took at least thirty years for a German publication to become known in France, and this was why it was safe to publish it in Germany first (Konrad Engelbert Oelsner, *An account of the life of Sieyes, member of the first National Assembly, and of the Convention* [London, 1795], iii). Kant's publisher in Königsberg also produced a French edition of the essay.

[31] Ruiz, "L'aube du kantisme en France," 165.

[32] Emmanuel-Joseph Sieyès, *Politische Schriften, 1788–1790: Vollständig gesammelt von dem deutschen Uebersezer nebst zwei Vorreden über Sieyes Lebensgeschichte, seine politische Rolle, seinen Charakter, seine Schriften*, ed. Konrad Engelbert Oelsner (1796), 1:cxvi.

[33] Ibid., 1:xxv.

[34] See, e.g., Charles-Guillaume Théremin to Antoine-Louis Théremin, 1 January 1796, in Ruiz, "Neues über Kant und Sieyès," 446; and Wilhelm von Humboldt to Friedrich Schiller, 23 June 1798, in Azouvi and Bourel, *De Königsberg à Paris*, 107–11.

and constitutional government.[35] Sieyès agreed with the Jacobins that the revolution had to achieve a united and sovereign nation. *What Is the Third Estate?* Sieyès's famous revolutionary pamphlet of 1789, had blocked a revival of the mixed regime as the preferred means for reining in absolute sovereign power. Sieyès had also opposed the idea of weakening this national sovereign will by allowing for a royal veto, on the English model. He insisted that a new French constitution needed to identify an ultimate decision maker if France were to avert internal disintegration and withstand external attack. However, Sieyès disagreed strongly with the Jacobins about how to unify France's sovereign national will. The Jacobins insisted on direct democracy with a universal franchise. As Sieyès warned, and as it in fact turned out, this democracy could only overcome its powerful centrifugal tendencies by appealing to a highly moralized patriotism. Despite the Jacobins' humanitarian ideals, this patriotism became thoroughly militarized in the emergency conditions that confronted revolutionary France. Ultimately, to hold France together, Jacobin democracy had to resort to a nightmarish reign of virtue.

Sieyès claimed that only representative institutions could create a unitary, popular sovereign will in a large and complex society with an extensive division of labor, like France. On three occasions (in 1789, 1795, and 1799), Sieyès tried and failed to establish his "representative system," a complex form of government involving a multitiered system of indirect elections that would start on the local level and ultimately produce a unitary representative of the national will. This process was designed to ensure that "the whole representative edifice is the unobstructed work of parish-based elections."[36] Sieyès was a critic of the fraternal conception of politics advanced by Saint-Just and Robespierre and embraced by Fichte in his early political writings. The contrast between the two is best captured by the distinction that Thomas Hobbes had made between "union" and "concord."[37] According to Hobbes's theory of the state, only the unitary will of the representative agent could transform an anarchic "multitude"

[35] See Gareth Stedman Jones, "Kant, the French Revolution and the Definition of the Republic," in *The Invention of the Modern Republic*, ed. Biancamaria Fontana, 155 (New York: Cambridge University Press, 1994). The account of Sieyès's political thought and the contrast with that of the Jacobins presented here are based on Hont, *Jealousy of Trade*, 447–528, originally published as "The Permanent Crisis of a Divided Mankind: 'Contemporary Crisis of the Nation State' in Historical Perspective," in *Contemporary Crisis of the Nation State?* ed. John Dunn, 166–231 (Oxford: Blackwell, 1995); and Sonenscher, introduction to Sieyès, *Political Writings*.

[36] Sieyès, *Views of the Executive Means Available to the Representatives of France in 1789* (1789), in *Political Writings*, 53.

[37] On the Hobbesian character of Sieyès's constitutional theory see Murray Forsyth, "Thomas Hobbes and the Constituent Power of the People," *Political Studies* 29, no. 2 (1981): 191–203; and Hont, *Jealousy of Trade*, 474–508. It was stressed at the time by Pierre-Louis Roederer, who translated Hobbes's *De Cive* while in hiding during the Terror; see Sonenscher, *Before the Deluge*, 330–31.

of individuals into a "people" capable of collective agency.[38] Hobbes described the opposite of such a "union" as "concord," which implied a community that was held together by a prepolitical moral consensus, that is, a theory grounded in an account of natural sociability. Sieyès himself coined a portentous term to describe what would result from an attempt to realize the politics of concord in a large and complex society like France: if the whole community tried to act as a sovereign directly, that would produce not a *ré-publique*—literally, a "public thing," or a government of laws according to the public will—but a *ré-total*.[39]

Sieyès elaborated his understanding of a republic in a famous exchange with Thomas Paine, which was published in the Paris journal *Moniteur* during the summer of 1791 and was quickly translated into German.[40] The topic of the exchange was ostensibly the relative merits of republics and monarchies, but Sieyès quickly transformed the shape of the debate. If a republic was a community with a public will, Sieyès argued, then monarchy was one possible form of the agent charged with executing it—one that he was prepared to argue was superior—and the alternative was properly called a polyarchy:

> Men who are willing to speak in precise terms will not permit themselves to suppose that Republicanism is the opposite of Monarchism. The correlative of *one* is *many*. Our adversaries are *Poliarchists—Policrates*; those are their true titles. When they call themselves Republicans, it should not be by opposition to Monarchy: they are Republicans, because they are for the public interest, and certainly we are so too.[41]

The only difference between monarchy and what Paine considered "republican" government was what Sieyès called "the manner of *crowning* the Government." A monarchical executive subordinated the entire administration to the ultimate decision-making power of a single individual's will instead of the majority of votes in a council or assembly. Sieyès compared the former to government "ending in a point" and the latter to government "ending in a platform."[42]

Sieyès's move effectively shifted the definition of a republic onto Hobbesian foundations. Where Paine had defined a republic as "a Government by Repre-

[38] Thomas Hobbes, *On the Citizen* (1642), ed. Richard Tuck, trans. Michael Silverthorne (Cambridge: Cambridge University Press, 1998), chap. 5; and Hobbes, *Leviathan* (1651), ed. Richard Tuck (Cambridge: Cambridge University Press, 1996), chap. 16.

[39] See Pasquale Pasquino, *Sieyes et l'invention de la constitution en France* (Paris: Jacob, 1998), 73–97, 175–76.

[40] See Wolfgang Mager, "Republik," in *Geschichtliche Grundbegriffe: Historisches Lexikon zur Politisch-Sozialen Sprache in Deutschland*, ed. Otto Brunner, Werner Conze, and Reinhart Koselleck, 5:608 (Stuttgart: Klett-Cotta, 1984); cited in Pasquino, *Sieyes et la constitution en France*, 229.

[41] Sieyès, "The Explanatory Note of M. Syeyes, in Answer to the Letter of Mr. Paine, and to Several Other Provocations of the Same Sort" (1791), in Sieyès, *Political Writings*, 172.

[42] Ibid., 169.

sentation," Sieyès maintained that representation was a means for creating a unitary public will out of a multitude of individual wills.[43] "When I speak of political representation, I go further than Mr. Paine," Sieyès wrote. "I maintain that every social constitution of which representation is not the essence, is a false constitution."[44] The debate between Sieyès and Paine was not a debate about the merits of republicanism, but about the best form of republican government—in other words, whom the constitution should charge with executing the public will that represented the community: "I will permit the word 'Republic' to be taken as synonymous to 'Representative Constitution'; but I declare that, after having taken it in this sense, I shall feel a necessity of enquiring, after all, whether they would wish that our Republic should be Monarchic or Poliarchic. Let us then, if we can, establish the question in these terms—'In a good republic, is it better that the government should be Monarchic or Poliarchic?'"[45] In fact, it is possible that (as one of Sieyès's friends later claimed) the debate with Paine was not really about Paine at all: Sieyès was targeting his critics, Robespierre and Danton, who had attacked him on the grounds that his commitment to representation amounted to a call for the alienation of sovereignty and was therefore contrary to their understanding of Rousseau's republican principles.[46]

Sieyès's representative system suggested a development of Rousseau's political theory that was very different from the implementation proposed by the Jacobins. The opposition between the two tracked an important tension between Rousseau's account of popular sovereignty and his account of constitutional government. The Jacobins (again paralleled by the early Fichte) stressed Rousseau's powerful condemnation of power politics. They downplayed his far-reaching rejection of natural sociability in the *Discourse on the Origins of Inequality*. Instead, they focused on his famous strictures against the permanent alienation of popular sovereignty, or the permanent representation of the people by particular institutions or individuals. This kind of political order inevitably exhibited relations of domination rather than reciprocity. Rousseau had rejected the political institutions of European monarchies because he considered slavery and war to be the inevitable result of alienating individual rights to an absolute sovereign. A world in which alienated sovereignty turned the vast majority of humanity into slaves serving the distended ambitions of a handful of individuals was inevitably a world characterized by might rather

[43] For Paine's "Government by Representation," see "From Mr Thomas Paine to M. Emanuel Syeyes" (1791), in Sieyès, *Political Writings*, 165. Sieyès on creating a public will: "A community has to have a common will. Without this *unity* of will, it would not be able to make itself a willing and acting whole. It is also certain that this whole has no rights that are not connected to the common will" (Sieyès, *What Is the Third Estate?* [1789], in *Political Writings*, 134).

[44] Sieyès, "The Explanatory Note of M. Syeyes," in *Political Writings*, 168.

[45] Ibid., 172.

[46] Sieyès, *Political Writings*, 164.

than right. The conclusion drawn by Robespierre and many others was that all the vices of the ancien régime would soon reassert themselves unless the new constitution gave the people a direct voice in governing.

However, Rousseau had also insisted on the need to preserve a strong distinction between sovereignty and government—between the sovereign people and the public officials whom it appointed to govern. Otherwise, Rousseau warned, it would be impossible to maintain a distinction between right and might. This is why, as Rousseau famously put it, democratic government was fit only for gods.[47] In a democracy, there was no longer a popular sovereign that was distinct from the government and therefore available to judge the legality of its actions. A democratic government would have to judge itself—and as Sieyès had warned, to require the large, diverse, and unequal population of a country like France to serve as the judge of its own godliness was to create a *ré-total*. According to admirers of Sieyès like Oelsner and Karl Friedrich Kramer (a former professor at Kiel who also undertook to publish Sieyès's works), it was therefore Sieyès who was the true inheritor of Rousseau's politics. In this view, the kind of egalitarian democracy demanded by Robespierre and his allies was a tyranny of the majority, incapable of realizing Rousseau's ideal of a government of laws in a modern European state. By contrast, Sieyès had greatly improved upon Rousseau's account of constitutional government because he had shown that carefully designed representative institutions could institutionalize popular sovereignty without reproducing all the pathologies of absolutism.[48]

Sieyès's representative system was an attempt to adapt Rousseau's ideal of a government of laws to the circumstances of a country like France. Rousseau's *Social Contract* required the people itself to assume the sovereignty of an absolute monarch. The people had to institute positive laws in order to secure individual rights, as well as appoint an agent to execute these laws. For the people to form a unitary sovereign will without submitting to external domination, each citizen had to see the duties created by the laws as having been self-imposed in his or her own interest. "The commitments which bind us to the social body are obligatory only because they are mutual, and their nature is such that in fulfilling them one cannot work for others without also working for oneself," Rousseau wrote. "Why is the general will always upright, and why do all consistently will each one's happiness, if not because there is no one who does not appropriate the word *each* to himself, and think of himself as he

[47] Rousseau, *Social Contract*, 92 (bk. 3, chap. 4).

[48] Sieyès, *Politische Schriften*, 1:vii–viii. Kramer described Sieyès as "perfecting [Rousseau's] system" in a letter to Sieyès in May 1795, cited in Dominique Bourel, "Un regicide ambassadeur à la cour des Hohenzollern," in *Contribution à l'histoire de la Revolution et de l'Empire*, ed. Hervé Brouillet, 279 (Paris, Atelier d'Impression de l'Armée de Terre 3, 1989). For further background on Kramer, see Alain Ruiz, "Un admirateur allemand de Sieyès: Karl Friedrich Cramer," *Revue d'Histoire Diplomatique* 88, no. 3 (1974): 259–311.

votes for all?"[49] At bottom, Rousseau's *Social Contract* was a theory of Hobbesian union rather than concord; the unifying sovereign will was represented in each individual member of the people by the feeling that the laws expressing the general will were self-authored.[50] This is why Rousseau sometimes referred to the "general wills" of citizens in the plural: each citizen had to realize that a commitment to his or her own well-being was a commitment to secure equal rights for everybody.[51]

Rousseau's theory of popular sovereignty therefore required a demanding act of self-representation. Individual citizens had to conceive of themselves as members of the sovereign. Rousseau himself stressed that establishing and maintaining this link between the individual citizen and the general will was an arduous task. Unlike his Jacobin admirers, Rousseau notoriously rejected the notion that the natural foundations of society could be distinguished from the highly unnatural corruption of natural independence that had given birth to despotism.[52] As a result, he was acutely aware that such a connection between individual and community could be forged only under very stringent conditions. In other words, there could be a general will only in a society that went to great lengths to maintain a high degree of social and economic equality—a society that cultivated intense sentiments of patriotism in its citizens so that the laws were "graven not in marble or in bronze, but in the hearts of the Citizens; which is the State's genuine constitution."[53] It was hard enough to see how these requirements could be satisfied in a small and isolated community that enjoyed external security and a high degree of material equality (as well as the legislative services of an exceptional founding genius), let alone in a large society facing formidable military threats and marked by an extensive division of labor with correspondingly greater inequality.[54] Liberty, Rousseau echoed Montesquieu, was not something that could be achieved everywhere.[55]

For citizens to enjoy their liberty by maintaining the sovereignty of the laws, Rousseau's theory demanded that they distinguish these laws from the acts of the government appointed to execute them. Legislation, as Rousseau defined it, was the act of imposing the obligation on each individual to respect others' rights. Laws applied the collective will of the community to each member of the community, where the collective will was to secure everyone's rights.

[49] Rousseau, *Social Contract*, 61–62 (bk. 2, chap. 4).

[50] Ibid., 50–51 (bk 1, chaps. 6–7).

[51] Ibid., 57 (bk. 2, chap. 1); Jean-Jacques Rousseau, *Emile, or On Education* (1762), ed. Alan Bloom (New York: Basic Books, 1979), 85, 461. On this point, see Richard Dagger, "Understanding the General Will," *Western Political Quarterly* 34, no. 3 (1981): 369–70.

[52] Saint-Just, "De la nature, de l'état civil de la cité ou les règles de l'indépendance du gouvernement," in *Oeuvres complètes*, 929.

[53] Rousseau, *Social Contract*, 81 (bk. 2, chap. 12).

[54] Ibid., 115–16 (bk. 3, chap. 15).

[55] Ibid., 100 (bk. 3, chap. 8).

But for this collective will to remain general—for it to remain recognizable by each individual as his or her own will—Rousseau specified that it could not address particular cases or act on particular individuals. "The essence of the political body," Rousseau explained, "consists in the concurrence of obedience and freedom, and that the words *subject* and *sovereign* are identical correlatives whose idea is combined in the single word Citizen."[56] If the law were to address a particular case, it would be experienced not as a concurrence between the individual and whole but as a relation of domination between two unequal and partial entities. To maintain this concurrence, a sharp distinction had to be drawn between the sovereign agency that legislated (the people) and the subordinate agency that was created to apply the law (the "executive power," which is what Rousseau called "government").[57] Rousseau was adamant that these two agencies had to remain distinct if the coercive force of the laws was to strike each citizen as self-authorized. "If it were possible for the Sovereign, considered as such, to have the executive power," Rousseau warned, "right and fact would be so utterly confounded that one could no longer tell what is law and what is not, and the body politic thus denatured would soon fall prey to the violence against which it was instituted."[58] To avoid this danger, the people "can and must be represented in its executive power, which is nothing but force applied to Law." Rousseau claimed that if his distinction between law and the application of law were taken seriously, "very few Nations would be found to have laws."[59]

Rousseau realized that this crucial constitutional distinction was particularly difficult to maintain in a democratic government. This difficulty is reflected in Rousseau's criticism of Athenian democracy. "When the people of Athens appointed or cashiered its chiefs, bestowed honors on one, imposed penalties on another," Rousseau noted, "the people no longer had a general will properly so called; it no longer acted as a Sovereign but as a magistrate."[60] However, the problem was not limited to democracies. Whatever the form of government, its personnel had to be appointed and replaced by the popular sovereign. Appointing particular individuals to be magistrates was an executive act rather than a legislative act. Rousseau's theory therefore contained an unavoidable demo-

[56] Ibid., 111 (bk. 3, chap. 13).

[57] Ibid., 82 (bk. 3, chap. 1).

[58] Ibid., 116 (bk. 3, chap. 16). In a later work, the *Letters Written from the Mountain*, Rousseau said one could describe a people as free, regardless of the form of its government, so long as "in the one who governs it one does not see the man, but the organ of the Law" (*Oeuvres Complètes*, ed. Bernard Gagnebin and Marcel Raymond [Paris: Gallimard, 1964], 3:842).

[59] Rousseau, *Social Contract*, 115–16 (bk. 3, chap. 16). Another striking (and important) indication of how sharply Rousseau drew these distinctions is that he classified declarations of war and peace as acts of government rather than acts of sovereignty (ibid., 58 [bk. 2, chap. 2]). Rousseau also made this claim repeatedly in the *Letters Written from the Mountain*.

[60] Rousseau, *Social Contract*, 62 (bk. 2, chap. 4).

cratic moment in the formation of a government. Having identified themselves as members of the sovereign, citizens would also have to transform themselves into magistrates in order to appoint their chiefs. Rousseau described this moment as the "sudden conversion of sovereignty into democracy."[61] Without this democratic moment, the distinction between sovereignty and government could not be maintained and right would be confounded with fact.

Rousseau also demanded that this democratic moment recur at regular intervals in order to prevent all the pathologies of absolutism from reemerging over time. Once instituted, the government could not represent the people in perpetuity; nor could a government be entrusted to reconvene the people of its own volition. Rousseau insisted that the people had to provide for its reemergence as the sovereign by legislating the suspension of all government and the convocation of constitutional conventions at regular intervals. Rousseau famously criticized the English for thinking they were free, even though they were "free only during the election of Members of Parliament; as soon as they are elected, [the people] is enslaved, it is nothing."[62] Ultimately, Rousseau himself was strikingly pessimistic about the prospect of achieving a republican constitution in modern European conditions.[63] The patriotic sentiments that activated the general will in the heart of each citizen could be incubated only under very exacting conditions. Rousseau concluded that this was impossible to achieve in a country like France. As Rousseau wrote to the physiocratic writer the marquis de Mirabeau in 1767, the task of finding "a form of Government that might place the law above man" was like "squaring the circle." If this was not possible—and Rousseau told Mirabeau that he did not believe "the

[61] Rousseau provided an interesting example of this conversion of the sovereign into a democratic form of government: Parliament resolving itself into a committee of the whole.

> This change of relation is not some speculative subtlety without example in practice: It takes place every day in the Parliament of England where the lower House on certain occasions turns itself into a committee of the whole, the better to discuss business, and thus becomes a simple commission rather than the Sovereign Court it had been an instant before; so that it subsequently reports to itself in its capacity as the House of Commons on what it had just settled as a Committee of the whole, and deliberates anew under one name about what it had already decided under another. (*Social Contract*, 117–18 [bk. 3, chap. 17])

[62] Although he cited Parliament as a model for the institution of government in the *Social Contract*, Rousseau pointed out that the English people had not secured itself against the alienation of its sovereignty (*Social Contract*, 114 [bk. 3, chap. 15]). Intriguingly, in the *Letters Written from the Mountain*, Rousseau wrote that "the Parliament of England is sovereign only in virtue of the Law and only by attribution and deputation" (*Oeuvres Complètes*, 3:824). But this attribution was seemingly permanent.

[63] "All things considered, I do not see that among us the Sovereign can henceforth preserve the exercise of its rights unless the City is very small" (*Social Contract*, 115–16 [bk. 3, chap. 15]). The only hope for republican government outside peripheral societies like Corsica would depend on some kind of federalism, which is alluded to but never discussed in the extant *Social Contract*.

children of Adam" could manage it—then the only recourse was to a Hobbesian despotism.[64]

Sieyès claimed that achieving constitutional government in a country like France required reintroducing representative institutions into Rousseau's social-contract theory. A large and populous society with an extensive division of labor could no longer form a general will through the direct union of individual wills in an assembly.[65] Instead, it had to appoint deputies or representatives to act on the community's behalf. In such a society, "representative" sovereignty (in the Hobbesian sense of the unification of the political community) had to be achieved through "representation" (in the familiar post-eighteenth-century sense of an electoral mechanism).[66] Rousseau had condemned representative institutions as antithetical to liberty in the *Social Contract*.[67] However, Sieyès claimed that admitting "government by proxy" did not amount to alienating the sovereign legislative will to a separate body. It was merely a delegation of "no more than a portion of the great common national will." The legislative power was "neither complete nor unlimited" and was exercised only as a trusteeship. The key was for the sovereign national will to create a "legislative constitution" in order to ensure that "it is not up to the body of delegates to alter the limits of the power with which it has been entrusted": "Thus the body of representatives entrusted with the legislative power, or the exercise of the common will, exists only by way of the mode of being which the nation decided to give it. It is nothing without its constitutive forms; it acts, proceeds, or commands only by way of those forms."[68]

[64] Rousseau to Victor Riqueti, marquis de Mirabeau, 26 July 1767, and "Government of Poland," in *Social Contract*, 270, 179. In his proposed constitution for Poland, Rousseau explored some methods for scaling up these patriotic sentiments and distributing them throughout the population of a large monarchy. But in his letter to Mirabeau, Rousseau starkly admitted that he had lost hope:

> If unfortunately this form cannot be found, and I frankly admit that I believe that it cannot be, then I am of the opinion that one has to go to the other extreme and all at once place man as much above the law as he can be, consequently to establish a despotism that is arbitrary and indeed the most arbitrary possible: I would wish the despot could be God. In a word, I see no tolerable mean between the most austere Democracy and the most perfect Hobbesism: for the conflict between men and the laws, which makes for a perpetual intestine war in the State, is the worst of all political States.

[65] Sieyès, *Views of the Executive Means* and *What Is the Third Estate?* (*Political Writings*, 48–49, 134).

[66] On the latter sense and an account of its emergence, see Bernard Manin, *The Principles of Representative Government* (Cambridge: Cambridge University Press, 1997).

[67] However, Michael Sonenscher has argued that Rousseau's account of Roman institutions in book 4 of the *Social Contract*, as well as his proposed constitution for Poland and other later writings, suggests a willingness to experiment with representation (introduction to Sieyès, *Political Writings*, liii–lvi). This may have some bearing on Oelsner's declaration that he much preferred the Rousseau of the "Government of Poland" to the Rousseau of the *Social Contract*—a preference that it is easy to imagine others in his orbit sharing (Sieyès, *Politische Schriften*, 1:viii).

[68] Sieyès, *Views of the Executive Means* (*Political Writings*, 48–49).

Sieyès further claimed that the sovereign power of creating the constitution should also be exercised through representative means. In *What Is the Third Estate?* he called this the "constituting power" (*pouvoir constituant*) in contrast to the "constituted power" (*pouvoir constitué*) exercised by the legislative and executive branches.[69] In Rousseau's account, the people authored its constitution in popular assembly. Instead, Sieyès proposed that the nation appoint "a body of extraordinary representatives" to serve as "a surrogate for an assembly of that nation." This body would be entrusted with the special power of determining the constitutional forms of both the legislative power and the executive power. Sieyès stressed that the special representative body exercising the nation's constituting power was not itself part of the constitution: "It is a surrogate for the Nation in its *independence* from all constitutional forms."[70] In *What Is the Third Estate?* Sieyès suggested that any part of the constituted government (including the executive) would have a right to convoke such an extraordinary representative body.[71] Since France did not yet have a republican constitution, Sieyès's hope was that the Estates-General called by Louis XVI (and when that became impossible, the representatives of the third estate alone) would become a constitutional convention that would transfer sovereignty from the monarch to the nation.[72]

Sieyès's approach eliminated democratic "provisional government" as a necessary stage in Rousseau's political theory. It claimed that representatives of the constituting power were already in place and would determine the constitution on behalf of the sovereign nation. The government would then be appointed through the representative institutions defined in the constitution rather than via the direct democratic participation of the nation: in other words, the constitution would not be ratified by direct popular vote, but would set off a cascade of new elections beginning at the local level and building up to the national representative. "Gradually it will be possible to see the various parts of the active constitution rising up on genuinely national foundations," Sieyès promised in *Views of the Executive Means*; and likewise it was "simply a

[69] Sieyès, *What Is the Third Estate?* (*Political Writings*, 135–39, 154).

[70] Ibid., 139.

[71] "Because recourse to a judge is always open to a litigant, or, rather, because anyone carrying out someone else's will is obliged to consult the author of the initial delegation either to clarify the conditions of the trust or to communication about circumstances that call for the new trust" (Sieyès, *Political Writings*, 142–43).

[72] It is noteworthy that, like Rousseau, Sieyès also made good use of the example of the English Parliament. Where Rousseau's reference to Parliament in the *Social Contract* purported to demonstrate how the democratic sovereign could convert itself into a democratic government, Sieyès envisioned that the representatives of the third estate could transform themselves into representatives of the sovereign's constituting power, and pointedly noted that Parliament had proved itself incapable of doing so during the regency crisis of 1788 (Sieyès, *Political Writings*, 138, 140).

matter of establishing a good system of *national* representation to get a good *legislative* constitution."[73]

Kant's discussion of a republican constitution in his essay on perpetual peace adopted the implementation of Rousseau's theory proposed by Sieyès. According to Kant's definition, a republican government exercised the absolute power of the state according to a public will. Despotic government, on the other hand, substituted the private will of the ruler for the public will expressed by the law. Republican government had to be established by a constitutional procedure that distinguished the executive from the legislative power. Kant's definition of the constitution echoed Sieyès's references to Rousseau's version of Hobbesian union: a constitution was "an act of the general will, whereby the multitude becomes a people."[74]

Kant's discussion of the difference between a republican constitution and a democracy is notoriously confusing, thanks to a cloud of terminology that is bewildering even by Kant's standards, but it merely retraced Sieyès's move to represent the people's constituting power.[75] What Kant described as "the highest state power" (*oberste Staatsgewalt*) was the power of the ruler of a despotic state, which, in some forms, might give the state a constitution and institute a republican government. There were three kinds of agent who might perform this function—one, many, or all—and Kant proceeded to discuss the suitability of each to the task. Kant claimed that it was impossible for an entire people to govern itself in accordance with its own laws. If every citizen became a magistrate, Kant warned, it would no longer be possible to maintain the representative character of sovereignty. Kant effectively denied that a people that converted itself into a democratic executive would be able to convert itself back into the sovereign legislator. As members of the democratic executive, individuals would no longer be able to identify themselves as representatives of the sovereign general will.

Kant's assessment of the other two candidates for representing the constituting power was more hopeful. Aristocracies and monarchs were perfectly capable of forming despotic governments that expressed the private will of the rulers rather than the public will of the entire community. However, it was at least possible for these agents, especially monarchs, to view themselves as

[73] Sieyès, *Views of the Executive Means* (*Political Writings*, 52–53).

[74] Kant, *Perpetual Peace*, 101.

[75] To make things worse, these terms are often inconsistently translated—but German readers of the time struggled to decipher the passage as well. See also Jeremy Waldron, "Kant's Theory of the State," in *Toward Perpetual Peace, and Other Writings on Politics, Peace, and History*, ed. Pauline Kleingeld, trans. David L. Colclasure (New Haven, Conn.: Yale University Press, 2006), 179–200; and Stedman Jones, "Kant, Revolution and Republic." After all the criticism of early reviewers, Kant greatly simplified the terminology of regime analysis in his 1797 *Rechtslehre* and no longer defined a republic in opposition to a democracy.

representatives of the people's sovereignty rather than actual rulers. This is the point of Kant's praise of Frederick the Great, who famously declared that he was merely the "first servant" of the people.[76] Aristocracies were less likely to transform themselves into the authors of republican constitutions, Kant claimed, since, internally, an aristocratic regime was a democracy of aristocrats. So Kant concluded that a monarch was the best candidate for a ruler who someday might implement a republican constitution and appoint a republican government. If aristocracies and especially monarchs could at least pay lip service to the idea that they were merely servants of the people, then there was hope that, given a suitable international environment, gradual reforms could make this a reality. Should this transformation take place, Kant specified, the republican government that resulted would have to draw on something like Sieyès's representative system. "If the type of government is to accord with the concept of right, the representative system is part of [*gehört zu*] it," Kant wrote. "The republican form of government is possible only in this system, and the form of government will be despotic and violent without it, no matter what the constitution is."[77] An indirect electoral process would produce a meritocratic system of ranks; the head of state would appoint the ministry or administration. A monarchy with a republican-spirited ruler might then become a republic with a monarchical government.

The Citizen of Fréjus, the Philosopher of Königsberg, and the Professor at Jena

Early on, Kant's essay on perpetual peace met with a decidedly mixed response. Wilhelm von Humboldt wrote to Friedrich Schiller that the work seemed "not very important,"[78] and its success in France appeared to be limited to narrow circles of enthusiastic German émigrés.[79] German periodicals gave the essay mixed reviews. On the one hand, Kant's essay met with a strong conservative reaction that viewed perpetual peace as a dangerous utopian idea.[80] As the next chapter will show, Friedrich von Gentz was among these who redirected Kant's

[76] Frederick II, *The Refutation of Machiavelli's Prince: Or, Anti-Machiavel* (1740), trans. Paul Sonnino (Athens: Ohio University Press, 1981), 34–35.

[77] Kant, *Perpetual Peace*, 102.

[78] Wilhelm von Humboldt to Friedrich Schiller, 30 October 1795, in A. Dietze and W. Dietze, eds., *Ewige Friede? Dokumente einer deutschen Diskussion um 1800* (Munich: Beck, 1989), 125.

[79] Letter from someone unknown in Basel to Christoph Martin Wieland, 10 December 1796, in Dietze and Dietze, *Ewige Friede?* 236.

[80] See, e.g., Friedrich Murhard, "Darf der Entwurf des ewigen Friedens ausgeführt werden?" (1797), in Dietze and Dietze, *Ewige Friede?* 248–50.

essay into an endorsement of quite a lot of the balance-of-power system.[81] Many other critical reviews objected that Kant's approach to perpetual peace strayed too far from humanitarian principles and retained far too much of the old regime. Some suggested that Kant had strayed dangerously close to apology for and even flattery of kings by ruling out any right to resistance, equating democracy with despotism, and endorsing monarchy.[82]

Herder was among these latter critics of Kant's essay. In the tenth collection of his *Letters for the Advancement of Humanity* (1797), Herder reflected at length on the subject of perpetual peace. Earlier, Herder had vehemently rejected Kant's Hobbesian dictum that "man is an animal who needs a master." Here, he renewed and extended this earlier criticism of Kant. Herder now claimed that any effort to turn a theory of the state based on this principle into a republican ideal was merely a new and eye-catching mask for the cold-blooded doctrine of reason of state. History, Herder complained, had too often been written "under the rule of an alleged positive law *according to reasons of state*." For all its deceptive appeals to "good of the fatherland" and "honor of the nation," such history was guilty of forgetting humanity, "which, according to it, lives merely *for the state*, that is, for kings and ministers." Herder suggested that a republican ideal like Kant's retained this deceptive character:

> We have gradually escaped from this fog too—but another dazzling phantom rises in history, namely, the *calculation of undertakings towards a future better republic, towards the best form of the state, indeed of all states*. This phantom is uncommonly deceptive in virtue of the fact that it obviously introduces into history a nobler yardstick of merit than the one that those arbitrary reasons of state contained—indeed even

[81] Friedrich von Gentz, "Über den ewigen Frieden," in Kant, *Zum ewigen Frieden: Ein philosophischer Entwurf; Texte zur Rezeption, 1796–1800*, ed. Manfred Buhr and Steffen Dietzsch, 250–91 (Leipzig: Reclam, 1984). Gentz's essay appeared in December 1800, but there had been rumors as early as November 1795 that he was intending to write a review against Kant's essay in the *Berlinische Monatsschrift* (Johann Gottfried Carl Christian Kiesewetter to Immanuel Kant, 5 November 1795, in Dietze and Dietze, *Ewige Friede?* 126). Kant's attack on Mallet du Pan in *Perpetual Peace* may have been directed at Gentz, who had translated du Pan in 1794; see Faustino Oncina Coves, "De l'antimachiavéllisme de Kant au machiavélisme de Fichte," in *Fichte lecteur de Machiavel: Un nouveau Prince contre l'occupation napoléonienne*, ed. Ives Radrizzani, 50 (Basel: Schwabe, 2006).

[82] See, e.g., Friedrich Wilhelm von Schütz, "Kommentar über Kants ewigen Frieden," *Neuer Niedersächsischer Merkur* 1 (1797): 17–26, 68–74, reprinted in Kant, *Zum ewigen Frieden*, 135–142; [Hermann Heynich], "Immanuel Kants philosophischer Entwurf zum ewigen Frieden. Fortgesetzt von Hermann H . . . ch," *Germanien* (1797): 37–112, reprinted in Kant, *Zum ewigen Frieden*, 143–82 (see especially 168–72); and, anonymous, "Ewiger Friede und Widerstandsrecht des Volkes" (1796), in *Beyträge zur Geschichte der französischen Revolution*, ed. Paul Usteri, 6:385–95 (Nendeln, Liechtenstein: Kraus Reprint, 1972).

> blinds with the names of 'freedom,' 'enlightenment,' 'highest happiness of the peoples.' Would God that it never deceived![83]

Since no form of government could suit every nation "at once, in the same way," Herder explained, "a history that calculates everything in the case of every land with a view to this utopian plan in accordance with unproved first principles is the most dazzling *deceptive history*." Whereas he showered praise on Las Casas, Fénelon, the abbé de Saint-Pierre, Montesquieu, Bernadin de Saint-Pierre, and others whom he considered to be humane prophets of peace, Herder was evidently disinclined to include Kant in this tradition.[84] "Many works of our time will be read twenty years later as well- or badly-intentioned fever fantasies," Herder concluded; "maturer minds already now read them that way."[85]

Fichte's response to Kant's essay diverges strikingly (and revealingly) from the critical reactions of Herder and others. When the first edition of Kant's essay appeared in the autumn of 1795, Fichte had just begun to deliver a new lecture series on natural right at Jena. In the summer of 1795, Fichte's ill-advised campaign to suppress the riotous student fraternities at the University of Jena had forced him to discontinue his public lecture series "Morality for Scholars" and temporarily to flee Jena in order to escape the stones that were being thrown through his windows.[86] One of the results of his forced retreat to the nearby village of Osmannstädt was a new series of lectures on natural right, the first part of which was published as his *Foundations of Natural Right* in March 1796 (the second part followed in September 1797). Fichte must have decided to write a review of Kant's essay immediately upon receiving it, because his anonymous review appeared in January 1796 in *Philosophisches Journal einer gesellschaft Teutscher Gelehrten*, which Fichte was soon to coedit.[87] In his review, Fichte

[83] Herder, *Philosophical Writings*, 412–13. The editors of both the Deutscher Klassiker Verlag and the Cambridge University Press editions suggest that this criticism is aimed at Kant's "Idea for a Universal History from a Cosmopolitan Point of View" (1784), but there is no reason to suppose it refers to a work from a previous decade rather than to *Perpetual Peace* (1795); see John Pizer, "The German Response to Kant's Essay on Perpetual Peace: Herder contra the Romantics," *Germanic Review* 82, no. 4 (Fall 2007): 343–68.

[84] Herder, *Philosophical Writings*, 386.

[85] Ibid., 412–13.

[86] See Fichte, *Early Philosophical Writings*, 25–28. Fichte's complaints were the occasion for Goethe's quip that having stones thrown through one's window was an unpleasant way to learn of the existence of the "not-I." See also La Vopa, *Fichte*, 261–68.

[87] Johann Gottlieb Fichte, "Rezension" (1796), in Kant, *Zum ewigen Frieden*, 93–101. Later citations to this work refer to Fichte, "Review of Immanuel Kant, Perpetual Peace: A Philosophical Sketch," which is a translation by Daniel Breazeale (*Philosophical Forum* 32, no. 4 [Winter 2001]: 311–21). See also Breazeale, "'More than a Pious Wish': Fichte on Kant on Perpetual Peace," in *Proceedings of the Eighth International Kant Congress, Memphis, 1995*, ed. Hoke Robinson, 1:943–59 (Milwaukee, Wis.: Marquette University Press, 1995); and Jean-Christophe Merle, "La réception du *Projet de paix perpétuelle* par Fichte: La critique d'un Kant prisonnier du droit des gens," in ibid., 2:893–900. The *Philosophisches Journal einer gesellschaft Teutscher Gelehrten* was founded and

was concerned to claim that his lectures had already developed precisely those claims in Kant's essay that had so dismayed Herder and other critics.

Fichte's review endorsed Kant's divergence from the fraternal conception of politics, which he himself had espoused in his earlier writings. What the review prefigures is that Fichte's *Foundations of Natural Right* fits into the same development of Rousseau's political philosophy suggested by Kant's *Perpetual Peace.* Like Kant's, Fichte's new theory of the state was also closely linked with Sieyès. Fichte was involved in the circles that promoted Kant in France. In fact, in the spring of 1794, Fichte served as an intermediary to help find a publisher for the German edition of Sieyès's works, which were translated by Johann Gottfried Ebel and accompanied by an essay on Sieyès by the battlefield-touring journalist and chief enthusiast of the Sieyès-Kant axis, Konrad Engelbert Oelsner.[88] Oelsner had many Swiss connections, and shared at least one friend in common with Fichte: Gerhard Anton von Halem, who deemed Sieyès and Fichte to be saying much the same thing about the kinds of representative institutions necessary for constitutional government.[89] Fichte himself seems to have felt this affinity and made an effort to link up with Sieyès, as reported by Johann Rudolf Steck, a Bernese student at Jena. Steck wrote to the Bernese professor of philosophy, Johannes Samuel Ith (also an acquaintance of the Fichtes), in the fall of 1796: "[Fichte] has become very aware of Sieyès's works, and believes what is indeed really unmistakable: if both of them have proceeded from the same point, so they both have the same goal and [worked] from the same perspective. He has asked me to acquaint [Sieyès] with his discoveries if possible and I will do my best; partly to make the language powerful enough that I can transplant these discoveries into foreign soil in a free excerpt, and partly as to finding some access [to Sieyès], in which regard of course I now have a contact who would give me some support."[90]

edited by Friedrich Niethammer, Fichte's colleague at Jena, and Fichte later became a coeditor. The editorial board included Fichte, Erhard, Wilhelm von Humboldt, Maimon, Rienhold, Schiller, and Schulze. Its mission was "the completion of philosophy as the science of the ultimate bases of human knowledge"; see Fichte, *Gesamtausgabe*, pt. 1, 3:93. Fichte's lecture list for the summer of 1796 promised to continue "his lectures on Kant's book on perpetual peace" as well as his own text on natural right (ibid., 3:297; cited in Salvi Turró, "Réception de *La paix perpétuelle* par Fichte," in Goddard and Rivera de Rosales, *Fichte et la politique*, 196).

[88] Fichte, *Lettres et Témoinages*, 49–51. Fichte was lecturing in Zürich during the spring of 1794 when Oelsner fled there from Paris to escape the Terror. But in any case, they belonged to similar circles in Switzerland.

[89] For Oelsner's Swiss connections, see Droz, *L'Allemagne et la Révolution française*, 64. Halem wrote of the link between Fichte and Sieyès in a letter to Johann Friedrich Herbart, 14 March 1797, in Fuchs, Lauth, and Schieche, *Fichte im Gespräch*, 1:412.

[90] Steck to Ith, ca. fall 1796, in Fuchs, Lauth, and Schieche, *Fichte im Gespräch*, 6.1:228. Ith was also an acquaintance of the Fichtes; see Marie Johanne Fichte to Johann Hartmann Rahn, 26 October 1793, in Fichte, *Gesamtausgabe*, pt. 3, 2:7. The way Fichte relates himself to Sieyès is comparable to similar remarks he made about Kant: Fichte took himself to be surpassing the letter of Kant's phi-

It is less clear whether Sieyès, for his part, ever became aware of Fichte. But a report did reach him in June 1796 that an article describing Sieyès's admiration for German culture had been read aloud by a certain professor during his lecture at Jena—"the citadel of German thought"—and that "such applause had never been heard at any German assembly from the Rhine to the Vistula."[91] A potentially more serious awareness and much more profound convergence is hinted at by Fichte's eminent colleague at Jena, Wilhelm von Humboldt (1767–1835).[92] In May 1798, Humboldt was invited to give a presentation on the latest developments in German philosophy at the Institut National in Paris.[93] Sieyès was present at the seminar, as was a former student of Fichte's from Jena whom Humboldt had brought along for support. Though Humboldt was mostly disappointed with the response he got from the French, he found Sieyès to be the exception. "He expressed things which sounded simply like Kant or Fichte," Humboldt wrote to Schiller afterwards. "On that occasion he expressed Kantian ideas, and even more Fichtean ideas."[94] This affinity between Sieyès and Fichte continued to register many decades later. In the 1830s and 1840s, it was still possible, from one political perspective, to denounce Sieyès as a dangerous "man of political speculation" by referring to him as "the Fichte of the French Revolution."[95] Or, from another perspective, it was equally possible to dismiss Fichte's *Closed Commercial State* as a "period piece" that had added nothing to Sieyès's "constitutional illusions."[96]

---

losophy and expressing its spirit. See, e.g., Fichte's draft of a letter to Reinhold, 20 February 1793, in Fichte, *Early Philosophical Writings*, 363.

[91] Reinhard to Sieyès, 4 June 1796, cited in Marcelle Adler-Bresse, *Sieyès et le Monde Allemand* (Lille: Atelier Reproduction des thèses, Université de Lille III, 1977), 1:58. The article in question was an interview of Sieyès by Cramer that appeared in the periodical *Frankreich im Jahr 1796. Aus den Briefen deutscher Männer in Paris*

[92] On Fichte's influence on Humboldt's seminal work on language, see Jere Paul Surber, *Language and German Idealism: Fichte's Linguistic Philosophy* (Atlantic Highlands, N.J.: Humanities Press, 1996), 5–6, 111–12. Humboldt became famous as a theorist of liberalism as well as a statesman, educator, and philosopher of language when his treatise *The Limits of State Action* (1792)—published in part by Friedrich Schiller in 1793—was published in full in the 1850s and noticed by John Stuart Mill, who drew his motto for *On Liberty* (1859) from it. On the salience of Humboldt's views on freedom and the state for Fichte's *Closed Commercial State*, see Douglas Moggach, "Freedom and Perfection: German Debates on the State in the Eighteenth Century," *Canadian Journal of Political Science* 42, no. 4 (2009): 1014–19.

[93] Azouvi and Bourel, *De Königsberg à Paris*, 105–112.

[94] Humboldt to Schiller, 23 June 1798, in Azouvi and Bourel, *De Königsberg à Paris*, 107, 111. See also Jacques Guilhaumou, "Sieyès, Fichte et la liberté humaine (1774–1794)," *Chroniques Allemandes* 2 (1993): 113–130. Fichte himself had entered into discussions with the abbé Gregoire about publishing a work on the relationship between the critical philosophy and the French Revolution, but nothing came of the project, which is discussed in Johann Franz Jakob Brechtel to Franz Bernhard Meyer von Schauensee, 24 October 1795, in Fichte, *Lettres et Témoinages*, 57.

[95] Franz Joseph von Buss, *Geschichte und System der Staatswissenschaft* (Freiburg, 1839), 1:ccxc.

[96] Busse, *Fichte und seine Beziehung zur Gegenwart*, 2:111.

Fichte was also reevaluating his views on Rousseau. Fichte had devoted the fifth lecture of his series "Morality of Scholars" to a careful treatment of Rousseau's *Discourse on the Arts and Sciences*; and Fichte and his students at Jena were actively involved in an effort to publish a new German translation of and commentary on the *Social Contract*.[97] The translator was an official in the French-occupied Rhineland named Franz Wilhelm Jung. Jung received considerable assistance on the project, including textual notes on the *Social Contract*, from Fichte; in exchange, Jung tried to put Fichte in charge of designing a new educational system for the Rhineland and to arrange a potential exile for him there as Fichte's position at Jena became increasingly precarious.[98] Jung's translation was eventually published in 1800, and his introduction made a point of stressing the compatibility between Rousseau's political philosophy and the kinds of representative institutions proposed by Sieyès, Kant, and Fichte and, he claimed, embodied in the French Constitution of 1799.[99]

Fichte's review of Kant's *Perpetual Peace* was punctuated by three outbursts of original exposition in which Fichte claimed to give a more systematic account of the essay's theoretical foundations and a clearer picture of its political implications. The new theory of the state intimated through these outbursts also reflected a new approach to the problem of perpetual peace. For Fichte, perpetual peace could no longer be construed as a matter of clearing away the debris created by a world of rapacious and despotic states, leaving the foundations for a fraternal community of nations. In fact, Fichte now held, there were no such foundations. States were a necessary and permanent feature of social life, and perpetual peace was now a question of how to pacify the state. As we

[97] Isaak von Sinclair to Franz Wilhelm Jung, 12 August 1794, in Fuchs, Lauth, and Schieche, *Fichte im Gespräch*, 6.1:64. The letter even points to the key interest in the question of representation: Fichte had been consulted on how to translate *souverain* into German (Sinclair reported that Fichte agreed with his worry that *Oberherr* was a dangerous choice because it was too easily construed as a physical individual and hence as a monarch).

[98] Unfortunately Fichte's notes on the *Social Contract* seem to be lost. Fichte wrote that Jung was welcome to use them for his edition so long as they were used anonymously. If the *Social Contract* were still to exercise an influence on public opinion, Fichte continued, it needed to be carefully examined and extensively edited. It was a great work that had greatly advanced the cause of humanity—it was simply the case that humanity had continued to progress. It was a worthy task, Fichte concluded, but one for which he himself did not have time (Fuchs, Lauth, and Schieche, *Fichte im Gespräch*, 3:138–41). Fichte was very close to heading for Mayence in 1799 when the controversy over charges of atheism cost him his professorship and forced him into exile (a fate that he compared to Rousseau's). Fichte was reluctant to head for Prussia, which he considered an ignorant backwater; he feared a rising tide of reaction and continued to hope that France would succeed in sparking a revolution somewhere in Germany. Even when he did finally leave for Berlin (possibly after some pressure from Reinhold and others not to go to France), he postponed a decision on where to go permanently until Easter 1800; even in 1803, he was still contemplating Strasbourg as an option (Fichte, *Lettres et Témoinages*, 85–109).

[99] Ibid., 109. See Jean-Jacques Rousseau, *Vom gesellschaftlichen Vertrage oder über die Grundsätze der Staatslehre-Neu übersetzt* (Frankfurt am Main, 1800).

shall see, Fichte's *Closed Commercial State* was a significant discussion of an important dimension of this problem. But in the first instance, pacifying the state was a matter of constitutional theory, approached in a Rousseauian idiom. The way to stop states from acting like insatiable monsters bent on enslaving their own citizens and dominating the world was to define the institutions that would transform them into governments of laws.

Fichte's review placed great emphasis on Kant's assertion that peace was not a natural condition, but could be achieved only in a civil state. Fichte claimed that in *Perpetual Peace* as well as in his earlier writings, Kant had only gestured at the foundations of his theory of right, and then sketched the results. At the heart of Kant's political theory, Fichte observed, was his provocative but not yet fully elaborated proposition that "*All human beings who can reciprocally influence one another must adhere to some civil constitution* [*bürgerliche Verfassung*]": in its absence, all had the right to treat others as enemies, even without prior harm.[100] Fichte's first concern, and the occasion for the first of his outbursts, was to establish that he had already fully worked out this controversial approach to rights himself and had presented it in his lectures on natural right before reading Kant's essay.

> In the course of his own investigations of natural right, and on the basis of principles independent of the hitherto familiar Kantian one, the present reviewer arrived at these same conclusions, as well as at the Kantian results discussed below; he also discovered the proof of these same conclusions and publicly presented them in his lectures prior to obtaining this book. Perhaps the reviewer may therefore be allowed to add a few words aimed at mitigating in a preliminary way the appearance of strangeness, which, given the prevailing manner of thinking, must cling to these propositions.[101]

Fichte explicated Kant's claim that everyone must adhere to a rightful constitution with what Daniel Breazeale has described as "a remarkably condensed sketch of some of the main features of the theory of right that he was propounding in his lectures and would soon publish in his *Foundations of Natural Right*."[102] People could coexist freely, Fichte argued, only if they all limited their own activity in such a way that others could also continue to exist and act freely. It made sense to talk about rights only in the context of such a relationship between people. It was meaningless for one person to claim a right against another wherever such a relationship of mutual self-limitation was impossible or whenever it was not reciprocal. It was therefore impossible to have a rightful

[100] Fichte, "Review of Perpetual Peace," 315.
[101] Ibid.
[102] Ibid., 312 (Breazeale's introduction to the translation).

relationship without the state, because in the absence of the state, it was always uncertain whether this relationship was (and would continue to be) recognized by everyone. This uncertainty and insecurity could be overcome only by furnishing an external guarantee, which in turn could be accomplished only by creating a state.[103]

Fichte claimed that Kant had also arrived at the conclusion that necessarily followed from this argument: "As everyone can easily infer from the foregoing, it follows, according to Kant's theory, that there is no 'natural right' in the proper sense of the term, no rightful relationship between human beings, except under a positive law and under some authority, and that the condition of being in a state is the sole, true natural condition or state of human beings."[104] Fichte's disavowal of natural rights, which he restated with great panache in his *Foundations of Natural Right*, represents a major shift from the rights theory that he had articulated in 1793–94. Formerly, Fichte had ascribed natural rights to individuals on the basis of their moral personality, their status as moral agents. Society was a voluntary association of individuals who had chosen to fulfill their duty to cultivate themselves as moral beings cooperatively, by exercising their social drive to form a division of labor. From this perspective, as Fichte's notorious remark about the difference between society and the state (and the theoretical superfluity of the latter) made clear, the state was merely a contingent means for protecting the natural rights due to moral beings. The state of nature was defined by the moral law. A sufficiently moral citizenry could theoretically get along perfectly well without the reinforcement furnished by positive laws and the political machinery to judge and enforce them.

In the *Foundations of Natural Right*, Fichte sharply criticized attempts to define rights in terms of the conditions for moral autonomy. He repeatedly emphasized the importance of distinguishing between the kind of justice he denoted as rights and the universal morality of unconditional duty.[105] By no means did Fichte deny that there was such a universal morality, but he now based his theory of rights on a significantly less moralized notion of what it meant to be a person.[106] "In the domain of natural right, the good will has no role to play," Fichte wrote. "Right must be enforceable, even if there is not a single human being with a good will; the very aim of the science of right is to sketch out just such an order of things."[107] In short, Fichte was now committed to following the example of the *Social Contract*, "taking men as they are, and the laws as they can be," and his new theory of right adhered to the kind of distinction between law and morality that Rousseau had described in the *Social Contract*:

[103] Ibid., 315–16.
[104] Ibid., 316–17.
[105] Fichte, *Foundations of Natural Right*, 10–14, 50–51.
[106] Neuhouser, "Right and Morality"; Ferry, "The Law and Ethics in Fichte."
[107] Fichte, *Foundations of Natural Right*, 50.

> What is good and conformable to order is so by the nature of things and independently of human conventions. All justice comes from God, he alone is its source; but if we were capable of receiving it from so high, we would need neither government nor laws. No doubt there is a universal justice emanating from reason alone; but this justice, to be admitted among us, has to be reciprocal. Considering things in human terms, the laws of justice are vain among men for want of natural sanctions; they only bring good to the wicked and evil to the just when he observes them toward everyone while no one observes them toward him. Conventions and laws are therefore necessary to combine rights with duties and to bring justice back to its object. In the state of nature, where everything is common, I owe nothing to those to whom I have promised nothing. I recognize as another's only what is of no use to myself. It is not so in the civil state where all rights are fixed by law.[108]

Fichte's *Foundations of Natural Right* took up the same perspective.

> There is no *natural right* at all in the sense often given to that term, i.e. there can be no rightful relation between human beings except within a commonwealth and under positive laws.—*Either* there is thoroughgoing morality and a universal belief in such morality; and furthermore, the greatest of all coincidences takes place (something that could hardly occur, even if everyone had the best intentions), namely, the claims made by different human beings are all compatible with one another. In this case the law of right is completely impotent and would have nothing at all to say, for what ought to happen in accordance with the law happens without it, and what the law forbids is never willed by anyone.—For a species of perfected moral beings, there is no law of right. It is already clear that humankind cannot be such a species, from the fact that the human being must *be educated* and must *educate himself* [*sich erziehen*] to the status of morality; for he is not moral by nature, but must make himself so through his own labor.
>
> *Or*—second possibility—there is no thoroughgoing morality, or at least no universal belief in it. In this case the external law of right exists, but can be applied only within a commonwealth. Thus, natural right disappears.
>
> But what we lose on the one side, we recover on the other, and at a profit; for the state itself becomes the human being's natural condition, and its laws ought to be nothing other than natural right realized.[109]

[108] Rousseau, *Social Contract*, 66 (bk. 2, chap. 6). For "taking men as they are, and the laws as they can be," see ibid., 41.

[109] Fichte, *Foundations of Natural Right*, 132–33.

A rightful relationship, as Fichte defined it, was contingent on reciprocity and was concerned only with human activity in the natural world that affected other human beings.[110] Without a prior basis for concord, or communal solidarity based on trust in each other's preexisting moral dispositions, human relations were subject to nothing beyond individual consent.

In Fichte's terms, it was impossible to claim a right to another's gratitude, trust, or honesty, though these could certainly be moral obligations.[111] "In the doctrine of right there is no talk of moral obligation," Fichte wrote. "Each is bound only by the free, arbitrary decision to live in community with others, and if someone does not at all want to limit his free choice, then within the field of the doctrine of right, one can say nothing further against him, other than that he must then remove himself from all human community."[112] A "species of perfected moral beings" would have no need for rights—but only so long as they were able to resolve all present and future conflicts through compromise alone. The moment judgment and coercion came into play, trust could not survive, and disputes would be impossible to resolve without uniting individuals by placing them under a common judge.[113] Human beings were obviously not a perfectly moral species, nor were they in a position to trust one another so deeply as to resolve disputes without ever having recourse to judgment and coercion. Justice was not arbitrary—as we shall see later, Fichte still held that there was a correct way to determine the mutual limitations of activity that created rights—but it could only be determined through positive laws.

This reorientation of Fichte's theory of rights is also evident in the qualifications he added, late in 1795, to his earlier remark that the state was at least theoretically superfluous to society. As the abbé Barruel's reaction illustrated, Fichte's public lectures at Jena had gained him considerable notoriety, and rumors spread that he had proclaimed the imminent disappearance of all kings and princes. It was to dispel these rumors and clear his name that Fichte had published the texts of his first five public lectures as *Some Lectures Concerning the Vocation of the Scholar* in September 1794.[114] A Danish translation of these lectures was published in 1796, and Fichte contributed several new notes to that edition. In commenting on the notorious passage about the superfluity of government, Fichte now introduced a major qualification to his earlier text.

> But if it is impossible for either party to be convinced—which is something which may easily occur, despite the sincere intentions of each—then what is right remains in dispute, and one of the parties suffers a

[110] Ibid., 102.
[111] Ibid., 125, 172.
[112] Ibid., 11–12.
[113] Ibid., 123–25.
[114] Fichte, *Early Philosophical Writings*, 139.

> wrong. But what is right should never remain in dispute, for there ought not be any wrong. Beyond this there must also be an infallible and supreme judge to whom one is duty-bound to submit oneself. And there must be positive laws, since judgment can only be passed according to law. And there must be a constitution, since this supreme judge could not be appointed except in accordance with a rule. Thus, to the extent that the state is related to human fallibility and is, in the first instance, that which puts an end to human quarreling over questions of right, then the state is completely necessary and can never cease to exist.
>
> But to the extent that the state is related to an evil will, to the extent that it is a compulsory power, then its final aim is undoubtedly to make itself superfluous, i.e., to make all compulsion unnecessary. This is an aim which can be achieved even if goodwill and the confidence in it do not become universal. For if everyone knows on the basis of long experience that every act of injustice will surely bring misfortune and that every crime will surely be discovered and punished, then one may expect that, on grounds of prudence alone, men will not exert themselves in vain, nor will they willfully and knowingly bring harm upon themselves.[115]

On the one hand, Fichte claimed, the state was a necessary and permanent feature of social life; even moral people could not trust one another to serve as judges and prosecutors in their own cases. On the other hand, a lawful state could make its subjects behave justly—and its laws could become "nothing other than natural right realized"—without relying on the moral disposition of its population.

These claims were notably absent from Fichte's engagement with Rousseau and Kant in his earlier writings. Fichte's *Contribution to correct the judgment of the public about the French Revolution* was written in 1793 in response to August Wilhelm von Rehberg, a Hanoverian official whose condemnation of the French Revolution sought to enlist Rousseau on the counterrevolutionary side. Rehberg's *Examinations of the French Revolution* had described Rousseau's *Social Contract* as a pure moral theory that later French followers had mistakenly attempted to put into practice, with disastrous results. In Rehberg's interpretation, Rousseau's general will was the law of universal moral reason. It could not determine social arrangements in the real world, where people did not behave morally. According to the theory of natural rights that constituted Fichte's response in 1793, all social arrangements were subject to individual conscience, and individual consent to positive laws could be withdrawn at any time. This position obviously remained vulnerable to the charge that theory

[115] Ibid., 157n.

was not applicable to practice. It also brought Fichte into considerable tension with Rousseau's political theory as well as his actual moral theory. Unwilling to concede Rousseau to the counterrevolutionaries, Fichte was reduced to evading open confrontation. "I do not want to investigate here what Rousseau said or thought," Fichte wrote in 1793. "I only ask what Herr Rehberg had to say."[116]

Fichte's revised theory of the state approached the problem of theory versus practice very differently, by developing a much stronger distinction between morality and right. Fichte presented himself as fully developing a position that had merely been hinted at by contemporaries like Johann Benjamin Erhard and Salamon Maimon as well as by Kant himself.[117] Fichte echoed Rousseau's *Social Contract*: the purpose of the state was to unite utility and justice: "In the sphere of right, there is no way to bind human beings together other than through the insight: whatever you do to the other, whether good or bad, you do not to him, but to yourself."[118]

Fichte's *Foundations of Natural Right,* and his note to the Danish edition of the *Vocation of the Scholar,* followed the argument that Kant memorably applied to a "nation of devils" in the first supplement to his essay on perpetual peace.[119] It was not true, Kant claimed, that human beings were too self-interested to achieve a republican constitution, or that "a constitution of so sublime a nature" could be achieved only "within a state of *angels*." On the contrary,

> nature comes to the aid of the universal and rational human will, so admirable in itself but so impotent in practice, and makes use of precisely those self-seeking inclinations in order to do so. It only remains

[116] Fichte, *Gesamtausgabe*, pt. 1, 1:238. See Philonenko, *Théorie et praxis*, esp. 202–5.

[117] In the preface to the *Foundations of Natural Right*, Fichte cited Johann Benjamin Erhard's "Devil's Apology" (1795) and Salomon Maimon's "On the First Grounds of Natural Right" (1795), both of which had appeared in the *Philosophisches Journal einer gesellschaft Teutscher Gelehrten*, as "excellent hints" that, together with Kant's *Perpetual Peace*, suggested the approach to natural right that he had fully developed. Richard Schottky characterized this as a Hobbesian trend in 1790s German political thought ("Untersuchungen zur Geschichte der staatsphilosophischen Vertragstheorie," 310ff.); Luc Ferry referred to "a certain Machiavellisation" of Fichte's theory of law and politics ("Law and Ethics in Fichte," 184). See the exchange between Ludwig Heinrich von Jakob, *Antimachiavel, oder über die Grenzen des bürgerlichen Gehorsams: Auf Veranlassung zweyer Aufsätze in der Berl. Monatsschrift, Sept. und Dec. 1793, von den Herren Kant und Genz* (Halle, 1794); and Paul Johann Anselm Feuerbach, *Anti-Hobbes, oder ueber die Grenzen der höchsten Gewalt und das Zwangsrecht der Bürger gegen den Oberherrn* (Erfurt, 1798). As Richard Tuck and others have claimed, such a distinction was central to the seventeenth-century natural jurisprudence of Hugo Grotius and his followers, and was retained by Rousseau, despite his great criticisms of that tradition: see Tuck, *Philosophy and Government, 1572–1651* (Cambridge: Cambridge University Press, 1993); and *Rights of War and Peace.*

[118] Fichte, *Foundations of Natural Right*, 172. Compare the claim that the populace will behave rightly "because what is right is bound up with what is advantageous to them" (153).

[119] Note that the second appendix was not added until the second edition of the essay; Fichte's review was written about the first edition.

> for men to create a good organization for the state, a task which is well within their capability, and to arrange it in such a way that their self-seeking energies are opposed to one another, each thereby neutralizing or eliminating the destructive effects of the rest. And as far as reason is concerned, the result is the same as if man's selfish tendencies were non-existent, so that man, even if he is not morally good in himself, is nevertheless compelled to be a good citizen. As hard as it may sound, the problem of setting up a state can be solved even by a nation of *devils* (so long as they possess understanding).[120]

Once selfishness was contained and made lawful in this way, it was possible to imagine the eventual moralization of social relations. "We cannot expect their moral attitudes to produce a good political constitution," Kant wrote of his nation of devils. "On the contrary, it is only through the latter that the people can be expected to attain a good level of moral culture."[121] Fichte made the same claim in the *Foundations of Natural Right.*[122] It was not possible to participate in the kind of moral commerce that Fichte had passionately portrayed in his earlier works without becoming a citizen of the state first. The path toward becoming "true men," as Fichte had put it in his public lectures, had to pass through citizenship before transcending it. "Humanity separates itself from citizenship in order to elevate itself with absolute freedom to the level of morality," Fichte wrote in the *Foundations of Natural Right*, "but it can do so only if human beings have first existed within the state."[123]

Fichte's new approach to the problem of perpetual peace was based on the same theory of unsocial sociability as Kant's. As he announced in his review of Kant's essay, and repeated in the preface to the *Foundations of Natural Right*, Fichte claimed to have produced a systematic deduction of this theory and consequently to have arrived at a better account of a republican constitution than Kant. (Given Steck's report about Fichte's opinion of Sieyès, discussed above, it seems likely that Fichte felt similarly about the relationship between his own rights theory and the account of natural right that Sieyès had sketched in his 1789 *Preliminary to the Constitution*.)[124] Fichte's 1796 treatise derived rights from the conditions of freedom understood as conscious, self-directed activity. Fichte claimed that to act self-consciously, or to ascribe to oneself the capac-

[120] Kant, *Perpetual Peace*, 112.

[121] Ibid., 113.

[122] See the very striking statement of this in the context of penal law (Fichte, *Foundations of Natural Right*, 237–38).

[123] Ibid., 178–79.

[124] Steck to Ith, ca. fall 1796, in Fuchs, Lauth, and Schieche, *Fichte im Gespräch*, 6.1:228. See Sieyès, "Annerkenung und erklärende Auseinandersetzung der Rechte des Menschen und des Bürgers," in *Politische Schriften*, 1:427–60. Sieyès's 1789 commentary on the rights of man and citizen had also been reprinted together with Oelsner's *Life of Sieyes* (1795).

ity to determine one's own ends, one had to realize these ends in the external world. The primary condition for consciousness was "an ongoing reciprocal interaction, dependent only on the person's own will, between the person and the sensible world outside of him."[125] A direct and inherently limitless relationship between the individual will and the natural world was constitutive of personhood. Fichte captured this relationship between the individual will and nature most succinctly in his essay on the origins of language, which appeared in April 1795 as his first contribution to the *Philosophisches Journal einer gesellschaft Teutscher Gelehrten.* "It is fundamental to man's very essence that he seeks to subjugate the power of nature," Fichte wrote. "The first expression of his own power is directed toward nature in order to shape it to his own ends."[126]

The relationship between the individual's will and the natural world that Fichte described was essentially unbounded. Although the *Foundations of Natural Right* described this relationship in the confusing terminology of "original rights," Fichte made it clear that this was merely a speculative exercise.[127] There were no inherent limits to this relationship between man and nature: "If—as occurs in the deduction of original right—a person in the sensible world is thought of as isolated, then (as long as he does not know of any person outside himself) he has the right to extend his freedom as far as he wills and can, and—if he so desires—the right to take possession of the entire sensible world. His right is actually infinite (if original right can be an actual right at all), for the condition under which such a right would have to be limited is absent."[128] Like Hobbes, then, Fichte described a natural right of each to all—which is to say, no natural right at all, since Fichte held that collisions of activity were ultimately inevitable and nobody could make a better claim to any particular sphere of activity than anybody else.[129]

[125] Fichte, *Foundations of Natural Right*, 183.

[126] Johann Gottlieb Fichte, "On the Linguistic Capacity and the Origin of Language" (1795; in Surber, *Language and German Idealism*, 121). Compare Fichte, *Foundations of Natural Right*, 9: "What is contained first and foremost in the concept of freedom is nothing but the capacity to construct [*entwerfen*], through absolute spontaneity, concepts of our possible efficacy [*Wirksamkeit*]; and the only thing that rational beings ascribe to one another with necessity is this bare capacity. But if a rational individual, or a person, is to find himself as free, then something more is required, namely, that the object in experience that is thought of through the concept of the person's efficacy actually correspond to that concept; what is required, therefore, is that something in the world outside the rational individual follow from the thought of his activity."

[127] "There is no condition in which original rights exist; and no original rights of human beings" (Fichte, *Foundations of Natural Right*, 102).

[128] Ibid., 111.

[129] The "natural right to everything" is not really a right in Fichte's terms, because Fichte defined rights as a kind of relationship between people in which each individual limited his or her own relationship to nature in such away that it did not come into conflict with another's relationship to nature. It was impossible to talk about rights outside the context of this relationship, or in conditions where this relationship could not be achieved (see *Foundations of Natural Right*, 51). Note that

Like Rousseau, however, Fichte rejected the claim that human beings were so thoroughly unsociable as to lack any aptitude for society at all. In his essay on the origin of languages, Fichte criticized this Hobbesian conclusion.

> How, on the other hand, does a human being originally act when he encounters another human being? Does the relationship exist between them in the primitive state of nature as obtains between a human being and nature? Would they go about trying to enslave one another, or, if they do not think they have enough strength to do so, then mutually flee from one another?
>
> We will assume that this would be the case: then surely no two human beings would be able to live in proximity to one another; the stronger would enslave the weaker if the latter did not flee as soon as he saw the former. But if this happened, would they have ever entered into society, would the earth have become populated through them? Their relation would have been exactly as Hobbes described it in the state of nature: a war of all against all. And yet we find that men agree with one another, that they mutually support one another, that they stand with one another in a social alliance. The reason for this phenomenon must lie in the nature of man himself: in the primordial nature of man a principle must be discernible which makes him behave differently toward others of his own kind than he behaves toward nature.[130]

Empirical evidence could always be gathered to support theories of both natural sociability and unsociability, Fichte concluded. The only way to account for human sociability was to identify an a priori principle that could vindicate a minimal other-regarding capacity.[131] It is a key feature of Fichte's transcendental deduction of consciousness that intersubjectivity is coeval with subjectivity itself.[132] In Fichte's account, one needed to be recognized as a person by another person in order to recognize oneself as a person in the first place. The development of self-awareness was logically dependent on the exercise of an other-regarding capacity, which Fichte further claimed it was possible to find empirically. In the *Foundations of Natural Right*, Fichte located this minimal

this is not entirely straightforward in Hobbes either, since strictly speaking there is no right and wrong in the state of nature: "To this warre of every man against every man, this also is consequent; that nothing can be Unjust. The notions of Right and Wrong, Justice and Injustice have there no place" (Hobbes, *Leviathan*, 90); see Schottky, "Untersuchungen zur Geschichte der staatsphilosophischen Vertragstheorie," 200–4. Fichte claimed that prior occupation could produce an exclusive right only within the context of an existing agreement of mutual self-limitation—and of course that agreement could not withstand uncertainty and diffidence without the state (*Foundations of Natural Right*, 120).

[130] Fichte, "On the Linguistic Capacity," 121–22.

[131] Ibid., 122.

[132] Fichte, *Foundations of Natural Right*, 64, 80–81.

other-regarding capacity in the natural ability to recognize that the human form differed from the other objects that one encountered in the world.

> The rational observer is completely unable to unite the parts of the human body except in the concept of *his equal*, in the concept of freedom given to him by his own self-consciousness. In order to be able to think something here, the rational observer must supply the concept of himself, because none is given to him; but with that concept he can now explain everything. Every animal *is* what it is: only the human being is originally nothing at all. He must become what he is to be: and, since he is to be a being for himself, he must become this through himself. Nature completed all of her works; only from the human being did she withdraw her hand, and precisely by doing so, she gave him over to himself. Formability, as such, is the character of humanity. Because it is impossible to superimpose upon a human shape any concept other than that of oneself, every human being is inwardly compelled to regard every other human being as his equal.[133]

As Fichte described it in his essay on the origin of languages, the human effort to bend nature to its will followed an authentically Hobbesian logic. The results of the human encounter with nature depended on the relative power of the two parties. Human beings either domesticated or fled from animals; they either conquered nature or reacted with fear to signs of nature's awesome power, like thunder. But Fichte claimed that this was not the only basic response of human beings to one another. Rather, human beings could naturally recognize each other as potential collaborators in the subjection of nature to reason.[134] As Fichte claimed in the *Foundations of Natural Right*, the most basic response of human beings to one another was neither flight nor domination, but reciprocal communication:

> Surely there is no human being who, upon first seeing another human being, would immediately take flight (as one would in the presence of a rapacious animal) or prepare to kill and eat him (as one might do to a beast), rather than immediately expecting reciprocal communication. This is the case, not through habituation and learning, but through nature and reason, and we have just derived the law that makes it the case.[135]

This communicative capacity was the basis for the narrowest of natural rights: to be recognized as someone who was capable of entering into a contractual

[133] Ibid., 74.
[134] Fichte, "On the Linguistic Capacity," 121.
[135] Fichte, *Foundations of Natural Right*, 75.

relationship. A particularly clear statement of this minimal natural right appears (rather significantly) in Fichte's description of cosmopolitan right. In this, Fichte echoed Kant: upon landing on a foreign shore, the only right that the uninvited foreigner could claim from the local inhabitants was bare hospitality:

> He has that original human right which precedes all rightful contracts and which alone makes them possible: *the right to every other human being's expectation to be able to enter into a rightful relation with him through contracts.* This alone is the one true human right that belongs to the human being as such: the right to be able to acquire rights. This, and only this, right must be granted to everyone who has not expressly forfeited it through his actions.[136]

Fichte held that a moment of mutual recognition was logically presupposed by personhood and that a capacity for this recognition existed empirically. But he also stressed that as far as a theory of right was concerned, to remain in community after that moment was a purely voluntary act.[137] Human beings were obviously capable of seeing one another as things as well as persons. They could form and maintain a community only if they all decided never to treat one another like things and to guarantee this, they would have to form a state.

Fichte's account of minimal sociability—the *Aufforderung* (summons), or as he also called it, *Erziehung* (upbringing)—served a function that Rousseau had assigned to the sentiment of pity. Rousseau had declared in his *Discourse on the Origins of Inequality* that "all the rules of natural right" could be derived from man's asocial relationship to nature as modified by a minimal other-regarding capacity—the principles of *amour de soi-même* and *pitié*—"without its being necessary to introduce that of sociability."[138] As we shall see, a major feature of Fichte's engagement with Rousseau, beginning with his critique of Rousseau's *Discourse on the Arts and Sciences* in his public lectures at Jena, and issuing in *The Closed Commercial State*, was his revision of the process by which natural right could be re-created in society. Human rationality, for Fichte as for Kant, was not inextricably intertwined with the awakening of the kinds of social emotions whose corruption had been so acutely analyzed by Rousseau. But Fichte followed Rousseau in claiming that the first step in re-creating natural right had

[136] Ibid., 333.

[137] Ibid., 81.

[138] Jean-Jacques Rousseau, "Discourse on the Origin and Foundations of Inequality Among Men" (1755), in *The Discourses and Other Early Political Writings*, ed. Victor Gourevitch (Cambridge: Cambridge University Press, 1997), 127. See also the famous passage in note 15:, "Self-love [*amour de soi-même*] is a natural sentiment which inclines every animal to attend to its self-preservation and which, guided in many by reason and modified by pity, produces humanity and virtue" (218). Like Rousseau, Fichte pursued this claim into a theory of language.

to be unconditional subjection to the state in exchange for exclusive rights and mutual protection.[139]

Like Sieyès and Kant, Fichte applied Rousseau's constitutional theory to the circumstances of a large and populous country. His second outburst in his review of Kant's essay on perpetual peace was to claim that he had done a better job of this than Kant—and in particular that he had produced a better account of the separation of legislative and executive powers, which was the distinguishing characteristic of republican government according to Kant: "In the opinion of this reviewer, this proposed separation of the legislative from the executive power has never been made with sufficient precision, or at least it has been exposed to many misinterpretations. The reviewer believes that the power that it is to be posited in opposition to the executive is capable of being specified more precisely."[140] In the *Foundations of Natural Right*, Fichte claimed he had resolved the ambiguities (or at least the appearances of ambiguity) in Kant's discussion of the separation of powers by providing what was, "so far as I know, the very first strict deduction, based on pure reason, of the absolute necessity of representation within a commonwealth."[141] Representation was "not just a beneficial and prudent arrangement," Fichte claimed, "but one that the law of right demands absolutely."[142]

In fact, Fichte's deduction of representation retraced Rousseau's distinction between sovereignty and government, repeating his warning that right and fact

[139] In *Foundations of Natural Right*, Fichte reworked Rousseau's contract theory very closely. In the second part of the *Foundations* (which appeared in print in 1797), Fichte broke it down into a property contract, a mutual-protection contract, a unification contract, and a transfer contract. In property right, as Rousseau put it, "one respects not so much what is another's as what is not one's own" (*Social Contract*, 54–55 [bk. 1, chap. 9]); see also Rousseau's definition of natural right in the "Discourse on the Origin of Inequality": do your own good with the least possible harm to others, which differs from a rich account of natural right in that it says "you must not do X," not "you must do Y." As Fichte explained, the negative character of the common will about property made it easy to verify whether individuals were in compliance with it: they merely had to refrain from acting to violate another's property. But protecting another was a positive act, and a problematic one at that, since the required reciprocity would never be present in a single instance of protection. The only way to resolve this difficulty was to make the promise of mutual protection consist in entering the state. Fichte construed the bond between individual wills as each individual's uncertainty about who would be the protector and who the protected. Fichte claimed that the imagination reacted to such uncertainty by wavering or oscillating (*schweben*) between images. Since one could easily imagine oneself on either side of the contract, the contract effectively created a whole that could always be identified with any one of its parts. For this state-person to come into being, all had to transfer their power to a separate agency, which would represent it; see *Foundations of Natural Right*, 165–77. Fichte also covered the same territory in the first part of the treatise (85–101). Both passages culminate with explicit references to Rousseau, (98, 177).

[140] Fichte, "Review of Perpetual Peace," 317.

[141] "In this work it was evidently not Kant's intention to give an exhaustive treatment of the subject" (Fichte, *Foundations of Natural Right*, 14).

[142] Ibid., 14, 141.

would be confounded if the populace both legislated and governed. The law (or, as Fichte also put it, "the constitution") reflected the general will, the rule of reason, which required equal rights for all.[143] These mutually imposed limits on individual freedom acquired their authority only on the basis of consent. However, the laws did not automatically determine the extent of justice. The law did not say "*how far* each person should limit his own freedom," which was "the issue of property in the widest sense of the term"; nor did the law determine how far a criminal's freedom should be limited in order to punish a violation of another's freedom.[144] Fichte held that the material outcome of the laws was not arbitrary; the substantive content of equal rights for a particular population was determined by the nature of things, not by the will of the majority. The people itself could not be trusted to determine the content of justice because, as Fichte put it, nobody could ever serve as his own judge, and there was nobody on earth in a position to judge whether the people had applied its laws (let alone to punish the people if it had not).[145] The only way to create a government of laws, then, was to appoint a subordinate agency to govern in the name of the people and to ensure that the people remained in a position to judge the government's actions.[146] In fact, Fichte claimed, it was only through the creation of such a representative agency that a multitude of individuals could become a unitary actor called "the people": "The community [*das Gemeine*] may not exercise the right of punishment immediately and by itself, for by doing so it would be the judge in its own case, which is never permissible. The community must, accordingly,

[143] Fichte explicitly defined the law of equality in terms of Rousseau's general will (ibid., 98).
[144] Fichte, "Review of Perpetual Peace," 317.
[145] Fichte, *Foundations of Natural Right*, 139–40.
[146] Fichte's argument is summed up nicely at the end of the introduction to the treatise:

> But then who is to proclaim the common will (which is, of course, completely determined by the nature of the matter) concerning both the rights of individuals and the punishment of those who overstep their rights? Who, then, is to clarify and interpret that necessary decree of nature and of the law of right? No one would be more ill-suited than the masses, and by aggregating individual votes one is likely to obtain a very impure version of the true common will. This task can belong to no one other than he who constantly oversees the whole and all of its needs, and who is responsible for the uninterrupted rule of the strictest right; in other words, it can belong to no one other than the administrator of the executive power. He provides the content of the law, which is given to him by reason and by the circumstances of the state; but the law gets its form, its binding power for the individual, only through the individual's consent, not specifically to this determinate law, but to be united with this state . . .
>
> The administrator of the executive power is the natural interpreter of the common will concerning the relationship of individuals to one another within the state; he is the interpreter, not exactly of the will that the individuals actually have, but rather of the will that they must have if they are to exist alongside one another; and this is so, even if not a single person should, in fact, have such a will (as one might well assume to be the case from time to time). (*Foundations of Natural Right*, 16, 142)

transfer the exercise of the right of punishment to a single individual or to an entire body [*Corps*], and it is through this separation that the community first becomes a *people* [*Volk*] (plebs)."[147] Like Sieyès and Kant, and unlike his earlier self, Fichte followed Rousseau in developing a new version of Hobbes's theory of the state as union rather than concord.

Fichte's interpretation of Rousseau led him to reject the idea that the separation of the executive and legislative powers was the distinguishing characteristic of republican government. The executive power, Fichte claimed, was properly understood as the entire edifice of the "state authority," which included the judicial and legislative branches as well as the "*potestas executiva in sensu strictiori*" ("the executive power in the narrower sense").[148] All these "*pouvoirs*" were "parts of one and the same public power"—Fichte's equivalent of what Sieyès had called the "public establishment."[149] Separating a judicial power from an executive power was "completely futile, and is possible only in appearance" because either the executive would be obliged to execute the judicial verdict, in which case the judiciary would be the real power, or the executive would veto the verdict, in which case it would have the ultimate power.[150] In authentically Rousseauian fashion, Fichte construed civil legislation as an exercise of executive power, or as the application of the laws: "Since those who administer the executive power are charged with presiding over right in general and are responsible for seeing to it that right prevails, it must be left up to them to care for the means by which right is to be realized, and therefore even to draft the ordinances themselves, which are not really new laws but only more determinate applications of the one fundamental law, which states: these particular human beings are to live alongside one another in accordance with right."[151] Consenting to the laws meant consenting to the government's determination of their content. "One only has to say 'I want to be a part of this state,'" Fichte wrote in his review of Kant's essay, "and one thereby says everything."[152] Fichte elaborated in *Foundations of Natural Right*: "Each person subjects himself to the law by declaring: I want to live with you people, and to do so in accordance with *all* the just laws that might ever be given in this state."[153] Fichte claimed that "no

[147] Fichte, "Review of Perpetual Peace," 318. I have modified Breazeale's translation where it somewhat confusingly reads "a nation or a people" for *Volk*; see Fichte, *Gesamtausgabe*, pt. 1, 3:225.

[148] Fichte, *Foundations of Natural Right*, 135–36.

[149] Ibid., 142.

[150] Ibid. A good illustration of Fichte's point is furnished by *Worcester v. Georgia* (1832), the occasion for the famous challenge President Andrew Jackson is said to have issued to Chief Justice John Marshall: "Mr. Marshall has made his decision; now let him enforce it."

[151] Fichte, *Foundations of Natural Right*, 142. Compare Rousseau's claim that if his distinction between law and the application of law were taken seriously, "very few Nations would be found to have laws" (*Social Contract*, 115–16 [bk. 3, chap. 16]).

[152] Fichte, "Review of Perpetual Peace," 318.

[153] Fichte, *Foundations of Natural Right*, 142.

one would be more ill-suited than the masses" to determine "the true common will." Putting this up to a popular vote would make justice more rather than less arbitrary. Rather, it was "the administrator of the executive power"—the one who "constantly oversees the whole and all of its needs, and who is responsible for the uninterrupted rule of the strictest right"—who was the "natural interpreter" of the general will.[154] Every executive act should immediately become law (as Fichte suggested, every exercise of public power was a *Tathandlung*, a "fact-act," or the *Wissenschaftslehre*'s term for a reality-constituting act of the mind).[155] It would then be up to the people to judge whether these acts were indeed general and consistent enough that each individual could recognize them as his or her own will.

To keep the government accountable to the constitution, the sovereign people had to be capable of passing judgment on its own representative. However, once a government had been formed, Fichte wrote, "from that point onward, the populace as such no longer exist; the people are not a people, not a whole, but only an aggregate of subjects."[156] It was impossible for the people to hold its representatives accountable unless it was somehow capable of reconstituting itself independently of its representatives' will: "The populace, as such, do not have a separate will and cannot actualize themselves as the populace, until they have detached their will from the will of the executive power and retracted their declaration that the executive power's will is always their own."[157] As Hobbes memorably put it in *De Cive*, the people was like a sleeping monarch who remained sovereign even though he might hand over the reins of power while asleep—so long as he did not fail to wake up.[158]

Fichte rejected the solution to this problem described in the *Social Contract*: namely, Rousseau's insistence that the people could ensure it would wake up by assembling in person on a fixed schedule determined by the constitution.[159] Fichte objected that a regularly scheduled constitutional referendum was suitable only for a small republic, and even there its regularity would encourage

[154] "He is the interpreter, not exactly of the will that the individuals actually have, but rather of the will that they must have if they are to exist alongside one another; and this is so, even if not a single person should, in fact, have such a will (as one might well assume to be the case from time to time)" (ibid., 16).

[155] Ibid., 100, 138.

[156] Ibid., 155.

[157] Ibid., 149.

[158] Hobbes, *On the Citizen*, 100 (chap. 7, art. 16). Many in the eighteenth century picked up this Hobbesian view of popular sovereignty, including James Wilson in America. See Gordon Wood, "The American Revolution," in *The Cambridge History of Eighteenth-Century Political Thought*, ed. M. Goldie and R. Wokler, 621–22 (Cambridge: Cambridge University Press, 2006). Herder brought up the idea of "nations falling asleep" as the origins of tyranny in *Ideen zur Philosophie der Geschichte*, bk. 9, chap. 4; see Herder, *Another Philosophy of History*, 124.

[159] Rousseau, *Social Contract*, 110–12 (bk. 3, chaps. 12–13).

disorder and cheapen the dignity of the proceedings. Instead, Fichte proposed that the people exercise its sovereign power of judging the government through an institution that he called the ephorate. (In a footnote, he specified that what he had in mind was rather more like the Roman tribunate than the Spartan magistracy—and indeed the institution he described closely followed Rousseau's account, in book 4 of the *Social Contract*, of the Roman tribunes as constitutional watchdogs.)[160] Fichte's ephors could not hold any executive power themselves, nor could they themselves pass judgment on the executive, since this would create a two-headed government without a supreme interpreter of the laws and would fail to fulfill the conditions for rightful relations. Rather, the ephors would possess only a strictly negative power: the right to issue an "interdict" to dissolve the entire government. Once an interdict was issued, the people would have to assemble (in groups large enough to resist the executive power, if necessary) and judge whether the executive or the ephors had violated the general will. Fichte claimed that the question posed to the people was sufficiently narrow and the criteria for judging were sufficiently well-defined for a clear verdict to be delivered: the people merely had to decide whether the executive had acted inconsistently and made an unjust exception to the laws or had committed some other transgression of comparable magnitude (such as threatening the independence of the ephors). The populace could be expected to deliver the correct verdict "because what is right is bound up with what is advantageous to them." Whatever exercise of public power they decided to permit would become constitutional law.[161]

Fichte's development of Rousseau's constitutional theory paralleled the efforts of Sieyès and Kant to preserve Rousseau's distinction between sovereignty and government, or the laws and their execution. The ephorate was intended to ensure that citizens could remain free even as subjects of the state: it ensured that citizens were dependent only on impersonal laws, of which they were both subjects and coauthors, and not on the arbitrary will of whoever might be wielding public power. Fichte's ephorate was linked with Sieyès in this Rousseauian context by Gerhard Anton von Halem, who was also a friend of Oelsner. Writing to a Swiss student at Jena in March 1797, von Halem noted that

[160] Fichte, *Foundations of Natural Right*, 151. Ephors appeared prominently in Calvinist resistance doctrine, as evidenced by Althusius, and the idea remained relevant for Rousseau (see book 4 of the *Social Contract* and letter 9 of the *Letters Written from the Mountain*). Ephors turn up in Federalist 63 (1788) and also figured in French constitutional debates of 1793. According to Wilfried Nippel, the model of a mixed constitution could be deployed to describe the parliamentary regime developing in the eighteenth century, but had difficulty accommodating the principle of judiciary independence. Checks and balances became a technical tool for the functioning of government, while constitutional guardianship was captured by the idea of ephors (Nippel, "Ancient and Modern Republicanism: 'Mixed Constitution' and 'Ephors,'" in *The Invention of the Modern Republic*, ed. Biancamaria Fontana, 6–26).

[161] Fichte, *Foundations of Natural Right*, 153.

although he had yet to read Fichte's new treatise on natural right himself, everything he had heard about Fichte's idea of an ephorate seemed to recall Sieyès's 1795 proposals for a "constitutional jury."[162] Von Halem was not thrilled with the idea. In the spirit of Rousseau's reply to Mirabeau, von Halem pointed out to his correspondent that any attempt to place the laws over men still amounted to setting up an institution that, like any other, would have to be occupied by men who would ultimately try to use their power to become masters of the laws. "Nonetheless," von Halem concluded, "what Sieyès and Fichte say is always exceedingly worth heeding."[163]

Fichte's theory of the state remained more radical than Kant's in its refusal to rule out all direct, popular political action as a matter of principle. By 1796, Fichte had backed away considerably from his earlier efforts to legitimate revolution. In 1793, Fichte had claimed that insensibly slow reforms were not the only path for historical progress. A violent revolution, he wrote in the preface to his *Demand for the Liberty of Thought*, could gain six centuries' ground at the cost of fifty years of suffering and misery, but at the risk of ending in a return to barbarism.[164] *The Closed Commercial State* was dedicated to a senior Prussian official and did not discuss violent revolution as an effective mode of advancing liberty.[165] But Fichte never went to the same lengths as many of his European and American contemporaries in their efforts to avoid the specter of the armed populace as a political agent.[166] The ephorate he described in the *Foundations of Natural Right* could be instituted from above, rather than from below, and it would normally achieve its aims by bargaining with the government. But the assembly of the people into a sovereign judge was explicitly described as a possible constitutional outcome.[167] Like Kant, Fichte followed the

[162] See Sieyès, *Politische Schriften*, 2:403–36; Pasquino, *Sieyes et la constitution en France*, 193–96.

[163] Gerhard Anton von Halem to Johann Friedrich Herbart, 14 March 1797, in Fuchs, Lauth, and Schieche, *Fichte im Gespräch*, 1:412.

[164] Fichte, *Gesamtausgabe*, pt. 1, 1:169.

[165] However, in 1799, Fichte still privately held that Germany's only hope of escaping the rising tide of reaction spreading from the east was for France to succeed in sparking a revolution in at least a part of Germany; see Fichte to Reinhold, 22 May 1799, in Fichte, *Lettres et Témoignages*, 91.

[166] See Manin, *Representative Government*.

[167] Fichte, *Foundations of Natural Right*, 152–53. Compare Federalist 63 (written by James Madison) on the ephorate:

> Lastly, in Sparta we meet with the Ephori, and in Rome with the Tribunes; two bodies, small indeed in numbers, but annually *elected by the whole body of the people*, and considered as the representatives of the people, almost in their *plenipotentiary* capacity. . . . From these facts . . . it is clear that the principle of representation was neither unknown to the ancients nor wholly overlooked in their political constitutions. The true distinction between these and the American governments lies *in the total exclusion of the people, in their collective capacity*, from any share in the *latter*, and not in the *total exclusion of the representatives of the people* from the administration of the *former*. (Alexander Hamilton, John Jay, and James Madison, *The Federalist Papers*, ed. Clinton Rossiter [New York: New American Library, 1961], 387)

Hobbesian logic that ruled out a right to revolution in principle: if there were no "people" without representation, any resistance was unlawful rebellion. But Fichte placed a greater emphasis on pointing out that the people itself could not rebel, and if the people was assembled, all government was silenced. If the people responded to some rebels by assembling and judging against its own government, Fichte was prepared to describe these rebels as "natural ephors" and to claim that formal legitimacy would follow: "It will become clear that the inciters' will contains the *content* of right, and it will acquire the *form* of right (which it still lacks) from the assent of the populace."[168]

Fichte's analysis of the forms of government was also less cautious than Kant's. Fichte endorsed Kant's attack on democratic government, since he considered the exercise of executive power by the people itself to be "a constitution fully contrary to right."[169] Like any regime that failed to distinguish between the laws and their execution, this kind of democracy was a form of unaccountable power and, therefore, a species of despotism. Unlike Kant, however, Fichte made it clear that there could be a legitimate kind of democracy, "a representative, and therefore rightfully constituted, democracy."[170] According to Fichte, any form of government was legitimate so long as the ephorate was present.[171] Within this rubric, Fichte's analysis of the forms of government eschewed Kant's obfuscating terminology and followed the same reasoning that Sieyès

[168] Fichte, *Foundations of Natural Right*, 160–61. If the revolution failed, the rebels were guilty, even if their cause was just: "They should have known their own nation better." "No people have ever risen up in unison like a single man—nor ever will—unless the injustice has reached an extreme," Fichte wrote; and if a premature revolution were somehow to succeed militarily, the result would be "the destruction and nullification of all right." Compare Kant: "It would be contrary to all political expediency, which in this case agrees with morality, to destroy any of the existing bonds of political or cosmopolitan union before a better constitution has been prepared to take their place" (*Perpetual Peace*, 118). On the other hand: "If, however, a more lawful constitution were attained by unlawful means, i.e. by a violent *revolution* resulting from a previous bad constitution, it would then no longer be permissible to lead the people back to the original one, even although everyone who had interfered with the old constitution by violence or conspiracy would rightly have been subject to the penalties of rebellion during the revolution itself" (118).

[169] Fichte, *Foundations of Natural Right*, 141.

[170] Ibid., 143. The same point was made in an anonymous 1796 review in the *Gothaische gelehrte Zeitungen*. This review faulted Kant's definition of democracy as the "self-administration of the legislative and executive power of the people taken in the strictest sense" for being "too narrow." This was wrong, the reviewer claimed, because "a representative democracy is also imaginable, namely one where the people has its highest powers administered in its name through executives it chooses from time to time" ("Rezension," *Gothaische gelehrte Zeitungen* 2, no. 5 [March 1796], reprinted in Kant, *Zum ewigen Frieden*, 80).

[171] "It is through the law (i.e. through the original will of the populace who give themselves a constitution), that each of these regimes obtains the force of right. All are rightful regimes as long as an ephorate is present; and all can produce and maintain universal right within a state, as long as the ephorate is efficacious and properly organized" (Fichte, *Foundations of Natural Right*, 144).

had deployed in his debate with Paine.[172] Like Sieyès, Fichte described a monarchical government as a system of public power that was responsible to a single ultimate administrator—a pyramid culminating in a single point—whereas a republican government culminated in a broad plateau:

> The only difference between a monarchy and republic is that, if there is no unanimity within the corps of persons [i.e., the government], the dispute is settled either by the unappealable decision of a life-long president (the monarch), or by some collective voice, such as a majority vote. In the latter case, the perpetual president is a mystical and often mutable person (i.e., those whose voices constitute a majority of votes and who decide the dispute without the possibility of appeal are not always the same physical persons).[173]

A "representative, and therefore rightfully constituted, democracy" was a government in which every public official was directly elected (the same could be said of an "elective kingdom"). In such regimes, the majority of the electorate formed the broadest of plateaus. Fichte also endorsed the various intermediate forms of "aristo-democracy" that would result from indirect voting systems like the one proposed by Sieyès, in which public officials appointed some of their own number. Strikingly, Fichte even managed to be less strident than Kant in his opposition to a hereditary aristocracy, so long as an ephorate was put in place immediately.[174]

Fichte's reworking of Rousseau's theory of the state ultimately suggested a kind of plebiscitary democracy. In this respect, Fichte was in tune with the dawning of the Napoleonic era and continued to share a great deal of common ground with his more radical republican contemporaries. Fichte had arrived at many of the same results as his friend Friedrich Schlegel (1772–1829), who had published a review of Kant's *Perpetual Peace* in the journal *Deutschland* during the spring of 1796.[175] Schlegel's review also drew upon Fichte's philosophi-

[172] For example, Fichte described the head of government as "highest regent," making the premise of popular sovereignty explicit (*Foundations of Natural Right*, 250). As many early readers of *Perpetual Peace* complained, the same premise was obscured by Kant's categorization of forms of sovereignty according to the number of officeholders. The revised regime analysis that appeared in Kant's *Rechtslehre* of 1797 went some distance in addressing the complaints of his reviewers.

[173] Fichte, *Foundations of Natural Right*, 143.

[174] In *Perpetual Peace*, Kant drew a contrast between hereditary aristocracy, which was a perverted system of privilege that "could never be approved by the general will of the people," and the political hierarchy of government officials that would be generated by the representative system, which was compatible with the law of equality (99–100n). Compare Johann Gottlieb Fichte, *The System of Ethics: According to the Principles of the Wissenschaftslehre* (1798), ed. Daniel Breazeale and Günter Zöller (Cambridge: Cambridge University Press, 2005), 339–40.

[175] Friedrich Schlegel, "Versuch über den Begriff des Republikanismus" (1796), in Kant, *Zum ewigen Frieden*, 104–20, translated as "Essay on the Concept of Republicanism Occasioned by the

cal system to repackage Rousseau's political theory and directed that ensemble into an extensive criticism of Kant's essay. Schlegel complained that Kant had distorted Rousseau by calibrating his definition of the republican ideal to the potential of a despotic monarchy to acquire a republican spirit. Schlegel was willing to endorse anything short of a hereditary regime—including, notably, a term-limited dictatorship—so long as the populace always exercised its sovereign "constituting power" (*konstitutive Macht*) directly.[176] Schlegel was even more open than Fichte to the prospect of a democratic revolution in Germany: a republican constitution had to originate in a fully democratic founding moment, as social contract theory stipulated, rather than filter down through the establishment of constitutional institutions like the ones described by Sieyès, Kant, or even Fichte.[177]

The distinguishing characteristic of Fichte's theory of the state is the depth and rigor of his effort to render plebiscitary democracy in the Rousseauian idiom developed by Sieyès and Kant—an idiom that maintained a strong distinction between a full account of civic friendship and the narrow kind of justice that could be achieved by the state in a nation of devils. The difference between Fichte and contemporary republicans who were otherwise quite close to him, like Schlegel, was evidently appreciated by Joseph Görres (1776–1848). Görres was then a hotheaded young journalist from the city of Koblenz in the Rhineland (like many of his generation, he later exchanged his radical republicanism for Catholicism). In 1798, Görres published an extensive essay on perpetual peace whose immediate goal was to persuade the French government to guarantee the newly acquired liberty of the Rhineland by annexing that territory to the French Republic. Görres was also concerned to push back against Kant's antidemocratic line, and his essay drew on a highly eclectic mélange of sources and idioms, including Rousseau, Sieyès, and Fichte, to do so.[178] But Kant was not the only target Görres identified: despite the admiration he professed for Fichte's views on religion, at the very outset of his essay Görres found it neces-

Kantian Tract 'Perpetual Peace,'" in *Early Political Writings of the German Romantics*, ed. Frederick C. Beiser, 93–112 (Cambridge: Cambridge University Press, 1996).

[176] Schlegel, "Essay on Republicanism," 104.

[177] Schlegel's support for democracy is notable for his insistence on fully universal suffrage, not just without property qualification but—in notable contrast to Fichte—also including women ("Essay on Republicanism," 102).

[178] Görres's appropriation of Sieyèsian terminology is the most striking: he described any "representative system" as a "polyarchic" aristocracy, in contrast to "democratic holarchy," or unmediated sovereignty of the nation; however, the former could take more or less republican or despotic forms depending on how the corporate elite of "Suffetes, Archons, Ephors, Patricians, Nobles, or Peers" was composed (Görres, "Der Allgemeine Frieden, Ein Ideal" [1798], in *Ausgewählte Werke*, ed. Wolfgang Frühwald [Freiburg: Herder, 1978], 1:20). He also wrote in the preface that he intended to send the work to Sieyès, and did send a copy to the Directory.

sary to indicate his disapproval of Fichte's views on politics.[179] For Görres, in other words, Herder's strictures against Kant's theory of the state were also applicable to Fichte's.

Toward *The Closed Commercial State*

Fichte's *Closed Commercial State* was an extension of a theory of the state that retained the Hobbesian as well as the republican strain in Rousseau's political philosophy. Fichte had certainly not abandoned the humanitarian ideals that he shared with Herder and many others. He continued to invoke the image of a cosmopolitan moral community in the *Vocation of Man*, the popular presentation of his philosophical system that he published the same year as *The Closed Commercial State*, and in many other writings.[180] But from the *Foundations of Natural Right* (1796) onward, Fichte held this vision at one remove and came to view the state as a necessary prerequisite for the creation of such a community: "In the state, nature re-unites what she had previously separated when she produced several individuals. Reason is one, and it is exhibited in the sensible world also as one; humanity is a single organized and organizing whole of reason. Humanity was divided into several independent members; the natural institution of the state already cancels this independence provisionally and molds individual groups into a whole, until morality re-creates the entire species as one."[181] The prior question—the question directly addressed by *The Closed Commercial State*—was how to create a republic: what could be done to achieve the reworked social contract Fichte had described, without imagining that the state existed in an imaginary vacuum or that it was already surrounded by other republics capable of cooperating to construct a legal international order. How could the state be reformed into a republic in a hostile and unjust international environment, and avoid the corruption of power politics? Fichte's *Closed Commercial State* addressed the conditions necessary to create a state that could avoid becoming an instrument of power politics. There had been states in Europe for only a very short time, Fichte wrote in his review of Kant's essay and repeated in *The Closed Commercial State*, and the present age was still characterized by attempts to create them.[182]

179 "With regard to religious matters I have nearly completely followed the distinguished discoverer of the *Wissenschaftslehre*, but in political matters I have differed markedly from him" (Görres, ibid., 1:8).

180 Johann Gottlieb Fichte, *Die Bestimmung des Menschen* (1800), trans. Peter Preuss as *The Vocation of Man* (Indianapolis, Ind.: Hackett, 1987), 85–90.

181 Fichte, *Foundations of Natural Right*, 176.

182 Fichte, "Review of Perpetual Peace," 320; and *Der geschlossene Handelsstaat*, *Gesamtausgabe*, pt. 1, 7:95. It is unusual, and perhaps significant, that the lectures on universal history Fichte pre-

Fichte's *Closed Commercial State* focused on an important aspect of the problem of creating a republic in an unlawful environment: international commercial rivalry and the constraints that it imposed on states whose survival depended on their economic success. This was the third question in Herder's 1792 letter, and the following chapters will show how Fichte grappled with Rousseau's and Kant's responses to it.

sented in 1804–5 described the present age as the third of five stages of history, rather than the final stage before the end of history; see Fichte, *Die Grundzüge des gegenwärtigen Zeitalters* (1806), *Gesamtausgabe*, pt. 1, 8:201, 206–7.

Chapter 2
Commerce and the European Commonwealth in 1800

Gentz's Review

Fichte's *Closed Commercial State* was a prominent target in the lengthy article on perpetual peace that Friedrich von Gentz published in the December 1800 issue of his *Historical Journal*.[1] Gentz (1764–1832) was a Prussian official who had studied under Kant in Königsberg and became famous for his 1794 translation of Edmund Burke's *Reflections on the Revolution in France*. He later moved to Austria, where he served as an important advisor to Klemens von Metternich and acted as secretary for the Congress of Vienna. In 1800, however, Gentz's patron was the British government, which had begun paying him to deploy his formidable eloquence in the major debates leading up to the end of the War of the Second Coalition against France.[2] Gentz's criticism of Kant's *Perpetual Peace* and his attack on Fichte's *Closed Commercial State* were linked to his opposition to the kind of peace settlement that was being promoted by Sieyès and the French foreign ministry.

In his review essay, Gentz mapped out contemporary debates about perpetual peace by using the contractual analogy implied by the idea of international relations as a state of nature. There were three basic approaches to this problem. One was to pursue the analogy to its logical conclusion and unify all humanity by creating a world state. Alternatively, a world in which humanity remained divided into multiple states could be pacified if these states were thoroughly separated and had nothing to fight over. The third approach was to qualify the analogy to some degree by introducing some form of international federation. Kant was obviously a theorist of international federalism, but Gentz complained that he had not said terribly much about how he thought such a

[1] Gentz, "Über den ewigen Frieden."

[2] See Murray Forsyth, "The Old European States-System: Gentz vs. Hauterive," *Historical Journal* 23, no. 3 (1980): 522. These debates are also discussed in F. H. Hinsley, *Power and the Pursuit of Peace: Theory and Practice in the History of Relations between States* (Cambridge: Cambridge University Press, 1963), 186–94; and Emma Rothschild, "Language and Empire, c. 1800." *Historical Research* 78, no. 200 (May 2005): 208–29.

federation should be organized.[3] Meanwhile, Gentz cast Fichte's *Closed Commercial State* as a radical proposal to achieve perpetual peace by separating nations, thereby removing all causes of conflict among them. Fichte had proposed that commerce between citizens of different states be made impossible, which Gentz regarded as cutting rather than solving the Gordian knot of the law of nations.[4] Economic and political isolation would certainly be an effective way of eliminating the violent turmoil produced by the European states system—the "republic" or "commonwealth" of Europe, in contemporary parlance. But Gentz charged that this would produce a stagnant peace without freedom, for to eliminate global commerce was to destroy the cosmopolitan wellsprings of progress and to condemn humanity to an eternal childhood.[5]

As Gentz saw, *The Closed Commercial State* ends by explicitly invoking the ideal of a peaceful community of independent republics. Fichte's analysis of commerce in *The Closed Commercial State* was an extension of his engagement with Kant's views on perpetual peace. Kant had suggested that European states could be reformed into republics once the pressures of war compelled them to institute a legalized and demilitarized international order. Kant had also claimed that the "spirit of commerce" (*Handelsgeist*) could ultimately serve to reunite a divided humanity and transform a reformed states system into a genuinely cosmopolitan order. Fichte's *Closed Commercial State*, a provocative reworking of this model, argued that the development of the modern European states system had thoroughly corrupted the "spirit of commerce." The result, Fichte claimed, was that international trade had itself become a formidable obstacle to the process of reforming European states into republics.

Fichte's *Closed Commercial State* linked the problem of perpetual peace to the problem of economic rivalry. To tame the European states system, Fichte claimed, it was necessary to address the transformation of the "spirit of commerce" into what David Hume had called the "jealousy of trade."[6] In this view, international markets had become an arena for the kind of competition and conflict between states that Hobbes had described as the state of war. Fichte's claim was that Kant's ideal could be achieved only once this corrosive combination of power politics and international trade had been neutralized. International trade could not serve as a means of forging the foundations of a cosmopolitan community if it remained subject to the logic of reason of state. In the autumn of 1800, this claim was unmistakably aligned with the anti-English arguments advanced by the French foreign ministry. These were publicized most effectively in a provocative book entitled *De l'état de la France à la fin de l'an*

[3] Gentz, "Über den ewigen Frieden," 270.

[4] Ibid., 254.

[5] Ibid., 267.

[6] David Hume, "Of the Jealousy of Trade," in *Essays: Moral, Political, and Literary*, ed. Eugene Miller, rev. ed. (Indianapolis, Ind.: Liberty Classics, 1987), 327–31; see also Hont, *Jealousy of Trade*.

VIII, which was written by Friedrich von Gentz's nemesis, a senior French official named Alexandre-Maurice Blanc de Lanautte, comte d'Hauterive (1754–1830).[7] D'Hauterive was a protégé of the eminent statesman Charles-Maurice de Talleyrand, and the peace settlement he proposed for Germany was closely associated with the foreign policy promoted by Sieyès. Fichte's *Closed Commercial State* took this vision of a future peace as its starting point. Whereas Kant's *Perpetual Peace* had appeared in the context of Sieyès's efforts to arrange Prussia's exit from the First Coalition against France in 1795, Fichte's book appeared when the shape of a future peace settlement was again being debated throughout Europe in the autumn of 1800.

Perpetual Peace and *The Closed Commercial State*

Like his earlier writings, Kant's 1795 essay on perpetual peace identified war as the catalyst that would eventually bring about the transformation of existing states into republics. To be sure, Kant deemed war a great evil and lamented that the state's need for constant military readiness retarded the advancement of culture by diverting precious resources and encroaching on individual liberty. But even more striking is Kant's emphasis that the ever-present fear that defined a Hobbesian state of war—the original impetus behind the emergence of settled political order in agricultural societies—could exert a positive effect on domestic politics. External pressure had compelled states to exhibit a basic respect for the humanity of their subjects. States had to develop internally in order to survive, and successful internal development required states to grant expanding civil liberties.[8] The same reasoning underpinned Kant's arguments against a world state, even though he acknowledged that creating one was the only way to engineer an unqualified exit from the international state of nature. A world state would be a "soulless despotism," an ungovernable monolith that would eventually degenerate into anarchy.[9] When he revisited the subject in 1798, Kant cited China's experience as an example of this fate. The absence of threats to China's security explained why it had lapsed into such a stagnant despotism and why its subjects had been "stripped of every vestige of freedom."[10] Kant concluded that for the time being, some degree of warfare was a necessary evil. "So long as human culture remains at its present stage," Kant wrote, "war is therefore an indispensable means of advancing it further; and only when

[7] Alexandre-Maurice Blanc de Lanautte, comte d'Hauterive, *De l'état de la France, à la fin de l'an VIII* (Paris, 1800), translated by Lewis Goldsmith as *State of the French Republic at the End of the Year VIII* (London: Jordan, 1801).

[8] Kant, "Idea for a Universal History with a Cosmopolitan Purpose," in *Political Writings*, 50.

[9] Kant, *Perpetual Peace*, 113.

[10] Kant, "Conjectures on the Beginning of Human History" (1786), in *Political Writings*, 232.

culture has reached its full development—and only God knows when that will be—will perpetual peace become possible and of benefit to us."[11] The gradual transformation of the European states system would increasingly exclude violence, but not by eliminating international rivalry altogether: "Unlike that universal despotism which saps all man's energies and ends in the graveyard of freedom," Kant wrote in *Perpetual Peace*, "this peace is created and guaranteed by an equilibrium of forces and a most vigorous rivalry."[12]

The initial tipping point in this transformation would arrive when the growth of trade and especially the financial revolution conspired to make warfare unsustainable. Kant subscribed to the common eighteenth-century view that public debt was a powerful but ultimately self-destructive tool and that a default was ultimately unavoidable.[13] Even the most plentiful state treasury was unable to fund the kind of war machine that could be supported by a public debt. But for all the positive economic side effects that a credit system might generate, sooner or later a state would necessarily confront a stark choice between servicing its debt and funding its military. Choosing the latter promised a constitutional crisis, while the former would deliver military catastrophe. Eventually, Kant wrote in 1793, "sheer exhaustion must eventually perform what goodwill ought to have done but failed to do."[14] States would be compelled to give themselves more republican constitutions and form an alliance to demilitarize the European states system. As Kant specified in the fourth preliminary article of his hypothetical treaty of perpetual peace, a reformed treaty system would have to eliminate modern war finance. In 1795, Kant famously looked to France as the agent that might set this process in motion: "If by good fortune one powerful and enlightened nation can form a republic (which is by its nature inclined to seek perpetual peace), this will provide a focal point for federal association among other states. These will join up with the first one, thus securing the freedom of each state in accordance with the idea of international right, and the whole will gradually spread further and further by a series of alliances of this kind."[15] Kant also anticipated that an impending international debt crisis and the ensuing peace settlement would lead to the creation of a legal international order.[16]

If war was the instrument that was ever so gradually transforming the European states system into a republican federation, commerce was the mechanism that would give it the potential to continue developing into a cosmopolitan

[11] Ibid.

[12] Kant, *Perpetual Peace*, 114.

[13] See Sonenscher, *Before the Deluge*.

[14] Kant, "On the Common Saying: 'This May Be True in Theory, but Does Not Apply in Practice'" (1793), in *Political Writings*, 90.

[15] Kant, *Perpetual Peace*, 104.

[16] Immanuel Kant, "The Contest of Faculties," in *Political Writings*, 189–90.

order. Only commerce could ultimately reunite humanity by counteracting geographic separation (itself frequently the result of warfare) and overcoming linguistic and religious differences. It was in this sense that Kant's essay on *Perpetual Peace* described commerce as the great counterweight to war: "Nature also unites nations which the concept of cosmopolitan right would not have protected from violence and war, and does so by means of their mutual self-interest. For the *spirit of commerce* sooner or later takes hold of every people, and it cannot exist side by side with war."[17] Kant condemned the "abuses" of cosmopolitan right committed both by non-European peoples who continued to live by plunder, like the Barbary pirates and the Bedouins, and by the European commercial states (*handeltreibenden Staaten*) that sought to exploit, conquer, and settle the rest of the world. Notably, he went so far as to praise China and Japan for "wisely" protecting themselves from such exploitation by the commercial states.[18] This stance echoed Kant's remark in his 1793 essay

[17] Kant, *Perpetual Peace*, 114.

[18] Ibid., 106–7. The late-eighteenth-century European conception of Japan as a closed commercial state is nicely illustrated by an earlier defense of its isolationist policies:

> Happy would have been the condition of men, if nature had so bless'd each Country with all the necessaries of life, that the inhabitants fully satisfied with their situation, should have no reason to entertain any thoughts of invading the rights and properties of others. History then would not have been fill'd with so many tragical events. Murdering and plundering of each other, ravaging and unpeopling of whole Countries, laying in waste and ruin publick and private, sacred and profane buildings, and many other calamities, the dreadful consequences of war, cruelty and ambition, would have been entirely unknown to mankind. Men, on the contrary, free from other business, would have been more attentive to promote their publick and private welfare, more diligent to cultivate the desart and barren places of their Country, more industrious in the improvement of arts and sciences, more bent upon the practice of vertue, more inclined to equity, freer from passion and self-interest, juster in rewarding the good and punishing the wicked, more careful in the education of children, more exact and mindful in the care and management of their private families: In a word, they would have made themselves and others happy, and in their several societies stood a pattern of a Government, the best that could be wished for, in imitation of the Japanese, who confined within the limits of their Empire enjoy the blessings of peace and contentedness, and do not care for any commerce, or communication with foreign nations, because such is the happy state of their Country, that it can subsist without it. (Engelbert Kaempfer, *The history of Japan, giving an account of the ancient and present state and government of that empire; of its temples, palaces, castles and other buildings; of its metals, minerals, trees, plants, animals, birds and fishes; of the chronology and succession of the emperors, ecclesiastical and secular; of the original descent, religions, customs, and manufactures of the natives, and of their trade and commerce with the Dutch and Chinese. Together with a description of the Kingdom of Siam*, trans. J. G. Scheuchzer [London, 1727], 2:54)

On Kaempfer, see David Mervart, "A Closed Country in the Open Seas: Engelbert Kaempfer's Japanese Solution for European Modernity's Predicament," *History of European Ideas* 35, no. 3 (September 2009): 321–29. The Japanese term *sakoku* (鎖国, or "closed country"), used to describe the isolationist policy of the Tokugawa shogunate, was coined by Shizuki Tadao, a Nagasaki interpreter,

"On the Common Saying: 'This May Be True in Theory, but It Does Not Apply in Practice,'" that in certain conditions, the legitimate "means of *securing the rightful state*" against external enemies might well have to include significant restrictions on commerce.[19] It also presaged the very argument that Fichte went on to develop at length in *The Closed Commercial State.*

In 1793, Kant distinguished between paternalistic government aiming to improve the welfare of the people, and patriotic government aiming to safeguard their autonomy, but he specified that legitimate measures undertaken by the latter "might include certain restrictions on imports, so that the means of livelihood may be developed for the benefit of the subjects themselves and not as an advantage to foreigners or an encouragement for their industry. For without the prosperity of the people, the state would not have enough strength to resist external enemies or to preserve itself as a commonwealth."[20] This remark has sometimes been dismissed as an aberration, but like Kant's praise of China and Japan, it shows that Kant did not exclude the idea of a closed commercial state as a transition strategy that might, in certain conditions, lie on the path toward perpetual peace.[21] The broader point Kant went on to stress in *Perpetual Peace*, however, was that abuses of the spirit of commerce, and the severe countermeasures that might be used to deal with them, would still not prevent the expansion of commerce around the globe. This process would eventually lead to the extension of international law beyond the confines of the European states system: "In this way, continents distant from each other can enter into peaceful mutual relations which may eventually be regulated by public laws, thus bringing the human race nearer and nearer to a cosmopolitan constitution."[22] Ultimately, Kant wrote, it was the connections forged by commerce that made it possible to imagine the further transformation of the international laws of a future European treaty organization into universal human rights: "The peoples of the earth have thus entered in varying degrees into a universal community, and it has developed to the point where a violation of rights in *one* part of the world is felt *everywhere.* The idea of a cosmopolitan right is therefore not fantastic and overstrained; it is a necessary complement to the unwritten code of political and international right, transforming it into a universal right of humanity. Only

---

in his 1801 Japanese translation of part of Kaempfer's treatise; see Tashiro Kazui, "Foreign Relations during the Edo Period: Sakoku Reexamined," *Journal of Japanese Studies* 8, no. 2 (1982): 283–84.

[19] Kant, "Theory and Practice," in *Political Writings*, 80.

[20] Ibid.

[21] Kant's remark is treated as an aberration in Samuel Fleischacker, "Values Behind the Market: Kant's Response to the *Wealth of Nations*," *History of Political Thought* 17, no. 3 (1996): 393.

[22] Kant, *Perpetual Peace*, in *Political Writings*, 106.

under this condition can we flatter ourselves that we are continually advancing towards a perpetual peace."[23]

Fichte commented on Kant's account of nature's "guarantee of perpetual peace" in the final outburst of original exposition that concluded his review of *Perpetual Peace*. Fichte's review endorsed the basic outline of Kant's model and retraced its entire trajectory. Exhaustion from conflict, along with commercial interests, would eventually lead to the establishment of rightful relations both within and among European states and between Europe and the other continents. Fichte drew on two ubiquitous themes of eighteenth-century historiography to substantiate Kant's claim that this process would not stop until it had encompassed all humanity. On the one hand, the "blossoming North American free state" would ensure that enlightenment and freedom came to "those portions of the world that have, until now, been oppressed."[24] Meanwhile, Fichte wrote, echoing philosophes like Voltaire, the balance of power achieved by the "great European republic of states" would ensure that the "workshops of culture" were safe from fatal disruptions like the barbarian invasions that had doomed the world of classical antiquity.[25] Once a European state had succeeded in giving itself "a constitution in accordance with right and reason," others would begin to emulate its success. Once states became republics, Fichte concluded, lawful relations among them would follow as a matter of course, since emanci-

[23] Ibid., 107–8.

[24] On development of the image of America in the 1770s and 1780s and its connection to Physiocracy see Durand Echeverria, *Mirage in the West: A History of the French Image of American Society to 1815* (Princeton, N.J.: Princeton University Press, 1968).

[25] Fichte, "Review of Perpetual Peace," 321 (I have amended the translation). Voltaire famously referred to Europe as "a great republic divided into many states" (*Le Siècle de Louis XIV* [1751; London, 1752], 1:6). See also Emer de Vattel's equally famous statement.

> Europe forms a political system, an integral body, closely connected by the relations and different interests of the nations inhabiting this part of the world. It is not, as formerly, a confused heap of detached pieces, each of which thought herself very little concerned in the fate of the others, and seldom regarded things which did not immediately concern her. The continual attention of sovereigns to every occurrence, the constant residence of ministers, and the perpetual negotiations, make of modern Europe a kind of republic, of which the members—each independent, but all linked together by the ties of common interest—unite for the maintenance of order and liberty. Hence arose that famous scheme of the political balance, or the equilibrium of power; by which is understood such a disposition of things, as that no one potentate be able absolutely to predominate, and prescribe laws to the others. (*The Law of Nations, or, principles of the law of nature, Applied to the Conduct and Affairs of Nations and Sovereigns* [1758; London: Robinson, 1797], bk. 3, sect. 47)

On narratives of the rise of civilization in Europe that culminate with the balance of power as the pinnacle of its achievements, see Karen O'Brien, *Narratives of Enlightenment: Cosmopolitan History from Voltaire to Gibbon* (Cambridge: Cambridge University Press, 1997); and J.G.A Pocock, *Barbarism and Religion*, vol. 2: *Narratives of Civil Government* (Cambridge: Cambridge University Press, 1999).

pated peoples would have no more to gain and plenty to lose from continuing wars begun by their former masters.[26]

Like Gentz, Fichte pointed out in his review that Kant had stopped short of describing the unification of humanity under a genuinely enforceable regime of international law. However, Fichte greatly accentuated the latent cosmopolitan connotations of Kant's model by describing "the federation of nations [*Völkerbund*] proposed by Kant for the preservation of peace" as "no more than an intermediary condition, through which humanity well may have to pass on its way to this great goal."[27] Fichte worked out this pointed interpretation of Kant's account of international right in the lectures that were published as *Foundations of Natural Right*. Fichte insisted on a more explicitly cosmopolitan theoretical starting point by formulating the idea of international right not in terms of the relations between states but in terms of the "rightful relation between their citizens." The only way for citizens of different states to have lawful relations with one another was for their states to enter into treaties to "mutually guarantee the security of the other's citizens, just as each guarantees the security of its own."[28] The purpose of the international confederation that Kant described was to protect this treaty system, or international right, from an unjust aggressor state. Like Kant, Fichte specified that this confederation (*Völkerbund*) did not amount to a world state (*Völkerstaat*), because it lacked coercive power.[29] However, Fichte went on to emphasize that this confederation would necessarily be called upon to pass judgment on alleged violations of treaties, both by members and nonmembers. Moreover, he went a key step beyond Kant in specifying that it would have to be capable of going to war not only to impose its judgments, but also to "annihilate" or "destroy" (*auszutilgen*) unjust aggressor states and transform their former subjects into members of the international community.[30] In this way, the expanding confederation would gradually shade into the unification of humanity under one judge: at the end of his sketch, Fichte compared the confederation's judgments of governments to those of the popular sovereign (or nation).[31]

[26] Fichte, "Review of Perpetual Peace," 321.

[27] Ibid., 319.

[28] Fichte, *Foundations of Natural Right*, 322.

[29] The normative basis of the coercive power of the state was the impossibility of lawful relations without it, Fichte explained, whereas "a state can exist in rightful relation even without this confederation." Therefore it was merely a "voluntary association, one certainly not based on coercion" (Fichte, *Foundations of Natural Right*, 329).

[30] On Rousseau's and Kant's sensitivity to the relationship between democracy and total war, see the recent discussion in Richard Tuck, "Democracy and Terrorism," in *Political Judgement*, ed. Richard Bourke and Raymond Geuss, 313–32 (Cambridge: Cambridge University Press, 2009).

[31] Fichte, *Foundations of Natural Right*, 331; see Pauline Kleingeld, "Six Varieties of Cosmopolitanism in Late Eighteenth-Century Germany," *Journal of the History of Ideas* 60, no. 3 (July 1999): 511–12. As Kleingeld describes, Fichte envisioned a league ultimately turning into a coercive juridi-

The main thrust of Fichte's final outburst in his review of *Perpetual Peace*, however, was to emphasize a point that remained very clearly within the spirit of Kant's essay: namely, that the very first step of Kant's model—the violent process of state formation and the gradual transformation of existing states into constitutional republics—was far from complete:

> The universal insecurity that accompanies every constitution that violates right is surely so striking that one would have to believe that human beings must long since have been moved to establish a state constitution in accordance with right through considerations of their own advantage, which alone can be the motive for establishing such a constitution. This, however, has not yet happened. The advantages of disorder must therefore still generally outweigh those of order. A considerable portion of humanity must still gain more than they lose from this general disorder, and those who only lose must nevertheless continue to hope that they will win as well. And this is indeed the case.[32]

If insecurity was the dynamic that could be expected to generate a republican order, Fichte observed, things had not yet gotten bad enough. Rather than the imminent demilitarization of the international order and an expanding circle of republican constitutional settlements, Fichte predicted mounting class conflict and cycles of intensifying imperialism and war until Europe resolved its "social question" and the rest of the world gained the wherewithal to end Europe's "commercial oppression." Until then, Fichte wrote, the formation of states, let alone their transformation into republics, had to be regarded as a work in progress.

> Our states, on the whole, are still young for states; the various classes [*Stände*] and families have still only partially consolidated their relations with one another, and all of them still retain the hope of enriching themselves by robbing from the others. The goods of our states are still by no means all utilized and distributed, and there still remains much to covet and to occupy. And finally, even when everything at home has been consumed, the commercial oppression of foreign nations and portions of the world opens up a constantly flowing and lucrative source of assistance. So long as this remains the case, injustice is far from being

cal power "with the authority to enforce federal law," though it is important to emphasize that this was a result produced by conflict and that Fichte retained Kant's premise that there was no such thing as a law above states or a legitimate authority to enforce it. See also Kleingeld, "Kant's Theory of Peace," in *The Cambridge Companion to Kant and Modern Philosophy*, ed. Paul Guyer, 497 (Cambridge: Cambridge University Press, 2006).

[32] Fichte, "Review of Perpetual Peace," 320.

> sufficiently onerous to permit one to count on the universal abolition of injustice.[33]

Fichte's claim that European states were "still young for states" became a fundamental premise of *The Closed Commercial State,* which closely echoed Fichte's 1796 review in its identification of "the source of the greatest part of the current abuses." "In modern Europe there were hardly any states for a very long time," Fichte wrote in 1800. "At present we are still living among attempts to form them."[34] As Fichte also pointed out, most European states were so far from acquiring republican constitutions that they had yet to attain the absolute sovereignty and bureaucratic uniformity to which they all aspired, but remained mismatched shards of former dynastic possessions.[35] The latter observation was particularly trenchant in late-eighteenth-century Prussia, which remained such a motley patchwork that government documents still commonly referred to it as "His Majesty's states and provinces" and which could be described—as some top ministers reputedly did—as "a federation of states."[36] As we shall see, it was hardly a coincidence that *The Closed Commercial State* used the inflammatory discourse of "natural borders"—deployed in the 1790s to justify France's annexation of the Rhineland—to make this point.[37]

The Closed Commercial State further extended the thrust of Fichte's review by claiming that the European states system could not begin to be pacified unless the nature of European trade was fundamentally changed. The book ended by describing "the perpetual peace among peoples" that would be achieved "once this system becomes universal." Like Kant, Fichte did not at all envisage perpetual peace as a static condition. On the contrary, closed commercial states would enter into "the freest mutual communication" with one another and engage in a robustly competitive race for scientific discoveries, technological advances, and legislative innovations.[38] In the popular presentation of his philosophy that Fichte also published in 1800, *The Vocation of Man*, Fichte likewise envisioned humanity ultimately becoming "capable of the most unrestricted communication with itself" and forging a truly cosmopolitan community in

[33] Ibid.

[34] Fichte, *Der geschlossene Handelsstaat, Gesamtausgabe*, pt. 1, 7:95.

[35] Ibid., 7:94.

[36] C.B.A. Behrens, *Society, Government and the Enlightenment: The Experiences of Eighteenth-Century France and Prussia* (London: Thames and Hudson, 1985), 29, cited in Brendan Simms, *The Impact of Napoleon: Prussian High Politics, Foreign Policy and the Crisis of the Executive, 1797–1806* (Cambridge: Cambridge University Press, 1997), 37. See also J. H. Elliot, "A Europe of Composite Monarchies," *Past and Present* 137 (November 1992): 48–71.

[37] On the idea of natural borders—still appearing as late as post–World War II discussions of the future of the Rhineland—see Sydney Seymour Biro, *The German Policy of Revolutionary France: A Study in French Diplomacy during the War of the First Coalition, 1792–1797*, 2 vols. (Cambridge, Mass.: Harvard University Press, 1957).

[38] Fichte, *Der geschlossene Handelsstaat, Gesamtausgabe*, pt. 1, 7:141.

which "everything useful which has been found at one end of the earth will immediately be communicated and known to all."[39] *The Closed Commercial State* began, however, with a dramatic restatement of Fichte's earlier denunciations of imperialism:

> Europe has a great advantage over the other parts of the world in trade. It acquires their forces and goods without furnishing anything near an equivalent in its own forces and products. Each individual European state, however unfavorable its balance of trade might be in relation to the other European states, nonetheless draws a certain advantage from this common exploitation of the rest of the world, and never renounces the hope of improving the balance of trade in its favor and drawing a still greater advantage—all things which assuredly it would have to renounce if it quit the great European commercial society [*Handelsgesellschaft*]. In order to eliminate this basis for refusal, it would have to be shown that a relation that is not founded on right and equality—like Europe's with the rest of the world—cannot possibly subsist: a demonstration which lies beyond the limits of my present project. However, even if this demonstration were carried out, it could always be said to me: 'This condition still endures at least for now—the submission of colonies to metropoles endures, the slave trade endures—and we will not live to see any of these stop. Leave us to take advantage of it as long as it lasts; the age when it ceases can find out how to manage. If necessary let them investigate whether they can take anything from your thoughts; we cannot even wish for your goal, so we hardly need any instructions on the means for realizing it.' I admit that I have no reply to that.[40]

The Closed Commercial State, as this striking passage indicates, was concerned with the earliest stage of the Kantian model of perpetual peace. It focused on the question of how to overcome the corruption of commerce by the development of the European states system. Fichte's fundamental claim was that the European trading system had been corrupted irrevocably by the still incomplete rise of states and that existing states could not be pacified until they had dismantled the remnants of the common market that predated their formation. The middle book of *The Closed Commercial State* developed this claim in a succinct yet sophisticated "contemporary history" of "the condition of commercial relations among presently existing states."[41]

[39] Fichte, *Vocation of Man*, 86.
[40] Fichte, *Der geschlossene Handelsstaat*, *Gesamtausgabe*, pt. 1, 7:44.
[41] Ibid., 7:91.

Fichte's History of Commerce

Fichte's historical model considered the development of modern European commerce from the conquest of Rome by Germanic tribes to the formation of modern states and their intensifying involvement in international markets. Fichte described European states as the product of Germanic kingship and mores combined with the influence of Roman law. After the fall of Rome in the West, Fichte explained, there was no longer any real civil authority. The concepts of state, subject, and authority could not be applied to this society of "half barbarians." Among the Germanic tribes that conquered Europe, kings were no more than leaders of armies that came together during times of war. Otherwise, the populace remained "without political bonds," and each was "his own judge and defender." Some capacity for arbitration was furnished by the relations of serf and lord, vassal and suzerain, which were the sole sources of social cohesion. But this was still a far cry, Fichte stressed, from the notion of a nation united by laws.[42] Indeed, these bonds were so weak that the same individual could be the vassal of one king and possess allodial lands in a second kingdom—which meant that in the event of a war between the two kings, he would have to fight "in person" for the first king, while simultaneously "standing his ground" as the owner of land on the other side. In sum, Fichte claimed, "they lived, in fact, in the state of nature."[43]

Fichte's Christendom was able to develop as a common market thanks to the universal use of gold and silver as a medium of exchange.[44] Commerce was limited in extent, but Fichte stressed that it remained a natural exchange between different regions with complementary natural endowments, unconstrained by any kind of geopolitical considerations. In other words, the reciprocity that Kant had called the "spirit of commerce" remained untainted by the competitive dynamics generated by the rivalry of independent states. Given Europe's common market and shared mores, and in the absence of states, Fichte found it possible to describe Europe as a single national community. Fichte drew a contrast with classical antiquity. Ancient cities were rigorously separated peoples for whom all foreigners were either enemies or barbarians. By contrast, Western Christendom formed a single nation of Germanic origin, held together by common mores, religion, and form of government. "No wonder," he observed, "that these populations, united by everything and without state constitutions (which are what especially separates humanity) to separate them, since there

[42] "*Weit entfernt, daß sie Zweck an sich, daß die Gesetze das eigentliche Bindungsmittel* der Nation hätten sein sollen" (ibid., 7:93). Note Fichte's use of "Nation" here rather than "Volk," to refer to the contractual idea of a population united under a common judge.

[43] Ibid.

[44] Compare John Locke's account of the state of nature in *Two Treatises of Government*, ed. Peter Laslett (Cambridge: Cambridge University Press, 1988), 293ff.

were none—no wonder they saw themselves as one nation, and behaved as one; no wonder they mingled, traveled, engaged in business and commerce, used each others' services, and that someone who arrived in another region believed he was still at home."[45]

According to Fichte, modern states began to form in Europe with the introduction of Roman law. The application of the Roman concept of imperator to modern kings and emperors led to the first appearance of "truly political concepts and institutions." Starting in France, which Fichte singled out as his model, monarchy developed as serfs and vassals gradually became subjects and their former lords became their judges. Fichte emphasized the contrast between this account of state formation (which, broadly speaking, followed Montesquieu's lead) and the juridical theory of the social contract. Modern European states were formed not through the "assembly and union of unassociated individuals under the unity of the law," as the model of the social contract supposed, but "rather through the division and fragmentation of a single, great, yet only weakly associated mass of men."[46]

Crucially, Fichte maintained that Europe's common market had not been fundamentally altered by the mere appearance of separate political units. The cosmopolitan or "national" character of the trading system was not diminished: every European continued to enjoy untrammeled natural liberty in trade. So long as the governments of particular states continued to fund themselves through the revenues from public lands, Fichte explained, they were just another set of individual actors within the "great commercial state" of Christendom. Like their own citizens, these governments were free agents in the state of nature, enjoying their natural liberty just like everyone else. Their commercial

[45] Fichte, *Der geschlossene Handelsstaat*, *Gesamtausgabe*, pt. 1, 7:93. Edmund Burke's nearly identical depiction in the first of his *Letters on a Regicide Peace* (1796) nicely illustrates that this was a widespread view of what Europe had been, and that it was not tied to any particular view of what it had since become and why: "From this resemblance in the modes of intercourse, and in the whole form and fashion of life, no citizen of Europe could be altogether an exile in any part of it. There was nothing more than a pleasing variety to recreate and instruct the mind, to enrich the imagination, and to meliorate the heart. When a man travelled or resided for health, pleasure, business or necessity, from his own country, he never felt himself quite abroad" (Burke, *Letters on a Regicide Peace* [1795–97], in *Select Works of Edmund Burke*, ed. Francis Canavan [Indianapolis, Ind.: Liberty Fund, 1999], 3:134). Herder's "The Origins of Modern Europe," in book 20 of his *Ideas toward the Philosophy of the History of Mankind* (completed in 1791), had also described Gothic Europe as a single commonwealth or commercial state (*Handelsstaat*). In chapter 1, "The Spirit of Commerce in Europe," Herder's narrative anticipated Fichte's in describing the trading networks linking the city republics of Gothic Europe as "an extensive commercial state" (*weitverbreiteter Handelsstaat*) stretching from the Mediterranean to the Baltic and from the Atlantic to the Black Sea, and as having been founded on "genuine principles of security and mutual aid" that were "probably a pattern for the future state of all the commercial nations of Europe" (Herder, *Ideen zur Philosophie der Geschichte*, 2:442–43; see also 2:479).

[46] Fichte, *Der geschlossene Handelsstaat*, *Gesamtausgabe*, pt. 1, 7:94.

relations were not constrained by any obligations; all were independently entitled to as much of others' surplus production as they could pay for with their own gold. Individual states and their citizens continued to trade freely throughout Europe and with other parts of the world. Only political constitutions now divided the population of Europe and qualified its cosmopolitan unity—a political division that was reinforced by the end of religious unity after the Reformation. Fichte presented modern commerce as a holdover that predated this division of Europe. "It is no wonder," Fichte proclaimed,

> that this separation, which occurred not long ago, is not yet completed; that notable traces of the former cohesion remain; and that a good portion of our concepts and institutions still seem to presuppose the perpetuation of this nullified cohesion.
>
> Among other things, our commercial system was also formed during that unity of Christian Europe, and at least its main features continue to the present age.[47]

The key turning point in Fichte's historical narrative was the introduction of national taxation. When governments began to collect taxes, they immediately acquired an interest in the wealth of their subjects: the wealthier their subjects, the higher the tax revenues. "In the government's conception," Fichte explained, "these taxpaying citizens were unified into a unity, into a single body, in whose prosperity [*Wohlhabenheit*] it was interested."[48] Since these national taxes were collected in the universal currency of the European commercial republic, the government's interest in the prosperity of its subjects amounted to an interest in their success in the international market. In short, promoting a positive balance of trade became a reason of state. This transformation of the relationship between states and their subjects was distinctly one sided, Fichte stressed, because individual citizens continued to regard themselves as independent commercial agents "without a common interest." The concept of a "national fortune" (*Nationalvermögen*) and "of a nation which has this fortune" had now become intelligible, but only in a significantly incomplete sense. The members of a nation remained fully autonomous commercial agents in a state of nature. A state in this half-anarchic condition "is indeed a nation united through laws and through a common judge, but in no way is it united through a common fortune." For a state to become a genuine national community, it would have to extract itself from commercial anarchy. Nature, Fichte hinted, had in fact pushed governments in this direction, forcing them unintentionally to expand their horizons by giving them "an interest through profit which they should already have for the sake of right."[49]

[47] Ibid., 7:94.
[48] Ibid., 7:100.
[49] Ibid., 7:100–1.

The half-anarchic condition of European nations and their lack of a "common fortune" did not pose much of a problem for states or their subjects so long as human needs remained simple and human industry still operated on a relatively small scale.[50] Initially, those who failed to succeed in European trade had little to fear:

> With the minor extent of industry there was no fear that the market would be closed off, that the producer and the merchant would suffer, or that they would encounter a lack of food; with the simple way of life and limited human needs, neither did the producer have to do without customary goods.[51]

However, as living standards began to climb, both individuals and states became exposed to the full implications of the undiminished "anarchy of trade."

> What transpires without great injustice or oppression among nations with a simple way of life is transformed with increased needs into the most fearsome injustice and the source of great misery.[52]

To become a relatively rich member of the great European commercial republic was to command a greater share of the product of others' labor. Naturally, everyone valued his own labor more than the labor of others and preferred that others spend their time working for him rather than the other way around. Fichte appropriated Hobbes's signature phrase to describe the resulting dynamic as "an endless war of all against all in the trading public, the war between buyers and sellers." Fichte echoed Rousseau in suggesting that the state of war described by Hobbes was a condition that was aligned with the intensification of the bonds of commercial society:

> This war becomes more and more violent, dangerous, and unjust in its consequences as the world becomes more populous, as the commercial state expands through adventitious acquisitions, as production and the arts increase, and as the quantity of goods that come into circulation increases and diversifies together with everyone's needs.[53]

The Hobbesian dynamic manifests itself in Fichte's mordant account of the "war" between producers and consumers over price. The consumer resorted to the rhetoric of free trade, Fichte charged, in order to extort the producer's merchandise: by "free trade," the consumer meant "the freedom for the producer to close off his markets, to find no outlet for his goods, and to sell his goods well

[50] Ibid., 7:94–95, 98.
[51] Ibid., 7:94–95.
[52] Ibid., 7:98.
[53] Ibid.

under their value out of necessity." To this end, the consumer demanded strong competition among producers and merchants and sought to compel the latter to sell "at the price his generosity still consents to offer." If the consumers were successful, "the working man gets poor and hard-working families waste away in misery and privation, or else emigrate away from an unjust people." For their part—whether in self-defense or otherwise—producers found devious ways of manipulating supply and increasing prices or lowering quality. The producer's counterstrategies played out in Hobbesian fashion: "Through them he places the consumer in danger of suddenly doing without his ordinary needs or of being obliged to pay extraordinarily dearly for them, and of finding himself indigent in other respects." Ultimately, Fichte stressed, natural liberty in commerce left everyone's livelihood at everyone else's mercy. "Nobody could guarantee the perpetuation of his condition through the perpetuation of his labor," he concluded, "because people want to be thoroughly free to destroy each other."[54]

The expansion of trade and industry also exposed states within the European republic to increasingly stark alternatives. If states never intervened in the commerce of their subjects, Fichte claimed, relatively rich states with a positive balance of trade would continually grow richer, while relatively poor states would become increasingly impoverished. In the former case, a state with a positive balance of trade would receive an influx of global currency. The population would use this surplus to purchase "superfluities" (*Entbehrliche*) from other members of the European republic—meaning that "the foreigner who can hardly meet his own basic needs is forced to work for its pleasures" and that this state "continuously augments its internal well-being at the cost of foreigners' well-being." Alternatively, the rich state's government would collect the surplus in tax revenue and use it to become more powerful.

A negative balance of trade would result in the outflow of global currency from a state and a consequent rise in prices. Either the government would become less powerful, or it would extract a greater proportion of the population's shrinking resources. If a relatively poor state did not succeed in intervening to reverse the balance of trade, it would fall into a terminal cycle of depopulation and capital flight, a scenario that Fichte described in lurid detail. Depopulation would enable the remaining inhabitants to export the raw materials that had sustained the former population; but as this trade expanded, fewer and fewer workers could be supported, and finally the harvest itself would be exported. Some additional revenue might then be generated from foreign speculation in the now depopulated and uncultivated lands, but eventually the state would sell itself for foreign subsidies. At this point, it would become no more than a "province of another state" and "a means to the other state's arbitrary ends"—the fate that Fichte would attribute to Germany after the Napoleonic conquests

[54] Ibid., 7:98–99.

in his *Addresses to the German Nation*.[55] This downward cycle would end with the complete desolation of the arts and of commerce. It would produce "savage descendants of a cultivated people," who had sold off their patrimony and their future. No longer capable of sustaining any greater industry, they would scratch out their meager living by peddling "timber, animal pelts, dried fish, and the like."[56]

Since the security of states had come to depend on the success of their populations in international markets, European states had not in fact refrained from intervening in these commercial relations. Rich and poor states alike were concerned to protect their tax bases and maintain their relative military power by shifting the balance of trade in their favor. They had adopted the same set of strategies to do so, regardless of whether they were trying to retard and reverse the decline of a poor nation or maintain and increase the prosperity of a rich nation. States began to discourage exports of raw materials and to encourage exports of manufactures. They imposed heavy tariffs or even outright prohibitions on the import of foreign goods while subsidizing their own exports. They sought to encourage agricultural productivity, attract skilled workers, import raw materials in order to reexport them with added value, and finally to gain the shipping trade of the great European commercial state.[57] The question for a contemporary history of Europe in 1800 was whether these policies had been successful in achieving their ends.

Doubtless, becoming a net exporter was a good way for a government to increase its tax revenues, or at least to combat their decline. Indeed, these measures were "not without favorable results," Fichte allowed, in stemming the losses of nations that were losers in commerce and in sparing them from descending into a horrific downward spiral.[58] Fichte insisted, however, that such mercantilist strategies would never succeed in maintaining or increasing a nation's standing. The problem was that these strategies could no longer be effective once they were adopted by all sides. It was clear, Fichte wrote, "that as soon as one government publicly follows these measures, and seeks to draw exclusive advantages for itself and its nation from its inclusion in a common commercial republic, all the other governments which are suffering as a result will most likely follow the same measures, if they are only a little wise."[59] Fichte took the position, which many eighteenth-century thinkers associated with David Hume, that a rich country could not hope to maintain its commercial predomi-

[55] Fichte, *Reden an die deutsche Nation* (1808–9), trans. Gregory Moore as *Addresses to the German Nation* (Cambridge: Cambridge University Press, 2008), 9; cf. 144.

[56] Fichte, *Der geschlossene Handelsstaat*, *Gesamtausgabe*, pt. 1, 7:103.

[57] Ibid., 7:104–5.

[58] Ibid., 7:107.

[59] Ibid., 7:106.

nance indefinitely.[60] Once any nation had achieved a favorable balance of trade, Fichte observed, all the others resorted to whatever means were necessary to weaken it and restore the equilibrium. If this goal could not be achieved by weakening the predominant power directly, then it would be accomplished at the expense of still weaker states. In such conditions, European commercial relations could no longer be characterized as the reciprocally beneficial exchange of commodities between regions with diverse endowments. Instead, states now vied for markets as they had previously fought over territory: "In addition to the hostile tendency that all states had against all others anyway, because of their territorial boundaries, a new one over commercial interest has arisen."[61] As Hume had famously proclaimed, commerce had become a "reason of state," another arena for the kind of guarded and watchful rivalry between gladiatorial sovereigns that Hobbes had described as the state of war.[62]

Fichte's account highlighted how this commercial rivalry had spun out of control, leading to world wars and spawning dangerously corrupt and depraved political ideologies.[63] Fichte cited the notorious example of the Dutch, who uprooted spice plants and dumped spices overboard in order to raise prices on the European market. The rush to empire was another example of how states were willing to inflict losses on themselves in order to cause still greater losses for their competitors. Such monopolistic and beggar-thy-neighbor policies were indicative of a "secret universal commercial war" that had escalated to overt warfare. "Thus halves of continents are bought in opposition to a people's political principles," Fichte noted, "because the war is actually directed against the commerce of those who were bought, to their detriment." In short, Fichte identified the commercial rivalry between states as the underlying source of interstate conflict in contemporary Europe: "Conflicting commercial interests are often the true cause of wars for which different pretexts have been furnished."[64] Conflicting mercantile interests gave rise to ideologies that spread these wars around the globe: "Eventually political concepts which could not be more dangerous were generated through these commercial interests, and these concepts generated wars, whose true reason was not concealed, but displayed openly." Mercantile interests had launched European states into bloody global wars over

[60] Hume's position was not, in fact, so straightforward; see Hont, *Jealousy of Trade*, 267–322, originally published as "The 'Rich Country–Poor Country' Debate in Scottish Classical Political Economy," in *Wealth and Virtue: The Shaping of Political Economy in the Scottish Enlightenment*, ed. Istvan Hont and Michael Ignatieff, 271–316 (Cambridge: Cambridge University Press, 1983).

[61] Fichte, *Der geschlossene Handelsstaat*, *Gesamtausgabe*, pt. 1, 7:106.

[62] Hume, "Of Civil Liberty" (1741), in *Essays*, 88–89. Hume's essay was originally entitled "Of Liberty and Despotism."

[63] Fichte, *Der geschlossene Handelsstaat*, *Gesamtausgabe*, pt. 1, 7:107, 117–18.

[64] Ibid., 7:106–7.

the "dominion of the seas," a doctrine that Fichte dismissed as an absurdity, and over the right to monopolize the lucrative trade with China and Japan.[65]

Fichte's indictment was that the way European states had responded to this predicament had failed to deliver security for either themselves or their subjects. This was to controvert Hobbes's famous remark in *Leviathan* (1651) explaining why the natural liberty of sovereigns was not completely analogous to that of individuals: "Because they uphold thereby the industry of their subjects, there does not follow from it that misery which accompanies the liberty of particular men."[66] Like Rousseau, Fichte declared outright that this was not the case for contemporary European states: "No state that counts on export to foreign markets [*auf Absatz an das Ausland*], and stimulates and directs the country's industry on account of it, can secure the duration of this market for its subjects."[67] Even extremely high tariffs, Fichte claimed, could not completely secure producers from foreign competitors who might someday find ways to flood the market or add value to their products. On the other hand, customers seeking to satisfy their needs remained dependent on the availability of imports and vulnerable to fluctuations in price.

The half anarchy of modern European states was no better than the complete anarchy that had preceded their formation, Fichte concluded, and yet it had introduced new problems. High tariffs caused prices to rise and therefore lowered the standard of living; an effective tax administration required the creation of an enormous bureaucracy, which lowered productivity. The taxes and tariffs imposed by states ultimately inspired a vague sense of resentment among their subjects, who had been joined by political constitutions but otherwise remained "free and autonomous members" of the "immense commercial republic"—indeed, states tacitly presupposed this fact by taxing their subjects in the global currency. This resentment of a dimly perceived but acutely felt injustice undermined the authority of the state and caused underground trade (encouraged by competing states) to flourish. In such conditions, Fichte observed, "cheating the government ceases to be a misdeed, and becomes a permissible and glorious act of self-defense against the common enemy. It becomes impossible for someone who does not want to participate in these general practices to continue to be industrious."[68] Fichte imagined a scenario in which outright civil war and a return to complete anarchy would soon follow. Governments would resort to increasingly draconian punishments in order to suppress these underground markets, but their searches and informants would only intensify the mutual mistrust. Haphazard enforcement would generate even more re-

[65] Ibid., 7:107.

[66] Hobbes, *Leviathan*, 90.

[67] Fichte, *Der geschlossene Handelsstaat*, *Gesamtausgabe*, pt. 1, 7:108.

[68] Ibid., 7:110–11.

sentment; the battle between smugglers and the government would escalate into open warfare; and a brutalized mob would make tax collectors disappear without a trace.[69]

Fichte's historical model delivered the insight that the European states system could be pacified only after commercial rivalry had been tamed. War was unavoidable, Fichte insisted, until the true causes of war had been eliminated:

> It has always been the privilege of philosophers to groan about wars. The author likes them no more than anyone else, but he believes that he realizes their unavoidability in present circumstances, and considers it impractical [*unzweckmäßig*] to complain about what cannot be avoided. If war is to be eliminated, the basis of war must be eliminated.[70]

Fichte claimed that a peaceful republican order could not emerge until states had eliminated the problem of jealousy of trade and that they could only do so by fully realizing the still-incomplete separation of Christendom into independent states:

> All institutions which permit or assume direct commerce [*Verkehr*] between a citizen and the citizen of another state fundamentally regard both as citizens of one state, and are relics and results of a constitution which has long since been overthrown. They are parts of a bygone world which do not fit into ours.[71]

In sum, states had to end the "anarchy of trade" just as they had ended political anarchy. The commercial state had to be "completed" (*geschlossen*), just as the juridical state had been.[72] The path to perpetual peace outlined by *The Closed Commercial State* required that states thoroughly extricate themselves from the competition for international markets and reorient their economies for domestic production.

Fichte's analysis of commercial rivalry effectively ruled out the supposition that global commerce could serve as the vehicle for the gradual reunion of humanity under a cosmopolitan constitution. Fichte echoed Rousseau and Herder in his scorn for the kind of "empty" cosmopolitanism that he attributed to international commerce. As some of Fichte's other writings claimed in greater detail, expanding international markets could not provide an adequate foundation for the kind of aesthetic education in morality that Kant and many others (including himself) envisioned.

[69] Ibid., 7:111.
[70] Ibid., 7:118.
[71] Ibid., 7:95.
[72] Ibid.

> The advantages of the extensive system of international trade—the mutual acquaintance of nations through voyages and trade—have been greatly extolled. Very well: if only we really were peoples and nations; if only a solid national education [*Nationalbildung*] existed somewhere that might combine peoples through their dealings with one another, and meld them together into something comprehensively and purely human. However, it seems to me that through our striving to be everything, and to be at home everywhere, we have become nothing, and find ourselves at home nowhere.[73]

In Fichte's analysis, the growth of global markets had distorted the development of culture by confounding the means for achieving material welfare with those for obtaining national glory. The result was the kind of nationalism (*Nationalhaß*) that Fichte associated primarily with the Anglo-French rivalry for preeminence.[74] Fichte proposed to eliminate such distortions by dismantling the international trading system. A closed commercial state could then allow the development of a healthy culture to proceed apace within its own borders:

> It is clear that in a nation which has closed in this way, whose members live only among themselves, and very little with foreigners, whose particular way of life, institutions, and mores are sustained by these regulations, who love their fatherland and everything of their fatherland with devotion, a higher degree of national honor and a sharply determined national character will develop very quickly. This will be a different, absolutely new nation. The introduction of the national currency is its true creation.[75]

Over and beyond the achievement of a healthy national culture, Fichte promised that the closing of the commercial state would in fact pave the way for the eventual reunion of humanity by achieving "humanity in one country": "The further perfection of all human affairs rapidly follows its course in it, separated from the remaining world."[76] The primary means for reuniting humanity once it had been divided successfully into closed commercial states was not commerce, but scientific and cultural exchange:

> There is nothing which entirely cancels all differences between positions and between peoples—and which belongs purely and simply to man as such, rather than the citizen—other than science [*Wissenschaft*]. Through it, and through it alone, men are and ought continually be

[73] Ibid., 7:141.

[74] Ibid., 7:118. Fichte developed this analysis of nationalism in greater depth in some of his later writings, including the *Patriotic Dialogues* and the *Addresses to the German Nation*.

[75] Fichte, *Der geschlossene Handelsstaat*, *Gesamtausgabe*, pt. 1, 7:139.

[76] Ibid., 7:133–34.

> connected, since in every other respect their separation into peoples is complete. Only science remains their common property, since they have divided all else among themselves. No commercial state shall cancel this connection; rather, it shall favor it, for the enrichment of science through the united energy of humankind even promotes its exclusive earthly ends. The treasures of foreign literature shall be imported by funded academies, and exchanged for domestic ones.[77]

Only under such conditions, Fichte maintained, could the natural trade of European Christendom be re-created artificially in a world of states. Once established, closed commercial states could safely engage in a complementary trade with one another so long as it was conducted by governments rather than private individuals, and without any motive for profit: "Among such states, destined by nature itself to a continuous bartering trade [*Tauschhandel*], a commercial treaty can be set up."[78] Fichte's example of such a mutually advantageous arrangement—the wine-growing countries of southern Europe could export their surplus wine to the north in exchange for surplus grain—elicited mockery from some contemporary readers who supposed that Fichte would find his exile in Prussia unbearable without a secure supply of imported wine.[79]

Prussia and the Anglo-French Debate of 1800

After a string of defeats in 1799, Napoleon's victory at the Battle of Marengo in June 1800 drove the Habsburgs out of Italy. Russia's rupture with Austria and Britain spelled the end of the second coalition against France, and the possibility of a peace settlement appeared on the near horizon. In the autumn of 1800, the French vision of a future peace was prominently put forward in d'Hauterive's *De l'état de la France à la fin de l'an VIII*. D'Hauterive's diplomatic career had begun in Moldavia and had taken him to New York after the French Revolution, where he served as the French consul. After losing this position over charges of financial improprieties, he made his living by farming outside New York until he was rediscovered by Talleyrand, who was also in exile. Both d'Hauterive and Talleyrand returned to Paris in 1798, where d'Hauterive was quickly promoted to the senior ranks of the French foreign ministry.[80] D'Hauterive remained a

[77] Ibid., 7:141.

[78] Ibid., 7:136.

[79] See, for example, Christian Gottfried Körner to Friedrich Schiller, 29 December 1800, in Fuchs, Lauth, and Schieche, *Fichte im Gespräch*, 2:423–24.

[80] See Alexis-François Artaud de Montor, *Histoire de la vie et des travaux politiques du comte d'Hauterive, comprenant une partie des actes de la diplomatie française, depuis 1784 jusqu'en 1830*, 2nd ed. (Paris: Le Clere, 1839). On d'Hauterive's time in New York, see also Rothschild, "Language and Empire."

close associate of Talleyrand, and his book was widely received as an official statement of French foreign policy. His peace plan, based on an analysis of the European trading system, quickly generated a spirited rebuttal from several pro-English writers, notably including Friedrich Gentz. In the context of this international debate, Fichte's analysis of commerce was closely aligned, against Gentz, with contemporary French criticism of England's commercial supremacy, like d'Hauterive's. Fichte's *Closed Commercial State* was a bold proposal for Prussia to pursue a pro-French strategy. It explained how Prussia could take advantage of a French-led reorganization of central Europe in order to transform itself into a prospective member of a pacified republican international order.

Like Fichte, d'Hauterive developed a historical account of the European states system that attributed the breakdown of European order to the rise of commerce and the outbreak of commercial rivalry. D'Hauterive's overtly polemical account was designed to counter the charge, made most famously by Edmund Burke, that France had ignited the wars of the 1790s through its egregious violations of the law of nations. On the contrary, d'Hauterive claimed, it was English trade policy that had already undermined the law of nations and ultimately sparked the chaos that had engulfed all Europe. D'Hauterive described England as the first state whose interests had come to be bound up entirely with the commercial interests of its traders. His icon for jealousy of trade was Oliver Cromwell, the lord protector of the English Commonwealth, whom he depicted as assuming the jealous posture of the Hobbesian sovereign with respect to commerce: "Cromwell was the real founder of the maritime system, the real author of the naval wars of Europe. He conceived the idea of fixing their industry upon a permanent state of conspiracy and war against the industry of others, of separating for ever their interests from the interests of Europe . . . He proclaimed the *Navigation Act*; by that bold and decisive measure placed the commerce of his nation in a position of constant jealousy and enmity with the commerce of all others."[81]

D'Hauterive claimed that England's rise to global dominance had thoroughly corrupted the European states system. England had elevated a "false and expensive principle of imitative emulation" into the guiding principle of its foreign policy. Its constant goal was to maintain and extend its commercial preeminence by whatever means necessary. D'Hauterive characterized this as a quest for universal monarchy in the form of commercial monopoly.[82] The effect

[81] D'Hauterive, *State of the French Republic*, 19.

[82] Ibid., 130. This happened to be the same charge that the English themselves had leveled against the Dutch during the Anglo-Dutch wars of the previous century; see Steven Pincus, "The English Debate over Universal Monarchy," in *A Union for Empire: Political Thought and the British Union of 1707*, ed. John Robertson, 37–62 (Cambridge: Cambridge University Press, 1995). D'Hauterive amplified the well-worn complaint by linking England's pursuit of commercial monopoly with its financial power. Claiming that England's "maritime system" could easily bring other states under

of England's new constellation of trade and war had been to "introduce into the political system of Europe a perpetual principle of disturbance, versatility, and agitation."[83] As other European states rushed to catch up with England, they found themselves less and less secure. Abuses multiplied, and by the eve of the French Revolution, d'Hauterive clamed, Europe had already been overcome by a "general disorganization," a lawless state of war. General war had arisen in the 1790s, then, not because France had acted like the rogue state described by the authorities on the law of nations, but because the common norms of European civilization had already been undermined. The fundamental cause of the war, d'Hauterive claimed, was "the uncertain and insecure position in which all the states of Europe, at the time of the French revolution, found themselves placed with regard to each another."[84] This insecurity was in turn a consequence of the vicious commercial rivalry that England had instigated and imposed on the rest of Europe. Jealousy of trade had destroyed the law of nations. The only order left in contemporary Europe was the rule of the stronger, and that was England. Ultimately, d'Hauterive argued, the real fault lay with those states that still failed to perceive that England represented the greatest threat to their security. He found this misperception to have been excusable a century earlier, when all Europe had aligned itself against Louis XIV during the War of the Spanish Succession, but that was no longer the case. "At present," d'Hauterive asked, "what illusion could have prevented the states of the continent from seeing that, in destroying, or but merely in weakening, France, the tendency must be blindly to subject all the interests of the political system of Europe to the movements of the maritime system, and the interests of all the maritime states to the almost arbitrary direction of a single power?"[85] D'Hauterive charged that English naval supremacy had allowed England's admiralty courts to substitute their own law for the old law of nations. Britain's Navigation Acts were a "law of perpetual war" that had gone unanswered.[86] They subordinated the general utility encapsulated in commerce to the particular interests of one powerful state. Many anti-English writers (including, as we have seen, Fichte) claimed that England's Navigation Acts were a legacy of earlier claims to "dominion of the seas." One French writer later went to some lengths to demonstrate that England's present efforts to justify its commercial supremacy were something

---

its sway once they were dependent on English capital, he deemed the political independence of the United States of America to be therefore meaningless.

[83] D'Hauterive, *State of the French Republic*, 26.

[84] Ibid., 29.

[85] Ibid., 67.

[86] Ibid., 171.

of a national tradition, which he traced back to John Selden's refutation of Hugo Grotius's classic defense of Dutch trade, *The Free Sea* (1609).[87]

Underlying d'Hauterive's polemics was the same claim that Fichte's *Closed Commercial State* made about commerce and perpetual peace: namely, that a permanent peace settlement could not be achieved until commercial rivalry had been eliminated. A new system of international right would not endure unless England's commercial hegemony was replaced by a new trading system. This new trading system would operate according to the principle of reciprocity rather than jealousy. In other words, it would embody the spirit of commerce rather than the spirit of conquest. D'Hauterive described this view of commerce as the legacy of Archbishop Fénelon. Fénelon had established that states could expand more through peaceful internal development, by providing expanding markets for one another's surplus products, than by trying to conquer one another's territory.[88] Even if this insight had not yet penetrated all the halls of power, d'Hauterive wrote, it was increasingly being acknowledged "that the most solid basis of the riches of one nation, is the riches of all those to whom it is allied by relations of commerce; that commerce is a vast organization which has a general life, and general interests; and that this life and these interests can receive no partial injury without exciting sympathy and pain in the whole aggregate."[89]

D'Hauterive's strategy for realizing Fénelon's principles was a revival of various French schemes dating from the previous round of systemic crisis and global war, in the 1740s and 1750s. His plan for ending England's commercial monopoly followed a script that had been outlined in 1756 by Victor Riqueti, the marquis de Mirabeau, in his wildly popular *L'Ami des Hommes, ou traité de la population*. Mirabeau had warned that Europe would descend into a new dark age if the ferocious rivalry among commercial states for dominion of the seas were not brought to a peaceful resolution.[90] He envisioned France becoming the arbiter of a system of treaties establishing mutual free trade and fraternity among all commercial states. France would vanquish England's monopolistic Navigation Acts by fighting a war to establish universal free trade once and for all. In doing so, it would be fighting for "the common cause of humanity" and would therefore become "the friend of mankind." The war would end with

[87] Joseph-Mathias-Gérard de Rayneval, *De la liberté des mers* (Paris, 1811), 1:vi–x. See John Selden, *Mare Clausam* (1635), trans. Marchamont Nedham as *Of the Dominion or Ownership of the Sea* (London: Du-Gard, 1652); and Hugo Grotius, *Mare Liberum* (1609), trans. Richard Hakluyt as *The Free Sea*, ed. David Armitage (Indianapolis, Ind.: Liberty Fund, 2004).

[88] D'Hauterive, *State of the French Republic*, 130–31.

[89] Ibid., 148.

[90] Victor Riqueti, marquis de Mirabeau, *L'ami des hommes, ou traité de la population* (1756; Paris: Guillaumin, 1883), 498.

France "imposing the yoke of humanity" and making "entry into the universal confraternity of trade" the basis of the new treaty system.[91]

In d'Hauterive's version of Mirabeau's "confraternity of trade," France and its allies would enact a "federal" act of navigation. Unlike a system of competing national navigation acts, which reflected national jealousies and hatreds, the fundamental purpose of this federal navigation act would be "to produce its own abolition, and that of all acts of the same nature." The Hobbesian "law of perpetual war" would be replaced by a Fénelonian "law of reciprocity," and the spirit of conquest would give way to the spirit of commerce. France and its partners would agree to exempt one another from commercial restrictions while collectively imposing them on England in order to thwart its bid for commercial monopoly and force it to join the new system of free trade. In this way, d'Hauterive promised, "the ideas of association being blended with those of prohibition, they will produce, by degrees, a general association, and, by a necessary consequence, the abolition of all the prohibitory laws."[92] Then commerce would be able to take up its natural function as the catalyst for a cosmopolitan order. D'Hauterive maintained that France was well positioned to impose this yoke of humanity on Europe and lay the foundations for a pacified international order. Following the lead of many French political economists since Jean-François Melon in the 1730s, d'Hauterive pointed out that England's power was relatively precarious: it was highly dependent on a command of export markets as well as a continuing faith in its strained financial system. By contrast, France was relatively self-sufficient and secure. Its successful political recovery from the turmoil of the revolution, and its recent military success on the Continent, now enabled it to lay the foundations for the new economic order.

The key prerequisite for overcoming England's economic dominance was a fundamental restructuring of the balance of power in Germany. This aspect of d'Hauterive's peace strategy also harked back to French thinking of the 1730s and 1740s.[93] The old European balance of power, based on the dynastic rivalry between the houses of Bourbon and Habsburg, had failed to respond to the dramatic rise of commerce, thereby leaving England to take full advantage of it. The fragmentary territories of the Holy Roman Empire remained a perennial source of instability. Germany's antiquated political landscape rendered it incapable of participating in the kind of commercial system envisaged by Fénelon. On the contrary, it offered many occasions for conflict and numerous opportunities for the English financial colossus to insinuate itself there in pursuit of its own interests. The map of Germany had to be redrawn so that it consisted

[91] Ibid., 505.

[92] D'Hauterive, *State of the French Republic*, 172.

[93] See François Labbé, "La rêve irénique du marquis de la Tierce: Franc-Maçonnerie, lumières, et projets de paix perpétuelle dans le cadre du Saint-Empire sous le règne de Charles VII (1741–1745)," *Francia* 18, no. 2 (1991): 47–69.

of several viable and secure states that would no longer serve as either pawns of English finance or prey for Habsburg and Hohenzollern expansionism. Such states would be capable of participating in the benefits of commerce and contributing to the construction of a new system of free trade: "By the advantages of navigation becoming more generally distributed, the interest of commercial independence might be more forcibly and universally felt."[94] D'Hauterive's message to Prussia, Russia, and Austria was to accommodate themselves to this plan or have it imposed upon them by force. He emphasized that French policy toward these powers was also geared toward integrating them into a future commercial order: the last peace settlement with Austria, the Treaty of Campo Formio in 1797, had granted Venice to the defeated Austrians with the intent of turning them into a maritime and commercial power.

D'Hauterive's peace plan and his vision of a reformed Germany was one variation on a strategy that was widely discussed in the 1790s.[95] This strategy was promoted with particular energy by Sieyès, who had taken a leading role in French diplomacy upon his reemergence into active political life in 1794. Equipping France to overcome England's naval supremacy was Sieyès's chief priority, as the Dutch republicans discovered to their dismay when they encountered him at the negotiating table in 1795.[96] The key to a permanent peace, Sieyès later wrote to Talleyrand, was to transform Germany into federations of republics. These federations would secure France's borders as well as "defend Germany from English commerce" and make the world safe for republicanism:

> Dare to establish, in northwest Germany from the Yssel or the Ems to the Baltic, a league or confederation as representative as possible, and then wage a war against Great Britain in which its fleets would be impotent, and you will have peace upon the sea, true peace, solid and permanent, for you and for all western Europe. Your agents abroad will then be able to show themselves to be republican without fear of hampering affairs, and, to speak the truth, the Republic will be recognized politically, morally and civilly.[97]

Sieyès was closely associated with the Treaty of Basel between France and Prussia, which broke up the first coalition against France and set the stage for a reorganization of Germany in April 1795. One Prussian admirer of Sieyès, Karl Friedrich Knesebeck (1768–1848), had even made an ill-advised and unauthorized attempt to push Prussia to the negotiating table by publishing a peace plan

[94] D'Hauterive, *State of the French Republic*, 116–17.

[95] Biro, *German Policy of Revolutionary France*, 2:622–29.

[96] Glyndon Van Deusen, *Sieyes: His Life and His Nationalism* (New York: Columbia University Press, 1932), 109–12.

[97] Sieyès to Talleyrand, 25 August 1798 and 26 January 1799, in Bailleu, *Preussen und Frankreich*, 1:486, 497.

in Sieyès's name.[98] According to the treaty, Prussia effectively ceded its possessions on the left bank of the Rhine to France, pending future compensation elsewhere in Germany under the auspices of a general peace settlement. France secured its "natural border" on the Rhine, and Prussia guaranteed the neutrality of northern Germany and focused on its expansion to the east. Although Knesebeck's pamphlet was unauthorized, it did reflect Sieyès's genuine interest in getting Prussia to play a constructive role in the broader transformation of Germany. In 1798, Sieyès himself embarked on a mission to Berlin as the "extraordinary ambassador" of France in order to propose such a Franco-Prussian alliance. One prominent aristocratic observer later remembered the provocative arrival of "the notorious Sieyès, a villainous-looking fellow," who made his first appearance at the Prussian court without a wig and wearing an "enormous tricolor sash." "A frightful omen," Friedrich August Ludwig von der Marwitz recalled, "of what we would experience eight years later" when the French army occupied Berlin.[99]

Not surprisingly, Anglophiles like Gentz were strongly opposed to the French peace proposals and objected to the analysis of commerce that informed them. D'Hauterive's book immediately provoked a series of impassioned responses from the British side. Gentz and his allies denied the French claim that commercial rivalry had poisoned the workings of the balance of power and turned the European states system into a monstrosity. Instead, they defended the view that commercial rivalry, along with limits on trade such as Britain's Navigation Acts, was a necessary feature of a world of independent states. In this view, it was not the explosive rise of commerce that had caused the collapse of the European states system, but the French quest for territorial expansion and Napoleon's pursuit of a quite old-fashioned form of universal monarchy. Gentz's *On the State of Europe Before and After the French Revolution* (originally published in 1801 and translated into English in 1802) sought to show that "the extension of the commercial and colonial system is by no means incompatible with the principles of the federal constitution of Europe."[100] England had merely

[98] *Europa in Bezug auf den Frieden. Eine Rede des Abt Sieyès, gehalten nach der Auflösung der Jakobiner in den geheimen Auschuss der Revolution am 12. Frimare im dritten Jahr der französischen Republik. London, im Dezember 1794*, discussed in Adler-Bresse, *Sieyès et le Monde Allemand*, 1:32–47. Adler-Bresse believed that Knesebeck probably got his information from a fellow Silesian, either Oelsner or Ebel. The pamphlet was very popular and went through several editions. A French translation (presumably made for Sieyès by one of his German friends) was left in Sieyès's papers. Later regretting what he had done, Knesebeck asked Oelsner to pass along his apology for abusing Sieyès's name. See also Otto Tschirch, *Geschichte der öffentlichen Meinung in Preussen vom Baseler Frieden bis bum Zusammenbruch des Staates, 1795–1806*, 2 vols. (Weimar, 1933).

[99] Friedrich August von der Marwitz, *Lebenschreibung*, ed. Friedrich Meusel (Berlin, 1908), 1:134–35. See also Bourel, "Un regicide ambassadeur."

[100] Friedrich von Gentz, *On the state of Europe before and after the French Revolution: Being an answer to the work entitled De l'état de la France à la fin de l'an VIII*, 5th ed. (London: Printed for J. Hatchard, 1804), 60.

exercised "the indisputable right of every nation to promote its domestic industry, by every method which does not actually injure others."[101] Far from undermining the balance of power and destroying the European states system, England's commercial success had helped uphold them against French aggression.

The most interesting of d'Hauterive's opponents was Thomas Brooke Clarke, a close associate of Josiah Tucker, the prominent English political economist. Clarke responded to d'Hauterive's analysis of commerce by recounting Adam Smith's history of European commerce from the third book of the *Wealth of Nations*. In this view, the original Gothic constitution of Europe had been overturned by a commercial revolution unintentionally unleashed by the feudal barons. Their taste for luxury had led them to transfer their wealth to the towns and therefore to lose their violent and tyrannical grip on society.[102] Commerce was rightly celebrated as the source of modern civil liberties, Clarke wrote, for it had "leveled the proud baron, freed kings from slavery, and people from oppression."[103] Clarke concluded that the "vicious remnants of the feudal system," and their rearguard action against the dawn of the commercial age, had caused the revolution in France and the "disorganization" of Europe. The relative absence of such remnants in England, in Clarke's view, explained why England had avoided a comparable upheaval.[104] A veteran of the debates about Anglo-Irish union, which had centered on the question whether England's wealth necessarily preordained its economic decline, Clarke dismissed French intimations that England's economy and finances were on the brink of collapse.[105] "The principles of the Gothic military system, and those of the commercial system, were at war with each other," Clarke concluded, "whereas the principles of the new military systems and of the commercial system are perfectly in accord."[106]

[101] Ibid., 298.

[102] Thomas Brooke Clarke, *A survey of the strength and opulence of Great Britain: Wherein it is shewn, the progress of its commerce, agriculture, population, &c.* (London: Cadell and Davies, 1801), 1–8; and Clarke, *An Historical and Political View of the Disorganization of Europe Wherein the Laws and Characters of Nations, and the Maritime and Commercial System of Great Britain and Other States, Are Vindicated Against the Imputations and Revolutionary Proposals of M. Talleyrand and M. Hauterive, Secretaries of State to the French Republic* (London: Cadell and Davies, 1803), 155ff.

[103] Clarke, *Strength and opulence of Great Britain*, 8.

[104] Clarke, *Disorganization of Europe*, 166–70.

[105] See Istvan Hont, "The 'Rich Country–Poor Country' Debate Revisited: The Irish Origins and French Reception of the Hume Paradox," in *David Hume's Political Economy*, ed. Carl Wennerlind and Margaret Schabas, 243–322 (London: Routledge, 2008). Interestingly, Clarke was writing to promote union to the Irish, so in a sense he was on the opposite side of that debate. He claimed that England and Ireland could form a Fénelonian free-trade confederation centered on England, much like the one Mirabeau envisaged as centered on France. The union of 1800 was a topic of much discussion in Gentz's *Historical Journal*.

[106] Clarke, *Disorganization of Europe*, 154–55.

Clarke also ventured a more fundamental defense of commercial rivalry as a manageable and even necessary feature of international politics. To do so, Clarke leaned particularly heavily on Emer de Vattel's *Law of Nations* (1758).[107] Clarke's defense of England's Navigation Acts was a close paraphrase of Vattel's description of the duties of states with respect to commerce.[108] According to Vattel, the law of nations gave priority to the self-preservation of states over their duty to practice mutual aid through commerce. In particular, Vattel accorded wide latitude to states in imposing certain kinds of restrictions on trade if these were considered necessary to maintain the balance of power. Clarke drew on Vattel to defend England against d'Hauterive's condemnations. England had done no more than what was necessary to maintain its independence and had not prevented commerce from continuing to play its integrative cosmopolitan role. In fact, Clarke argued, what d'Hauterive called the "maritime system" had accomplished "not the destruction but the preservation of the balance of power." It was really the military exploits of Louis XIV that had threatened to overthrow the European states system; only the maritime prowess of the English and Dutch, the premier commercial nations of Europe, had saved it.[109] The French Revolution had mounted an unprecedented challenge to the law of nations. Like Burke (who had also drawn on Vattel to make this argument), Clarke concluded that overcoming such an aberration required extraordinary means.[110]

In his 1800 review essay on perpetual peace, Gentz presented this Vattelian account of the European balance of power as the only true implementation of Kant's ideal. Kant, of course, had rejected the idea that "a permanent universal peace" could be achieved "by means of a so-called *European balance of power*."[111] In *Perpetual Peace*, he memorably branded Vattel, together with Grotius and Pufendorf, as one of the "sorry comforters" whose purportedly legal code could

[107] His refutation of d'Hauterive opened by citing Vattel's defense of free speech and his praise of England; see Vattel, *Law of Nations*, bk. 2, ch. 1, sect. 19, and bk. 1, ch. 3, sects. 23–24.

[108] According to Clarke:

> The laws of nature, and the rights of nations prescribe systems of commerce. The principles of these natural and moral obligations maintain, that men are bound mutually to assist each other. But this general obligation is subservient to a particular obligation of still greater force, which establishes the right of every nation to labour, first for its preservation, next, for its perfection. Hence every state has a right founded upon the laws of nature and of nations to form her system of commerce upon these principles, and to annex to it what conditions she pleases. For, the duty of a nation to itself is paramount to its duty to others. (*Disorganization of Europe*, 60)

The passage is a summary of Vattel's *Law of Nations*.

[109] Clarke, *Disorganization of Europe*, 143, 149–50.

[110] See Iain Hampsher-Monk, "Edmund Burke's Changing Justification for Intervention," *Historical Journal* 48, no. 1 (2005): 65–100; and David Armitage, "Edmund Burke and Reason of State," *Journal of the History of Ideas* 61, no. 4 (2000): 617–34.

[111] Kant, "Theory and Practice," in *Political Writings*, 92.

not be enforced in the anarchic realm of international power politics.[112] Gentz dismissed this uncompromising stance as a dangerous and irresponsible form of utopian moralizing. In the short term, an attempt to institute a genuinely legalized international order would not eliminate war but merely recast it in the guise of judicial enforcement. Existing models of international federations were not encouraging: the Holy Roman Empire was obviously a disaster, and Gentz doubted that the United States of America would last longer than fifty years (a fairly accurate prediction of the onset of the American Civil War). Finally, even if Europe were to be successful in creating a European union someday, this would not herald the arrival of perpetual peace, but the inauguration of an even greater field of conflict between Continental superstates.[113]

The only viable path to perpetual peace, Gentz concluded, was to restore and maintain "the natural European federal constitution." Since the fall of Rome, Europe had gradually been consolidated into a system of large and stable states that were increasingly capable of maintaining law and order through "regular and liberal" government. It was a serious error to confound the very recent corruption of the European states system with the "true theory of the balance of power." The abbé de Saint-Pierre's peace project could not be achieved through an international federation, but it could be approximated ever more closely by a system of multiple power blocs. Despite the occasional violence this system would produce, it would safeguard the diffusion of enlightened public opinion. Had it not been for the catastrophic disruption of the French Revolution, Gentz replied to d'Hauterive, this process could have delivered a resolution to the problem of jealousy of trade. "The governments of Europe were at length sufficiently convinced," he claimed, "that the internal cultivation of their respective states was a source of riches, power, influence, real glory, and even external splendour, far more productive than all the conquests and aggrandizements that war or negotiation can accomplish."[114] Europe had been about to witness

> true principles of commercial policy prevailing over all obstacles, and combating successfully the most deep-rooted prejudices. Men recovered from the rage for monopoly, as from a dream of the infancy of human industry; their former ideas of the importance of exclusive dominion in distant regions, were considerably diminished, and the value of colonial possessions began to be seen in its true point of view. The same rivalry indeed continued in full force between the commercial nations;

[112] Kant, *Perpetual Peace*, 103.

[113] Gentz, "Über den ewigen Frieden," 275.

[114] Gentz, *On the State of Europe*, 181. The progress of enlightenment was not limited to governments alone: "A more enlightened, liberal, and benevolent way of thinking, had at the same time spread through the great body of the people in almost every European country. Their eyes were opened to their true interests; not only this or that particular war, but all wars were become in the highest degree unpopular" (182–83).

> but it existed in a more reasonable manner, and was no longer excited by vain phantoms, but contended for solid advantages. This evidently led the way to peace among nations; mankind had already passed judgment upon wars of conquest: the moment was not far distant when they would have unanimously acknowledged the folly of commercial wars.[115]

It was France's explosive jealousy of England that had actually caused the downfall of the European states system. Gentz concluded by exhorting other Continental nations not to imitate this pernicious example: "An amendment of the interior administration of every state, a wise and liberal legislation, an increased attention to the interests of commerce and industry, and a studious improvement of the true sources of the wealth of nations . . . With such weapons, but with such only, may Europe combat Great Britain!"[116]

The debate between d'Hauterive and Gentz indicates the contours of the momentous strategic choice that was confronting Prussia when Fichte appeared in Berlin and wrote *The Closed Commercial State*. Since the Treaty of Basel in 1795, Prussia had managed to maintain its own neutrality as well as the neutrality of northern Germany, and Frederick Wilhelm III was inclined to keep things that way as long as possible. In 1799, however, Sieyès was not the only foreign emissary who had taken up residence in Berlin, seeking an alliance. Sieyès was competing with Count Nikita Panin, Thomas Grenville, and Josef von Hudelist, representatives of Russia, England, and Austria, who were all gathered in Berlin in an attempt to persuade Prussia to join the second coalition against France.[117] Gentz was a staunch advocate of joining the coalition, which very nearly happened (the king was persuaded to issue marching orders, only to change his mind at the last minute and return to neutrality). On the other side, a significant though ultimately less influential French faction at court advocated an alliance with France. This faction included Prince Heinrich (the king's uncle), a notorious Francophile who had prepared his own proposal for the reorganization of Germany.[118] As we shall see, one of the most prominent members of this faction was Carl August von Struensee, the finance minister to whom Fichte dedicated *The Closed Commercial State*.

Prussia's rivalry with Austria, its concern to retain its dominance over northern Germany during a future reorganization of Germany, and its eagerness to maximize its compensation for the territory lost to France on the left bank of the Rhine contributed to an extremely complex diplomatic situation.[119]

[115] Ibid., 182.

[116] Ibid., 353.

[117] Philip Dwyer, "The Politics of Prussian Neutrality, 1795–1806," *German History* 12 (1994): 359.

[118] Biro, *German Policy of Revolutionary France*, 2:622–30.

[119] Simms, *Impact of Napoleon*; and Philip Dwyer, "Prussia and the Armed Neutrality: The Invasion of Hanover in 1801," *International History Review* 15 (1993): 661–87.

Another element in Prussia's strategic calculations—one whose significance is often underestimated by historians, but was highlighted by Fichte's contemporary history—was the importance of commerce.[120] Prussia's power still rested entirely on its military prowess; it was, in a famous phrase, "not a country which has an army, but an army which has a country."[121] Frederick the Great had made an abortive attempt to begin participating in global commerce by establishing an East Asia company in 1750, to the great disapproval of the Dutch and British. Prussian merchants were always highly vulnerable to search and seizure by the British navy, which inflicted serious losses. Frederick later concluded that participation in global commerce was beyond Prussia's reach.[122] At the end of Frederick's reign, the comte de Mirabeau warned Prussia that it could not hope to sustain its military power without undertaking serious economic reforms.[123] France's appeals for an alliance targeted Prussia's commercial aspirations and included offers to allow Prussia to annex Hanover (still a possession, as fate would have it, of George III of England).[124] The acquisition of Hanover would not only consolidate Prussia's territory but also give Prussia a base from which it could develop into a commercial state. One of d'Hauterive's fellow propagandists in the debates of 1800, François-Xavier Auduoin (1765–1837), exhorted Prussia to do just that: "Having been the school of warriors in the north," Audouin wrote, "Prussia ought to become that of commerce" by taking over the great trading city of Hamburg and liberating it from England's economic sphere of influence.[125] However, as the Prussian government was acutely aware, to invade Hanover was to court a potentially ruinous conflict with England, which was also Prussia's largest trading partner.[126]

Ultimately, Sieyès's mission to Berlin failed to achieve any results. The Prussian government proved unwilling to negotiate even an accord to standardize weights and measures with France. By January 1799, an exasperated Sieyès

[120] Dwyer, "Prussia and Armed Neutrality," 664.

[121] Georg Heinrich Berenhorst, cited in T.C.W. Blanning, *The French Revolutionary Wars, 1787–1802* (London: Arnold, 1996), 8.

[122] Florian Schui, "Prussia's Trans-Oceanic Moment: The Creation of the Prussian Asiatic Trading Company in 1750," *Historical Journal* 49, no. 1 (2006): 143–60.

[123] Honoré-Gabriel de Riqueti, comte de Mirabeau, *Lettre remise à Frédéric-Guillaume II, Roi Regnant de Prusse, le jour de son Avénement au Trône* (Berlin, 1787), 47–48.

[124] Biro, *German Policy of Revolutionary France*, 2:891–93.

[125] François-Xavier Audouin, *Du commerce maritime, de son influence sur la richesse et la force des états, démontrée par l'histoire des nations anciennes et modernes; situation actuelle des puissances de l'Europe, considérées dans leurs rapports avec la France et l'Angleterre; réflexions sur l'armament en course, sa législation et ses avantages* (Paris, 1800), 2:83–84.

[126] On the long history of Prussia's unhappy neutrality, extending back to the Thirty Years' War, see Christopher M. Clark, *Iron Kingdom: The Rise and Downfall of Prussia, 1600–1947* (London: Allen Lane, 2006), 23–24, 293–305. Fichte later denounced this policy in his 1807 article on Machiavelli: "Über Machiavelli als Schriftsteller," in Fichte, *Gesamtausgabe*, pt. 1, 9:256–59.

wrote to Talleyrand that the chief obstacle to perpetual peace was actually Prussian intransigence:

> When I cast my eyes on the past, I cannot stop myself from thinking that the Republic could long since have been at peace with England and consequently with the continent, had it laid a hand on the King of England's important possessions in Germany. Who stopped us from doing so? Prussia. I look in the future and I assure myself by the most certain arguments that we cannot contain England, that we cannot guarantee a solid peace even on the continent, that we cannot acquire good political and commercial influence in the North, except through a skillful arrangement of the small states which encompass the Ems, Elbe, and Weser. Yet who will want to stop us from effecting this aspect of the plan which suits the interest of the Republic and, I dare say, of Europe? Prussia.[127]

Sieyès returned to France empty-handed at the beginning of June 1799. In the end, it was Russia's estrangement from Austria and Britain, and its growing rapprochement with France, that changed the strategic landscape and compelled Prussia to abandon its neutrality. By July 1800, Prussia had begun to tilt toward an alliance with Czar Paul I, who had conceived of his own ambitious project to impose a general peace on Europe through the offices of a "northern confederacy."[128] Paul also took aim at England's maritime dominance by calling for a revival of the League of Armed Neutrality, an international federation that had appeared in 1780 during the American Revolution. Championed by Catherine the Great, the League of Armed Neutrality had pooled its naval resources in order to defend neutral free trade from English and French efforts to limit commerce with their rivals. Catherine herself had likened the federation to the abbé de Saint-Pierre's project for perpetual peace.[129]

D'Hauterive and his allies made a point of emphasizing the congruence between the proposal for a revived League of Armed Neutrality and the French vision of a new kind of trading system. Their argument was laid out particularly

[127] Sieyès to Talleyrand, 8 January 1799, in Bailleu, *Preussen und Frankreich*, 1:496–97.

[128] See Hugh Ragsdale, "A Continental System in 1801: Paul I and Bonaparte," *Journal of Modern History* 42, no. 1 (1970): 70–89; and Ragsdale, "Russia, Prussia and Europe in the Policy of Paul I," *Jahrbücher für Geschichte Osteuropas* 31 (1983): 81–118.

[129] Isabel De Madariaga, *Britain, Russia, and the Armed Neutrality of 1780: Sir James Harris's Mission to St. Petersburg during the American Revolution* (London: Hollis and Carter, 1962), 157. Catherine's bilingual memorandum demands quotation: "Il n'y avait plus moyen de faire autrement, denn die Teutschen hassen nichts so als wenn die Leute ihnen auf die Nase spielen wollen . . . Le confrere Charles échauffe nos oreilles dans ce moment; je vous prie de nous prêter la vôtre pour écounter ce que nous allons lui dire et à d'autres aussi, denn das ist eben so raisonnable wie die Projekte des Abts von St. Pierre."

clearly in a pamphlet published in 1800 by Thomas Paine. Paine proposed the expansion of the League of Armed Neutrality into a more universal "Compact Maritime."[130] The original League of Armed Neutrality of 1780 had succeeded only in protecting neutral commerce, he claimed, because the old maritime balance of power had kept England's navy in check. Now that the old states system had been destroyed, a coalition of northern European neutral states was no match for England. More fundamentally, such a coalition would fail to transcend European power politics. Rather than inaugurating a legalized states system that could protect the general interest as encapsulated in commerce, it would merely constitute another partial interest within the existing system.[131] The only way to defeat England's current stranglehold on neutral commerce was to join France in instituting the kind of federal navigation act described by d'Hauterive. Should Paul I join the French Republic in bringing England to its knees through a continental embargo, Paine proclaimed, they would jointly be hailed as liberators of the entire "commercial world" and authors of the first genuinely legalized international order. Whereas Gentz had transmogrified the ideal of perpetual peace into a defense of the old European balance of power as the best way to approximate natural law, Paine and his French allies depicted the formation of a Franco-Russian concert of Europe as the inauguration of a Kantian regime of international right and hence the next step on the path to perpetual peace.[132]

The congruence between the Russian project and the French perspective on commerce and perpetual peace was also evident in Prussia, where it reportedly earned the support of Struensee. French and Russian interests also converged with respect to Prussia's occupation of Hanover. The eventual declaration of the League of Armed Neutrality by Russia, Denmark, Sweden, and Prussia in December 1800 provoked a strong English response. Since Prussia had no navy to contribute to the league, its allies demanded that Prussia blockade the rivers of northern Germany against English shipping and occupy Hanover. In April 1801, Prussia finally responded to mounting French and Russian pressure (as well as its own significant incentives) and marched into Hanover.[133] This resolution of Prussia's strategic dilemma proved remarkably short-lived. Within weeks, England had decisively destroyed the Danish fleet off Copenhagen, and

[130] Thomas Paine, *Pacte Maritime, adressée aux Nations neutres, Par un Neutre* (Paris: Imprimerie-Librairie du Cercle-Social, 1800). An American edition was published in Washington, D.C., in 1801.

[131] Compare Audouin, *Du commerce maritime*, 2:67.

[132] Compare, in this light, Paul W. Schroeder, "Did the Vienna Settlement Rest on a Balance of Power?" *American Historical Review* 97, no. 3 (June 1992): 683–706, and the ensuing responses; and James R. Sofka, "Metternich's Theory of European Order: A Political Agenda for 'Perpetual Peace,'" *Review of Politics* 60, no. 1 (Winter 1998): 115–49.

[133] Dwyer, "Prussia and Armed Neutrality," 666–69.

Paul I had been assassinated by a pro-English faction at the Court of St. Petersburg. The league collapsed, and Russia under Alexander I signed a treaty with England in June. Prussia, compelled to beat an inglorious retreat from Hanover, promptly returned to a strategic impasse that ended with its capitulation to Napoleon after its disastrous defeat at Jena in 1806.

Fichte's Contribution to the Debate

The analysis of commerce that Fichte presented in *The Closed Commercial State* was aligned with the fundamentally Fénelonian perspective that contemporary French writers were employing in their attacks on England. The central motif of *The Closed Commercial State*—its analogy between the juridical theory of the social contract and the commercial state—also appears in Audouin's *Du commerce maritime* (1800), a contemporary French attempt to persuade the neutral nations that a French-led embargo of England was a more effective means of liberating commerce than the League of Armed Neutrality. Universal free trade was no more likely to be achieved at one fell swoop than a universal republic, Audouin argued, but the initial step was to join France in creating a new trading system based on reciprocity. For the time being, complete commercial liberty could be achieved only among citizens of the same state. "The act of navigation," he wrote, "would be the primary foundation of a commercial constitution, just as essential to the well-being of a people as the political constitution is to its liberty."[134]

Some of the more polemical discourses employed by d'Hauterive and others to describe their peace projects also appear in *The Closed Commercial State*. In addition to declaiming against "dominion of the seas," Fichte applied the concept of natural borders in order to justify the annexation of neighboring territories. Rather than emphasizing military considerations, Fichte defined the concept by stressing economic complementarities: natural borders were not those that were most defensible, but those which were most conducive to achieving "productive independence and self-sufficiency" (*produktive Selbständigkeit und Selbstgenügsamkeit*). Existing territories of the "modern European republic" that failed to meet this test were therefore in a condition of "natural war."[135] It would hardly have been necessary to spell out the case of Hanover (or

[134] Audouin, *Du commerce maritime*, 2:67–70. The affinity is reflected in the trope that later developed of describing *The Closed Commercial State* as a statement of the theoretical principles underlying Napoleon's continental blockade. See, e.g., Johann Friedrich Eusebius Lotz, *Handbuch der Staatswirthschaftslehre* (Erlangen: Palm und Enke, 1821), 1:144–46; and I. H. Fichte's editorial note to Fichte's *Sämmtliche Werke*, 3:xxxix–xl.

[135] Fichte, *Der geschlossene Handelsstaat*, *Gesamtausgabe*, pt. 1, 7:117–18.

Poland) for a Prussian reader in the autumn of 1800. The sensational example that Fichte did provide was that France and the British Isles naturally formed one unit and would continue to fight until one side or the other succeeded in uniting them.[136] This remark helped earn Fichte a reputation as one of the most prominent Francophiles and Anglophobes in Prussia. Wilhelm Traugott Krug, Kant's successor at Königsberg, later described Fichte's *Closed Commercial State* as a work that was motivated less by "speculation alone" than by Fichte's evident "hatred of England and fondness for France."[137]

Another strong indication of *The Closed Commercial State*'s coordinates in contemporary debates about the future of the European states system is Fichte's dedication of the book to the Prussian finance minister, Carl August von Struensee. Struensee appeared on the list of eleven names of potential kindred spirits in Berlin that Sieyès's Prussian confidant (and Fichte's collaborator in the German edition of Sieyès's works), Konrad Engelbert Oelsner, had drawn up for Sieyès before his mission.[138] Sieyès found Struensee's company a welcome respite from the unpleasant atmosphere of the Berlin salons, which were dominated by hostile French émigrés and which, he complained to Talleyrand, contained no "men of the second order."[139] According to Austrian diplomats, Struensee had become "an intimate friend," and Sieyès dined frequently chez Struensee, surrounded by a handpicked circle of intellectuals, traders, and civil servants, all "men of the second order."[140] Sieyès himself reported to Talleyrand that Struensee was the only member of the Prussian government who was prepared to negotiate with him, but "although His Excellency has merit, he is never pardoned for not having been born noble, and the confidence he enjoys is not commensurate with the fiscal and commercial affairs with which he is charged."[141]

Sieyès left Berlin for Paris on 1 June 1799, having just been elected to the Executive Directory of the French Republic; Fichte arrived in Berlin one month

[136] Ibid., 7:118.

[137] Wilhelm Traugott Krug, *Allgemeines Handwörterbuch der philosophischen Wissenschaften nebst ihrer Literatur und Geschichte* (Leipzig, 1827), 2:518.

[138] Adler-Bresse, *Sieyès et le Monde Allemand*, 1:91. Adler-Bresse speculates there was a Masonic connection involved. On Fichte's encounter with Freemasonry, see Engelbrecht, *Johann Gottlieb Fichte*. Fichte first joined in Zürich in 1793, and joined a lodge in Berlin in April 1800, where he delivered a pair of lectures, only to resign in July when his efforts to make it a vessel for his own thought encountered resistance.

[139] Sieyès to Talleyrand, 6 April 1799, in Adler-Bresse, *Sieyès et le Monde Allemand*, 2:251.

[140] Josef von Hudelist to Johann Amadeus Franz de Paula, Baron von Thugut, 23 April 1799, in Adler-Bresse, *Sieyès et le Monde Allemand*, 2:450–51.

[141] Sieyès to Talleyrand, 10 August 1798, in Adler-Bresse, *Sieyès et le Monde Allemand*, 2:593–94. Sieyès's impression is confirmed by Marwitz's memoirs: "As a deist and an educated bourgeois," Marwitz sniffed, Struensee was "by no means unsusceptible to revolutionary principles" (*Lebenschreibung*, 1:88).

later, having lost his professorship at Jena during the atheism controversy. After Sieyès's departure and Fichte's arrival, French diplomats in Berlin continued to send reports of Struensee's positive disposition toward France and of his staunchly republican principles. "You have nobody against you but the aristocrats," Struensee famously told one of them in August 1799:

> The King and the people are obviously for France. The very useful revolution which you have made from the bottom upwards will be made gradually in Prussia from the top downwards. The King is a democrat in his way; he works without letting up to reduce the privileges of the nobility, and he will follow the plan of Joseph II in this regard, but by gradual means. In a few years there will no longer be a privileged class in Prussia. The nobles will be allowed to keep their ribbons, which often take the place of pensions and relieve our finances; but the need to live in comfort will encourage them to throw themselves into a more lucrative career, that of commerce and industry. As it is precisely from the French Revolution that these principles are derived, our aristocrats detest you, and they do not hide it.[142]

Struensee's bourgeois background and republican principles must have been highly attractive to the newly arrived Fichte, who was notoriously sensitive to aristocratic snobbery and whose republicanism remained as fervent as ever. Struensee's encounter with Sieyès points toward the link between Sieyès's vision of a republicanized international order and Fichte's *Closed Commercial State.* "If the war resumes," Sieyès had predicted to Talleyrand in August 1798, "you will end it only to see it resume again, and so forth, unless you adopt a plan of republicanization different from the one which has been followed, and combine it with the military operations."[143] As the following chapter will detail, Fichte's *Closed Commercial State* proposed a blueprint for "republicanization." It sought to explain how a German state like Prussia could take advantage of a reorganization of Germany in order to lay the economic foundation for a constitutional republic. (Fichte assured his publisher that after the upcoming peace settlement, the book would also attract interest in other countries, like Bavaria—a state that also figured prominently in French visions of a restructured Holy Roman Empire.)[144]

Fichte's acceptance of "military operations" as a prerequisite for "republicanization" is one of the key differences between *The Closed Commercial State* and Kant's *Perpetual Peace*. Kant's essay embraced the prospect of an expand-

[142] Otto to Talleyrand, 13 August 1799 in Bailleu, *Preussen und Frankreich*, 1:505.

[143] Sieyès to Talleyrand, 29 August 1798, in Bailleu, *Preussen und Frankreich*, 1:487.

[144] Fichte to Johann Friedrich Cotta, 16 August 1800, in *Gesamtausgabe*, pt. 3, 4:285–86.

ing federation of republics centered on France, but it explicitly ruled out conquest as a means of creating this federation. In the second appendix to his essay (which was added to the second edition), Kant maintained that no regime of international law could permit a large state to justify the annexation of small states whose territories intruded upon its own and posed a threat to its self-preservation. No such reason of state could pass the test of publicity, since to profess such principles openly would obviously be counterproductive.[145] Kant insisted that conquest had to be excised completely from the canon of a truly republican politics, lest it infect and compromise the integrity of a legalized international order. It was better to err on the side of being a "despotic moralist," whose excessive rigidity might lead to imprudence and failure, than to emulate the politicians whose excuses for unjust political practices threatened to "make progress *impossible*, and eternalize the violation of right."[146] More generally, Kant cautioned strongly against overly ambitious attempts to implement perpetual peace through voluntary political action. To aim directly for such a lofty goal was to overtax the human capacity for practical wisdom.[147] Instead, Kant counseled states to avoid committing fresh injustices and, above all, to allow the gradual diffusion of enlightened public opinion to continue unmolested.

In 1795, Kant limited his liaison with Sieyès to a discussion of how to introduce the critical philosophy into France. In 1800, Fichte wrote a philosophical account of republicanization that took "military operations" as its starting point and sent presentation copies to the king of Prussia and several of his most important ministers. In this respect, Fichte's *Closed Commercial State* was less a reworking of Kant's essay on perpetual peace than an updated version of Voltaire's joint project with Frederick the Great, the *Anti-Machiavel* (1740).[148] The *Anti-Machiavel* is often remembered as an unexceptional piece of hypocritical moralizing by an idealistic young prince who invaded Silesia and launched a world war the moment he ascended the throne. Yet it was also an attempt to update the pacific ideals that had been articulated by Fénelon and to apply them to the circumstances of a modern European state.[149] It, too, had been written in the context of contemporary French discussions about a reorganization of Germany by force.[150]

145 Kant, *Perpetual Peace*, 128.

146 Ibid., 119.

147 Ibid., 122–23.

148 François-Marie Arouet de Voltaire, *Anti-Machiavel* (1740), ed. Werner Bahner and Helga Bergmann, *Oeuvres Complètes*, vol. 19 (Oxford: Voltaire Foundation, 1996).

149 Voltaire described the *Anti-Machiavel* in this way in an anonymous review that he wrote himself and then had published together with the book (Voltaire, *Anti-Machiavel*, 493–500).

150 Labbé, "La rêve irénique."

The geopolitical premises for the implementation of *The Closed Commercial State* in 1800 had evaporated even more quickly than those of the *Anti-Machiavel* in 1740. As an effort to circumvent the cycles of class conflict and imperialism that Fichte had foreseen in his review of Kant's essay on perpetual peace, *The Closed Commercial State* was stillborn. But to dismiss all such efforts out of hand is a step that many in our own time remain conspicuously reluctant to take.

Chapter 3
Republicanization in Theory and Practice

Fichte's Proposal

On 16 August 1800, just over a year after his arrival in Berlin, Fichte wrote to his publisher, Johann Friedrich Cotta, to inform him that he had delivered a fresh manuscript to the printer in Leipzig. Fichte described the manuscript as the outcome of an idea that he had been contemplating since working on his treatise on natural right several years earlier: namely, "to draw up the necessary commercial constitution of a thoroughly rightful and rational state" and "to show how existing states can raise themselves to this constitution." Fichte cited the policy debates he had encountered upon arriving in Prussia as the impetus that had spurred him to carry out this project:

> The material is of contemporary interest especially for the Prussian state (as well as other countries, e.g. Bavaria). Prussia has long been seeking the right system of trade limits [*HandelsEinschränkung*], and is yet again deliberating over the introduction of paper money—all matters which I flatter myself to have clarified. It was actually the debates which I often encountered here in Berlin over such matters that provoked me into writing down my ideas on this subject. After the peace is concluded this subject will appear on the agenda in all states. The work acquires *scientific interest* in that it forms the transition from the natural-jurisprudential to the political investigations of the *Wissenschaftslehre*.[1]

Fichte had already articulated the principles of a just "commercial constitution" in the theory of property that he had developed in his 1796 treatise on natural right (and that we will examine in detail in the next chapter). The novelty of *The Closed Commercial State* lay mainly in its additional emphasis on showing "how existing states can raise themselves to this constitution." Fichte undertook this task primarily in the third and final book of *The Closed Commercial State*, entitled "Politics [*Politik*]: How the commercial relations of an existing state may be brought to the constitution demanded by reason, or, of

[1] Fichte to Cotta, 16 August 1800, in *Gesamtausgabe*, pt. 3, 4:285–86.

the closing of the commercial state." Fichte's *Closed Commercial State* presented what Sieyès had called a "plan of republicanization."[2] Writing to Talleyrand from Berlin in August 1798, a frustrated Sieyès had predicted that there could be no permanent peace unless France succeeded in imposing reform on the rest of Europe by force of arms. Fichte's *Closed Commercial State* proposed to take advantage of a French-led transformation of the European states system in order to lay the economic foundations for a constitutional republic in a state like Prussia, thereby enabling it to become a member of a peaceful international order.

As we have seen, Fichte joined contemporary French writers in identifying the main obstacle to reform as the external pressure exerted by the European states system, and in particular the perversion of international trade into an arena of Great Power rivalry. Fichte was also a strong critic of the inequality and loss of independence that he, like Rousseau, attributed to the development of the division of labor in modern Europe. Fichte claimed that a state like Prussia (and as his letter to Cotta suggested, a French-imposed peace settlement in Germany would expand the number of candidates) could neutralize the effects of the international environment by switching to a system of paper money and imposing extensive limits on international trade. This strategy would generate the breathing space as well as the resources to resolve the class conflict, which Fichte described as "the anarchy of trade" and likened to a Hobbesian war of all against all.

Fichte's letter to Cotta described *The Closed Commercial State* as a contribution to ongoing debates about how to reform Prussia. As contemporary critics (as well as later scholars) have been quick to point out, Fichte clearly did not have any formal training in the discipline of political economy as it was taught in contemporary German universities.[3] However, Fichte's earliest political writings had already reflected his keen interest in the subject, and as Fichte's dedication of *The Closed Commercial State* to the Prussian minister Carl August Struensee helps reveal, Fichte's contribution to ongoing Prussian debates was highly

[2] Sieyès to Talleyrand, 29 August 1798, in Bailleu, *Preussen und Frankreich*, 1:487.

[3] On this training and discipline, see Keith Tribe, "Cameralism and the Science of Government," *Journal of Modern History* 56, no. 2 (1984): 263–84; and Tribe, *Governing Economy*. Twentieth-century discussions of the political economy of *The Closed Commercial State* include Werner Krause, "Fichtes ökonomische Anschauungen im Geschlossenen Handelsstaat," in *Wissen und Gewissen: Beiträge zum 200. Geburtstag Johann Gottlieb Fichtes, 1762–1814*, ed. Manfred Buhr (Berlin: Akademie Verlag, 1962), 224–40; Hans Hirsch, "Fichtes Beitrag zur Theorie der Planwirtschaft und dessen Verhältnis zu seiner praktischen Philosophie," in *Der Transzendentale Gedanke: Die gegenwärtige Darstellung der Philosophie Fichtes*, ed. Klaus Hammacher), 215–30 (Hamburg: Meiner, 1981; Hirsch, "Fichtes Planwirtschaftsmodell als Dokument der Geistesgeschichte und als Bleibender Denkanstoß," *Fichte-Studien* 24 (2003): 165–77; and Richard Gray, "Economic Romanticism: Monetary Nationalism in Johann Gottlieb Fichte and Adam Müller," *Eighteenth-Century Studies* 36, no. 4 (2003): 535–57.

attuned to long-running pan-European discussions of the political economy of reform.[4] As we have seen, Struensee had been instrumental in pulling Prussia out of the war against France in 1795, had developed an intimate friendship with Sieyès during his visit to Berlin, and was known for his Francophile tendencies. Fichte's "plan of republicanization" in *The Closed Commercial State* was a radical version of the kind of monetary reform that Struensee spent his career trying to achieve. Struensee was also a published commentator on the broader European debate about the character of modern finance. In his works, he sought to moderate the widespread view of public debt as a profoundly dangerous invention of clashing war machines, one whose positive economic side effects were outweighed by the mortal risk it posed to civil liberties and political agency. Fichte was not the first to attempt to link Struensee to a much more radical vision of the transformative potential of a paper-money system: he was preceded in this role by a French visitor to Berlin who went on to become a leading statesman during the French Revolution: Honoré-Gabriel de Riqueti, the comte de Mirabeau (1749–91). The kind of vision that Mirabeau and Fichte attempted to share with Struensee had originally emerged in the context of early-eighteenth-century French efforts to recover from the wars of Louis XIV and catch up to Britain.[5] It remained potent throughout the century, and came to play a key role in the French Revolution. Fichte's *Closed Commercial State* was an attempt to articulate this vision with philosophical rigor.

Fichte's final claim in his letter to Cotta was that *The Closed Commercial State* extended his theory of rights and added a theory of politics to his comprehensive philosophical system, the *Wissenschaftslehre*. This ambition was signaled by the book's subtitle (which Fichte also spelled out in his letter to Cotta): it was to be "A Philosophical Sketch as an Appendix to the Doctrine of Right and an Example of a Future Politics." *The Closed Commercial State* reformulated the moral condemnation of power politics that Fichte had leveled in his earliest political writings and integrated it into the framework of his mature philosoph-

[4] A notable effort to examine the political economy of *The Closed Commercial State* in this context was undertaken by Léon in *Fichte et son temps* (2:58–120).

[5] Fichte alluded to this earlier context in the dedicatory epistle of *The Closed Commercial State*, dated 31 October 1800, when he likened himself to Isaac Casaubon (1559–1614), the celebrated humanist and religious refugee who won the admiration of both Henri IV of France and James I of England (Fichte, *Der geschlossene Handelsstaat*, *Gesamtausgabe*, pt. 1, 7:41). The king of Prussia had just granted Fichte asylum after he was exiled from Jena over charges of atheism. However, the reference to Casaubon also had the effect of associating Friedrich Wilhelm and Struensee with Henri IV and the duc de Sully—the idol of eighteenth-century French reformers and their Jacobite allies and his equally celebrated chief minister. Saint-Pierre had cast his *Projet pour rendre la paix perpétuelle en Europe* as the implementation of Sully and Henry IV's mythical peace plan. On the image of Henry IV as a counterpoint to that of Louis XIV, see Neal Johnson, *Louis XIV and the Age of the Enlightenment: The Myth of the Sun King from 1715 to 1789*, Studies on Voltaire and the Eighteenth Century 172 (Oxford: Voltaire Foundation, 1978).

ical system. Fichte had famously declared that the *Wissenschaftslehre* was both inspired by the French Revolution and the manifestation of its epistemological equivalent: it emancipated the mind from dogmatism just as the revolution had emancipated the individual from the involuntary social bonds of the ancien régime. The link between the two was Fichte's claim that the emancipation of the self could proceed only through constant collective striving to master the external world. As we have seen, Fichte came to argue that this collective activity could not be undertaken without the state—the very institution that, in its current form, presented the greatest obstacle to individual liberty. *The Closed Commercial State* responded to the insight that constitutional reform alone was not enough to tame the state: it was also necessary to neutralize the effects of the modern economy and the international environment. Fichte presented the book as an example of the philosopher's proper contribution to the collective creation of a moral world. It showed the politician how to strive toward perpetual peace.

Fichte's Implementation Strategy

Fichte's history of commercial relations identified the jealousy of trade as the real cause of war among modern European states. The rise of states had transformed commerce from a peaceful mode of mutually beneficial exchange into a competition for supremacy via domination of international markets. Fichte claimed that European states could not be pacified and transformed into republics until the jealousy of trade had been eliminated. The premise of Fichte's strategy was that a state could extract itself from commercial rivalry by seizing control of its monetary system. Complete control over the money supply would enable the state to nationalize all foreign trade and give it the resources to begin increasing its economic independence.

Fichte proposed that the state seize control of the money supply in one decisive step by removing all gold and silver currency from circulation and replacing it with a fiat currency, or a form of money whose value was backed solely by the word of the state. This radical measure had to be imposed as abruptly and unexpectedly as possible in order to minimize opposition. It was particularly crucial, Fichte stressed, that the new national currency (*Landesgeld*) not take the form of paper money. Instead, it had to be made of an unknown material that had no other conceivable use. Fichte held that the use of specie as a medium of exchange was in fact the result of a long-standing convention. This convention was a relic from the bygone era that predated the emergence of the sovereign state as the ultimate arbiter of social conventions among its citizens. However, Fichte observed, many people were blind to the purely conventional origins of the metallic standards, and they stubbornly clung to the false belief that the value of gold and silver as currency was somehow determined by their intrinsic utility. It was crucial to avoid doing excessive violence to this prejudice by forcing people to exchange their gold and silver coins for paper bills—even though Fichte imagined that if the original convention had happened to take a different form, the same people would be heard complaining that "this little bit of silver" could not possibly be worth as much as "my good paper."[6] Accordingly, Fichte specified that the new national money was to have as little intrinsic use value as possible: it was to function as a pure sign whose meaning was solely determined by the authority of the state. The new money had to be pretty to look at but cheap to make, and above all it had to be difficult to counterfeit. Fichte was particularly concerned that the state be vigilant about preventing counterfeiting by foreign governments, lest the value of the new national money be determined by any other interest than the sovereign legislative will.[7] Fichte somewhat ostentatiously declined to share his knowledge of this previously unknown and reliably counterfeit-proof material with the reading public.[8] Fichte's pronounced concern was not merely a personal quirk, but also a reflection of recent historical experience: counterfeiting the paper *assignats* issued by the French republic during the revolution had become a major industry for its enemies. During the failed English-supported invasion by royalist émigrés at Quiberon in Brittany during the summer of 1795, the French government confiscated billions in counterfeited *assignats* that had been printed in London.[9]

Fichte further proposed that the introduction of the new national currency coincide with the unqualified demonetization of specie. According to Fichte, this step is what distinguished his plan from various failed monetary experiments like the French *assignats*, which had circulated alongside specie and whose value therefore remained contingent on whether they could be redeemed for "real" money.[10] The decision to adopt the new national currency "should hardly depend on the good will of the subjects," Fichte wrote.[11] Rather, the state had to render "all silver and gold instantly and thoroughly useless to the public for every purpose except exchanging it into the new national currency; indeed, the new national currency becomes absolutely indispensable for life itself."[12] Fichte claimed that the state could carry out this exchange without

[6] Fichte, *Der geschlossene Handelsstaat*, *Gesamtausgabe*, pt. 1, 7:121.

[7] Ibid., 7:79, 82, 121–22.

[8] Ibid., 7:82, 121.

[9] Michel Bruguière, "Assignats," in *A Critical Dictionary of the French Revolution*, ed. François Furet and Mona Ozouf, trans. Arthur Goldhammer, 431 (Cambridge, Mass.: Harvard University Press, 1989).

[10] Fichte, *Der geschlossene Handelsstaat*, *Gesamtausgabe*, pt. 1, 7:125–26.

[11] Ibid., 7:121.

[12] Ibid., 7:124.

having to resort to an excessively severe regime of prohibition and punishment and without having to outlaw emigration. By requiring that taxes be paid in the new national currency, the state would furnish its citizens with the necessary incentive to exchange their specie, and the government could make the exchange rate less favorable as time went on.[13] Those who refused to exchange their specie for the new national money were free to emigrate, but they would not be permitted to liquidate their property before leaving. Emigrants would be permitted to receive interest on their property while abroad in the form of life annuities, Fichte proposed, but the property itself would revert to the closest living relatives who had not left the country.[14]

Fichte claimed that the introduction of a national currency presented the state with an opportunity to achieve greater economic independence. At the moment of the monetary transition, Fichte proposed, prepositioned state agents would purchase all foreign goods available throughout the state. Importers would be required to furnish them with an accurate inventory of their current stock under pain of severe penalty.[15] The state would then become an intermediary in all commercial transactions between its citizens and foreigners. Imports and exports would require official approval and would be priced in the national currency for citizens, but in hard currency for foreigners. The state would also assume all the rights and responsibilities of its citizens in international trade: the state was not strictly responsible for any personal debts to foreigners, but it could offer to pay enough to satisfy "the nation's honor."[16] Once the state had nationalized all foreign trade, it would be in a position to determine the domestic prices of goods independently from their price on the world market. The goal of manipulating these prices was not to increase the government's revenue—indeed, Fichte held that the government was bound to recompense merchants for the losses they might incur because of the transition. Rather, the goal was to achieve economic independence. The domestic price of foreign imports, which the state planned eventually to eliminate, would gradually rise, and every year the volume of foreign trade would diminish.[17]

Fichte claimed that achieving greater economic independence did not have to mean accepting a lower standard of living. In theory, he maintained, nobody could claim a right to a standard of living beyond what could be achieved given the local climate and the degree of development (*Kultur*) that one's fellow citizens had collectively achieved through their accumulated labor.[18] Historically, however, existing European states were all successors to a prior system

[13] Ibid., 7:79, 121.
[14] Ibid., 7:136–37.
[15] Ibid., 7:128–29.
[16] Ibid., 7:129.
[17] Ibid., 7:129–31.
[18] Ibid., 7:115.

of global free trade. Their citizens had all contributed to the "flourishing of this great commercial republic" and to the "animation of universal commerce." They had grown up under this system and had become accustomed to its advantages since birth: these advantages had become needs "indispensable for well-being" (*zum Wohlsein unentbehrliches Bedürfnis*).[19] Fichte claimed that citizens of existing states—even those that had begun to introduce restrictions on free trade—continued to enjoy the advantages of global trade with the tacit consent of their governments: such states still considered their subjects to be independent agents on the global market because they continued to demand its means of exchange for the payment of taxes.[20]

Fichte concluded that the citizens of a closing commercial state could rightfully lay claim to all the advantages that could be obtained by an "independent and free member" of the "vast commercial republic." Someone who lost the advantages of global trade because of natural causes would have no grounds for complaint, but for the state to take away these advantages would be to break a tacit promise and violate a right. Although this injustice might to some extent be "unavoidable," and although it might guard against much additional injustice, Fichte claimed that it was nonetheless an injustice—one that he suggested was dimly but correctly perceived by the populace, which tended to resent newly imposed tariffs and other more recent restrictions on trade more than it resented the traditional taxes on land.[21] A closing commercial state had to recognize its citizens' transitional right to the benefits of global trade. The only imports to be outlawed immediately were purely status-oriented goods, or luxuries, "which are merely and solely intended for opinion" and which Fichte claimed could not be regarded as constitutive of well-being.[22] In every other case, the government had to undertake a massive and intensive effort to establish domestic equivalents for as many of the advantages of global trade as possible: "The closing of the commercial state of which we speak is in no way a renunciation and a modest confinement to the narrow limits of our country's present production, but an energetic appropriation of our portion of all that is good and fine on the entire surface of the earth, insofar as we are able appropriate it—our due share, since for centuries our nation has certainly contributed its labor and artistry to this common possession of humanity."[23] Fichte emphatically rejected the notion that natural constraints would compel a closing commercial state to adopt a regime of severe austerity. The "plan of republicanization" described in *The Closed Commercial State* was not intended for an indigent society, nor was it aimed at a nation that had already been plun-

[19] Ibid.
[20] Ibid., 7:125.
[21] Ibid., 7:110.
[22] Ibid., 7:131; cf. 116.
[23] Ibid., 7:116.

dered by its more successful competitors. Rather, it was designed for a state that still commanded considerable wealth and was farsighted enough to use it to secure an advantageous withdrawal from global trade.[24] With sufficient investment, Fichte claimed, such a state could develop economically viable domestic substitutes even for raw materials from distant tropical climes. For example, he predicted, a northern European country could develop a perfectly viable substitute for cotton out of previously uncultivated native fibers. Fichte stressed that even Europe's staple cereals were the artificial results of millennia of agricultural innovation. "What can man not do," Fichte asked, "by cultivating the most insignificant plant?"[25]

Fichte claimed that the resources for this state-directed development project would come from the enormous hard-currency reserves generated by the monetary transition. These reserves would be used to fund an aggressive policy of technology transfers, centrally planned industrialization through import substitutions and upstream development, and investment in the development of synthetic substitutes for imported raw materials.[26] Fichte emphasized that the first state to implement such a monetary strategy would get the biggest boost; other states copying its successful example would find that the value of specie had greatly depreciated because of the previous closing state's spending.[27] However, none of these policies would be effective unless the closing state had been able to construct a sufficiently large and unified domestic market. A collection of disparate and fragmentary territories like Prussia could not become a closed commercial state without annexing neighboring territories. Fichte claimed that the closing commercial state could also use its immense hard-currency reserves to arm itself so effectively and hire so many foreign troops that the annexation would be "more a campaign of occupation than a war."[28] Population transfers and massive investment would rapidly integrate the annexed territories into the new national market.

Once a closing commercial state had completed its "campaign of occupation" and achieved its "natural frontiers," Fichte claimed that it would be in a position to disentangle itself completely from the existing European states system. The government would publish a declaration explaining its actions to all other states and guaranteeing that it would no longer seek to form any alliances or offer to mediate between other powers or attempt to expand its borders. Fichte claimed that the credibility of this guarantee would be assured by the constitution of the closed commercial state. Its economic institutions would prevent it from profiting from any further conquest, and its standing army

[24] Ibid., 7:128.
[25] Ibid., 7:133n; cf. Kant, *Perpetual Peace*, 110.
[26] Fichte, *Der geschlossene Handelsstaat*, *Gesamtausgabe*, pt. 1, 7:132–33.
[27] Ibid., 7:138–39.
[28] Ibid., 7:134.

would be replaced by a citizens' militia incapable of projecting any offensive military power.[29] According to Fichte, only states that had gone to these lengths to insulate themselves from the effects of interstate rivalry could safely allow themselves to engage in international commerce on a permanent basis. Among such states, commerce would take a strictly circumscribed and noncompetitive form: it would be limited to bilateral exchanges of complementary superfluities arranged by commercial treaties.[30] Competition between states would be limited to noncommercial forms of endeavor and cultural achievement like scientific discoveries, literary accomplishments, and legislative innovations.[31]

Fichte claimed that a monetary strategy for disengaging the economy from international trade would supply the means for resolving domestic class conflict. Like Rousseau, Fichte held that individual independence had been lost within the division of labor as it had developed in modern European societies. The expansion of the division of labor meant that many members of society no longer lived directly off the land. Instead, some significant part of the population had come to live by exchanging its labor or manufactured products for the agricultural surplus of landowners. This kind of society harbored a fundamental inequality because the landowner's labor was protected by property rights, whereas the livelihood of the worker and merchant depended on the willingness of landowners to exchange their surplus. Evaluating this inequality was a central concern of eighteenth-century political economy. As we shall see in the next chapter, the theory of property that Fichte developed in *The Closed Commercial State* was a sophisticated attack on the tradition of natural jurisprudence, which supplied the normative basis for these evaluations. Ultimately, Fichte argued, the logic of the social contract required the state to guarantee a right to work and to ensure that every working citizen's standard of living reflected the level of prosperity achieved by the nation. In existing European societies, he charged, only the landowner could be regarded as a rights-bearing citizen; the rest of the population were mere "metics [*Beisassen*] who must purchase the tolerance of the former for whatever price may satisfy him."[32]

To transform these metics into citizens, Fichte's plan of republicanization called upon the state to take control of the economy. The state would secure everybody's subsistence by prioritizing agriculture, and it would ensure that everybody shared in the nation's prosperity by regulating the expansion of all other production. "The superfluous must everywhere be subordinated to the indispensable or to what is difficult to dispense with," Fichte wrote, "equally so in the great economy of the state."[33] Fichte stressed the difference between his

[29] Ibid., 7:119, 138.
[30] Ibid., 7:136.
[31] Ibid., 7:141.
[32] Ibid., 7:85.
[33] Ibid., 7:60.

plan and the traditional republican demand for an agrarian law. An egalitarian redistribution of land would transform workers and merchants into independent landed proprietors, Fichte observed, but the whole society would be reduced to indigence. Reversing the long expansion of the division of labor beyond agriculture would yield only "a miserable nation, still half-left-behind in barbarism." Fichte's goal was not to reverse the expansion of the division of labor but to ensure that it did not take place at the expense of anybody's independence. The economy could not bestow ever-greater comfort and convenience for the few at the expense of ever-greater misery for the many. On the contrary, its growth had to translate into a less burdensome workload for all as well as access to a share of "the most human pleasures" available.[34] Even a simple worker toiling in the fields had a right to enjoy the best his society had to offer, to don his Sunday best and "return to an absolutely human existence" on his day of rest.[35]

The institutions Fichte proposed for realizing these principles were extended and idealized versions of traditional, ancien régime arrangements. The state would set food prices according to a nationally appropriate standard of basic subsistence, and it would guard against natural fluctuations in the food supply by operating public granaries. A farmer whose harvest exceeded the state's calculations would be given a production credit against future shortfalls, and the surplus would be either stored in a public granary or used to address a shortfall in another region. The state's debt would be cancelled during a subsequent bad harvest or, should that fail to happen, via a tax credit.[36] This system would prevent famine (still an immediate concern for a European state in 1800) and ensure that food prices remained stable (a perennial concern).

The philosopher-planners of a newly formed (or reformed) state ought to err on the side of producing an agricultural surplus, Fichte recommended, but a constant surplus was a sign that extra production could be shifted to the manufacturing sector.[37] The state would maintain the proper equilibrium between agriculture and the rest of the economy through a reformed system of guilds. "Abuses by guilds (the remnants of earlier barbarism and general incompetence) ought not to occur," Fichte had written in his treatise on natural right, "but guilds themselves must exist."[38] A system of labor quotas enforced by guilds would enable the state to limit the number of workers and merchants

[34] Ibid., 7:71–72.

[35] Ibid., 7:68.

[36] Ibid., 7:76–77. Such ideas date back to early agricultural societies; a very similar mechanism, dubbed the "ever-normal granary" during the New Deal, remained in operation in the United States until 1972. On eighteenth-century regulation of the grain market, see Steven Kaplan, *Bread, Politics and Political Economy in the Reign of Louis XV* (The Hague: Nijhoff, 1976).

[37] Fichte, *Der geschlossene Handelsstaat*, *Gesamtausgabe*, pt. 1, 7:77.

[38] Fichte, *Foundations of Natural Right*, 203.

authorized to operate in each industry, because these sectors of the economy could be allowed to expand only at the pace set by agricultural productivity. Guilds would also enable the state to control the supply of manufactured goods as effectively as it controlled the food supply. Fichte insisted that supply shortages could never be allowed to result in price increases. The state had to secure a progressively improving quality of life for all its citizens, just as it guaranteed their basic subsistence.

To provide this security, Fichte claimed that the state had to provide incentives (in the form of signing bonuses) and allocate more labor to any particular branch of industry that was failing to meet demand. It might also be possible, he suggested, for the state to replicate the granary mechanism in the manufacturing sector, stockpiling certain goods to guard against potential shortages.[39] Fichte also proposed extending the "just price" regime for subsistence goods to the rest of the economy. A national standard of subsistence could be determined by identifying what was necessary for the simple possibility of life "according to the general opinion of the nation," without reference to personal taste: for example, for some nations, this would be the amount of grain needed to make a certain quantity of bread. There was no corresponding national standard for living well, but Fichte claimed that it was still possible to calculate the value of all other goods by reference to the standard for subsistence. The value of a manufactured product would be determined by its opportunity cost: in other words, by how much of the national staple could have been produced in its place (taking into account the subsistence of the laborers during the time of production as well as the time necessary to educate them and so forth).[40]

Fichte's vision of a planned economy was predicated on the adaptation of his monetary strategy. To set prices and keep them stable, the state had to be able to eliminate all external influences on the money supply.[41] Public spending had to be funded by fixed annual taxes levied in the national currency.[42] As the quantity and value of production rose (as they certainly would in "a laborious and well-governed nation"), the state would increase the money supply accord-

[39] Fichte, *Der geschlossene Handelsstaat*, *Gesamtausgabe*, pt. 1, 7:61–62; cf. the strategic oil reserves instituted by many states during the second half of the twentieth century.

[40] Ibid., 7:65–67. For an earlier example of this kind of calculation, see François-Jean de Chastellux, *De la félicité publique, ou considérations sur le sort des hommes dans les differentes époques de l'histoire* (Amsterdam, 1772), 1:8–22. For an attempt to formalize Fichte's account of a planned economy, see Guido Pult, "Le modèle de planification de Fichte," in *L'état commercial fermé*, ed. Daniel Schulthess, 43–56 (Lausanne: L'Age d'homme, 1980).

[41] The only exception to this rule that Fichte allowed was personal savings, which were impossible to eliminate without injury, and which the state would have to take into account in its calculations. In the case of a newly reformed state, Fichte specified, this would include the case of *ancien regime* pensioners (Fichte, *Der geschlossene Handelsstaat*, *Gesamtausgabe*, pt. 1, 7:82–83).

[42] Ibid., 7:72–75.

ingly by issuing rebates to every household and lowering prices.[43] By following this path, Fichte promised, the state would be able to encourage growth without disrupting the equilibrium between agriculture and the rest of the economy. Nobody's pleasures would come at the expense of anyone else's subsistence, and everyone would share in the benefits of increasing prosperity: "The nature of things, the necessary will of all, and the law, are in agreement."[44]

Fichte described his monetary plan in considerable detail. A major section of *The Closed Commercial State* was devoted to explaining how the plan would transform an existing European state into a republic by enabling it to escape from the jealousy of trade and resolve class conflict. However, this was obviously not a complete "plan of republicanization." *The Closed Commercial State* did not venture into an explicit discussion of constitutional reform, such as Fichte had undertaken in his *Foundations of Natural Right* several years earlier. Newly arrived in Prussia as a refugee from Jena, Fichte addressed the constitutional question indirectly. *The Closed Commercial State* emphasized the catastrophic injustice and violence that would ensue if a state were to employ the kind of monetary strategy it described for nonrepublican ends.

> It is clear from what has been said that the system presented here—should it actually come to be implemented—would have to be accepted or rejected with all of its parts. No government may take the monetary operation described here as just a convenient way to enrich itself, omitting the troublesome business of closing the commercial state, regulating public commerce, fixing prices, and guaranteeing everyone's condition, but allowing itself to make more money arbitrarily, and to put the money into circulation the moment it needs more. Such a method would bring about the insecurity of property and an enormous disorder which would very quickly drive the people to despair and to rebel against the thoroughly unjust government.[45]

The government could be entrusted with control over money only if it were certain to use that control to disengage itself from power politics and redress inequality. A government that gained such a high degree of control over the money supply while remaining engaged in the existing international environment would quickly become a monstrosity. Corruption and undiminished (even increasing) military commitments would lead it to print too much money and trigger massive inflation—a process that Fichte described as outright theft from the populace.

[43] Note that increasing productivity was expected to accrue from increasing population and advancing technology only. Nobody was expected to work harder than the "general customs of the country" required (ibid., 7:135; cf. 7:71–72).

[44] Ibid., 7:80.

[45] Ibid., 7:123.

Preventing this outcome was the one redeeming feature of the existing international monetary system that Fichte was prepared to recognize. Specie was a form of property that could be held beyond the reach of even the most powerful government. Property in precious metals, "the source as well as the final result of all other property, was independent of governments—which, in this regard, found themselves, like the meanest of their subjects, standing under the general necessity—and guaranteed by the agreement of nearly all of humankind." A fiat currency like the one Fichte proposed would eliminate this precious cosmopolitan refuge. In the new system, Fichte acknowledged, "citizens' property in money is dependent on the unlimited will of their masters." The most powerful reason for objecting to his monetary strategy, Fichte imagined, was that it might serve to encourage abuse: "Making governments aware that they have this ability is an enterprise neither humane [*menschenfreundliches*] nor just, and the most one can hope for is that these ideas will be despised and ridiculed as unrealizable dreams, and nobody will ever be able to persuade himself that it could indeed be done."[46]

Fichte's reply to this objection echoed Rousseau. The only way to prevent abuse by the government was to ensure that its interest was aligned with the common good. Crucially, Fichte specified that the economic institutions he described were to be enshrined in constitutional law.[47] Whatever form it took, the government had to be distinguished from and subordinate to the laws. *The Closed Commercial State* does not at all represent an abandonment of Fichte's constitutional theory, but is rather an extension of it. As he had in his treatise on ethics of 1798, Fichte now loudly disavowed his earlier advocacy of violent revolution as a vehicle for reform. Existing constitutions were the unjust products of chance and circumstance, Fichte wrote in the opening pages of *The Closed Commercial State*, but they could not be destroyed suddenly without turning men into savages.[48] Rousseau had written of the need for a legislator—a great founder to give the people laws and realize the social contract. *The Closed Commercial State* was addressed to the administrator whom Fichte hoped would transform Prussia into a constitutional republic according to his script.

The Closed Commercial State and the Political Economy of Prussian Reform

Carl August Struensee was an important participant in the Prussian policy debates that Fichte encountered upon his arrival in Berlin. Widely respected for his technical mastery in the world of eighteenth-century finance, Struensee was

[46] Ibid., 7:126–27.
[47] Ibid., 7:122–23.
[48] Ibid., 7:51.

the elder son of a priest from Halle; he first achieved recognition as a promising mathematician and the author of a treatise on ballistics. It was his even more precocious younger brother, however, who launched his career in high politics by bringing him to Denmark and placing him in charge of its finances. Johann Friedrich Struensee had used his position as the young and insane king's physician, and the queen's lover, to gain control over the Danish government by 1770. The flood of dramatic reforms he immediately introduced—freedom of the press, religious toleration, agrarian reform and the liberalization of trade, abolition of torture—was abruptly halted by a palace coup in January 1772, which resulted in the younger's Struensee's spectacular trial and gruesome execution.[49] Narrowly escaping his brother's fate, Carl August Struensee returned to Prussia after a few months in a Danish prison. He reemerged into public view in 1776 by publishing a set of essays and translations of major works on finance and trade; he then joined the Prussian administration as the director of a provincial bank in 1777 and rose through the ranks until he became minister of customs, excise, trade, and industry, a position that he held from 1791 until his death, in 1804.

The Closed Commercial State was broadly aligned with Struensee's positions on the questions that Fichte had identified in his letter to Cotta: the advisability of monetary reform and the proper limits to trade. Struensee was a staunch advocate of monetary reform throughout his career. He made several determined efforts to modernize Prussia's monetary system and introduce a paper currency in the 1780s and 1790s, but none of them overcame the inertia that continued to plague the Prussian government until it succumbed to Napoleon in 1806. Struensee came closest to succeeding in 1794 as the skyrocketing costs of the war against France threatened to empty Prussia's treasury. Struensee actually won the king's approval for his proposal to introduce a paper currency backed by the assets of the Prussian trading company that he had previously directed, but the plan was stymied by the resistance of officials who remained in charge of the various government accounts, and ultimately came to nothing.[50]

At the same time, Struensee was ambivalent about liberalizing trade. He was sharply critical of the existing host of internal and external trade barriers, and he strongly supported several attempts to eliminate the prohibition on exporting grain—attempts that were repeatedly quashed by powerful military interests nervous about jeopardizing Prussia's strategic reserves.[51] Struensee argued that a system of public granaries could not possibly achieve the capacity necessary to stabilize prices and guarantee the food supply. However, he

[49] Franco Venturi, *The End of the Old Regime in Europe, 1768–1776: The First Crisis* (Princeton: Princeton University Press, 1989), 246–61.

[50] Willy Real, "Die preussischen Staatsfinanzen und die Anbahnung des Sonderfriedens von Basel, 1795," *Forschungen zur brandenburgischen und preussischen Geschichte*, n.s., 1 (1991): 53–100.

[51] Rolf Straubel, *Carl August von Struensee: Preussische Wirtschafts- und Finanzpolitik im Ministeriellen Kräftespiel (1786–1804/06)* (Potsdam: Verlag für Berlin-Brandenburg, 1999).

also rejected principled calls for a completely free market in subsistence goods, such as those made by the French Physiocrats and their German admirers. Instead, looking to the English agriculturist Arthur Young, Struensee explored how Prussia might adopt England's policy of export subsidies as an alternative method of stabilizing domestic food prices. Struensee was also a staunch defender of existing protections for domestic manufacturers. In a 1790 article in the *Berlinische Monatsschrift*, Struensee defended the justice of these protective measures against calls for free trade. An isolated individual might appeal to his natural liberty to buy whatever he wished, Struensee wrote, but the citizen of a state could not. The state was charged with encouraging population growth and protecting its citizens, so it had to give precedence to the livelihood of domestic manufacturers over their English or French competitors. Anyone who thought that Prussia could survive and prosper in modern Europe as a purely agrarian state, Struensee concluded, would do well to consider the fate of Poland.[52]

Struensee was actively engaged in these debates when Fichte arrived in Prussia and published *The Closed Commercial State*. (Notably, his collected works were also published in Berlin in 1800.)[53] In 1798–99, Struensee was appointed to the commission that the newly enthroned Friedrich Wilhelm III had created to examine Prussia's tottering finances and conduct a comprehensive review of its economic strategy. Once again, Struensee advocated the introduction of a paper currency and the elimination of export prohibitions, but he and his allies failed to achieve any results.[54] It was this defeat, combined with Struensee's redoubled efforts to protect Prussian manufacturers against what he considered to be English dumping, that led the eminent historian of Prussia's early reform movement, Otto von Hintze, to blame him for Prussia's inertia. While others have described Struensee as the predecessor of Stein, Hardenberg, and the next generation of reformers, who eventually brought about the regeneration of Prussia, Hintze singled him out as a defender of the status quo whose excessive caution doomed all hope of reform before 1806. Struensee "lacked every quality necessary in a reformer," Hintze wrote in 1896. Despite Struensee's friendship with Sieyès, and his notorious remark to a French diplomat that

[52] The question whether Germany ought to develop as a self-sufficient "agrarian"-based state or an export-oriented "industrial" state was again the subject of much debate at the turn of the twentieth century, and renewed attention was paid to Fichte's *Closed Commercial State* in this context; see Weber, *Fichte's Sozialismus*, 62–63. On these debates and her husband Max Weber's intervention in them after his study of Elbing (the same town where Struensee had begun his Prussian career as director of the local bank), see Keith Tribe, "Prussian Agriculture —German Politics: Max Weber, 1892–7," in *Reading Weber*, ed. Tribe, 85–130 (London: Routledge, 1989); and Max Weber, "Germany as an Industrial State," in ibid., 210–20.

[53] Carl August von Struensee, *Abhandlungen über wichtige Gegenstände der Staatswirthschaft*, 3 vols. (Berlin: Unger, 1800).

[54] Horst Petzold, *Die Verhandlungen der 1798 von König Friedrich Wilhelm III: Eingesetzten Finanzkommission* (Göttingen, 1912).

Prussia's top-down reforms would peacefully match the social leveling that the French Revolution had achieved through violence, Hintze deemed him not a reformer but "the most significant representative of the old Frederican system," who "systematically developed" that system "to its logical conclusion."[55]

Struensee's caution is perhaps understandable given his tragic experience in Denmark. It is less obvious, but necessary to explain, how Struensee repeatedly became a magnet for rather less cautious advocates of radical reform. A decade before his encounters with Sieyès and Fichte, Struensee had gained the admiration and close friendship of the comte de Mirabeau. The estranged son of a celebrated philosopher, Mirabeau had been a notorious philanderer, gambler, and financial speculator before the Revolution transformed him into a statesman and orator. He was also a prominent critic of the economic system that Frederick the Great had developed in Prussia. Mirabeau had visited Berlin at the very end of Frederick's reign to research what became a monumental eight-volume history of Prussia and to dabble in diplomatic intrigue (he also wrote a scandalous account of the Prussian court during the succession).[56] "This man very much ought to be looked after," Mirabeau wrote of Struensee to the French *contrôleur général des finances*, Charles-Alexandre de Calonne, in 1786.[57] In his 1787 open letter to Frederick the Great's successor, Friedrich Wilhelm II, Mirabeau publicly recommended Struensee as the only man in Prussia capable of pulling off the economic reforms that, in his opinion, were necessary to prevent it from collapsing.[58]

According to Mirabeau, Frederick had unquestionably been a great man, but the economic and political system he had created was "radically vicious."[59] His flawed system had been born of the imperative of forming a great military as quickly as possible in a fragmented and not terribly fertile land. Like his father, Frederick had resorted to whatever measures would extract precious metals from his subjects and deliver them to the army as quickly as possible. Taxes and tariffs were multiplied, privileges and monopolies proliferated, and wages and prices were micromanaged—all at cross-purposes to Frederick's efforts at

[55] Otto Hintze, "Prussian Reform Movements before 1806" (1896), in *The Historical Essays of Otto Hintze*, ed. Felix Gilbert (New York: Oxford University Press, 1975), 78.

[56] Honoré-Gabriel de Riqueti, comte de Mirabeau, *De la monarchie prussienne, sous Frédéric le Grand; avec un appendice contenant des recherches sur la situation actuelle des principales contrées de l'Allemagne*, 7 vols. (London, 1788); and *Histoire secrete de la cour de Berlin, ou correspondance d'un voyageur françois, depuis le mois de juillet 1786 jusqu'au 19 janvier 1787*, 2 vols. (London, 1789). Among the many acquaintances Mirabeau made in Berlin was Alexandre d'Hauterive, who was passing through on his way from Moldavia back to Paris (Artaud de Montor, *La vie du comte d'Hauterive*, 57–58).

[57] Comte de Mirabeau to Charles-Alexandre de Calonne, 31 July 1786, in comte de Mirabeau, *Histoire secrete de la cour de Berlin*, 1:71 (letter 9).

[58] Comte de Mirabeau, *Lettre remise à Frédéric-Guillaume II*, 284.

[59] Ibid., 269.

encouraging commerce and manufacturing. In the end, Mirabeau charged, Frederick's despotic style of governing through informal channels had saddled his successor with an ineffective bureaucracy as well as a backward economy hampered by a system of "fiscal robbery" and "systematic monopoly."[60] However, Mirabeau continued, Frederick had also provided his successor with the resources to recover from this dire predicament by leaving Prussia free of debts and even in possession of an ample war treasury.

Prussia was unique among the European powers in this respect, and during the American Revolution, the abbé Mably had predicted that Prussia's independence from modern finance would allow it to become the savior of Europe: once a general debt crisis had crippled the other states and raised the specter of military dictatorship everywhere else, Prussia alone would remain to restore Europe's liberty.[61] Mirabeau took the opposite line from Mably's austere republican moralizing. Prussia had to embrace modern finance in order to introduce sweeping economic, social, and political reforms, or it would certainly cease to be a great power. Military power could no longer be sustained without "permanent foundations." Prussia had to be transformed from an "armed camp" into "a stable and prosperous monarchy, founded on freedom and property."[62] Creating a bank and introducing a paper currency would stimulate an economy that was throttled by the scarcity of specie. The interest on money would provide a substitute for the existing system of stifling taxes and duties and create an opportunity for sweeping social and economic reform. (Mirabeau's court memoir hints that he, and possibly his allies in the French government as well, might have anticipated significant opportunities for themselves in the establishment of a future Prussian state bank.)[63] In concluding his letter to the king, Mirabeau nominated Struensee, who "will confirm all my principles," as the only man in Prussia who was capable of implementing such a monetary reform.[64]

The kind of monetary strategy that Mirabeau proposed for Prussia (and soon afterward was instrumental in convincing France to adopt) followed a path originally marked out by another scandalous gambler and financial speculator turned statesman, John Law (1671–1729). Law was a Scot who rose to become *contrôleur général des finances* in France during the regency of the duc

[60] Ibid., 273.

[61] Cited in Sonenscher, *Before the Deluge*, 251. Mably also extended the same kind of advice to the American revolutionaries.

[62] Comte de Mirabeau, *Lettre remise à Frédéric-Guillaume II*, 275. Mirabeau was not entirely exaggerating: Prussia's army was among the most powerful in Europe, but the state was only the tenth largest in area and thirteenth in population (Otto Busch, *Militärsystem und Sozialleben im alten Preussen, 1713–1807: Die Anfange der sozialen Militarisierung der preussisch-deutschen Gesellschaft* [Berlin: de Gruyter, 1962], 2; cited in Tribe, *Governing Economy*, 9).

[63] Comte de Mirabeau to Calonne, 7 November 1786 and 16 December 1786, in comte de Mirabeau, *Histoire secrete de la cour de Berlin*, 2:19–20 (letter 44) and 2:165–67 (letter 56).

[64] Comte de Mirabeau, *Lettre remise à Frédéric-Guillaume II*, 284.

d'Orléans.[65] Law persuaded the regent that his ambitious scheme for the introduction of paper money could solve the massive debt crisis that was the legacy of Louis XIV's many wars. Law built up his famous system between 1717 and 1720. This complex set of institutions sought to replicate the success of the Bank of England in promoting trade while enabling France to pay down its crushing debt. By expanding the money supply, it promised to generate a powerful economic stimulus, unlocking France's unrealized economic potential and replacing a vicious cycle of tax payments and debt service with a virtuous circle of investment, production, and trade. Law's system collapsed in 1720 after a spectacular wave of financial speculation (mirrored in England by the South Sea Bubble). Despite this collapse, Law's monetary strategy continued to exercise imaginations throughout the course of the eighteenth century. When Mirabeau, among others, sought to promote the transformation of the revolutionary *assignat* from a means of debt payment into a nationally circulating paper currency in 1790, the arguments he brought before the Constituent Assembly were a reprise of Law's.[66]

For many eighteenth-century observers, however, the failure of Law's experiment confirmed some of their worst fears about the political ramifications of modern financial innovation. Michael Sonenscher has recently revealed the extent to which such fears permeated eighteenth-century political analysis and political theory.[67] Montesquieu was one of Law's many critics. In his view, a credit-based monetary system like the one Law had tried to create threatened to give the state arbitrary control over its subjects' property and eliminate vital moderating influences on the behavior of the modern centralized state, making Law "one of the greatest promoters of despotism that had until then been seen in Europe."[68] Hume also worried that modern finance would ultimately result in an unprecedented form of despotism. The impracticality of Law's ambitious debt-reduction scheme confronted states with a potentially deadly dilemma.

[65] Law first developed his theory in Scotland in 1705 as a solution to the monetary crisis brought on by the failure of Scotland's bid to establish an independent commercial empire in Panama. Law proposed establishing a land bank that would increase the money supply by issuing paper money backed by landholdings, claiming that this would redress unemployment and the underutilization of resources. However, Law's proposal was caught up in intensive parliamentary debate about union between England and Scotland (even provoking a duel involving Andrew Fletcher of Saltoun) and subsequently dropped; see Antoin E. Murphy, *John Law: Economic Theorist and Policy-Maker* (Oxford: Clarendon Press, 1997), 67–75.

[66] Antoin E. Murphy, "John Law and the Assignats," in *La Pensée Économique pendant la Révolution Française*, ed. Philippe Steiner and Gilbert Faccarello, 431–48 (Grenoble: Presses universitaires de Grenoble, 1990); and Jean-Claude Perrot, *Une Histoire Intellectuelle de l'économie politique, XVIIe–XVIIIe siècle* (Paris: Éditions de l'École des hautes études en sciences sociales, 1992), 195–215.

[67] Sonenscher, "Nation's Debt and the Modern Republic" and *Before the Deluge*.

[68] Charles-Louis de Secondat, baron de Montesquieu, *The Spirit of the Laws* (1748), ed. Anne M. Cohler, Basia C. Miller, and Harold S. Stone (Cambridge: Cambridge University Press, 1989), 19 (bk. 2, ch. 4).

Faced with a vital national interest (like Britain's need to restore the European balance of power against France), the state's survival might require it to default on its ballooning war debts—but this would amount to expropriating its creditors. Hume initially echoed Viscount Bolingbroke in calling for a patriotic regime to be prepared to make this sacrifice for the greater good. However, he later came to the conclusion that this outcome could completely destroy civil liberty. If the debt grew large enough, Hume imagined, a voluntary bankruptcy would leave the government in complete control of its subjects' wealth. In such a nightmare scenario, "the whole income of every individual in the state must lie entirely at the mercy of the sovereign," Hume wrote, yielding a "degree of despotism which no oriental monarchy has ever yet attained."[69] Hume's pessimistic prognosis was taken up by Kant, among many others, and applied to the events of the French Revolution. In Kant's analysis, it was the French monarchy's failure to administer "the heroic medicine which Hume prescribes" that ultimately led to the creation, in democratic form, of the very despotism Hume had feared would result from a voluntary bankruptcy:

> It was thus a great error of judgment on the part of a certain powerful ruler in our own times when he tried to relieve himself of the embarrassment of large national debts by leaving it to the people to assume and distribute this burden at their own discretion. It was thus natural that the people should acquire legislative powers not only in matters of taxation but also in matters of government, for they had to ensure that the government would incur no new debts by extravagance or by war. The monarch's ruling authority thus disappeared completely; for it was not merely suspended but actually passed over to the people, to whose legislative will the property of every subject was now submitted.[70]

Struensee was among those who denied that the political future of modern finance was necessarily so bleak. One of Struensee's first publications was a German translation of Isaac de Pinto's *Traité de la circulation et du credit* (1771), an influential defense of public debt by a prominent Portuguese-Jewish financier in Amsterdam.[71] Pinto (1717–87) had argued that, within limits, rising public debt did not necessarily foretell the kind of stark dilemma that Hume

[69] David Hume, "Of Public Credit," in *Essays*, 359; see Sonenscher, "Nation's Debt and the Modern Republic," 83; see also Hont, *Jealousy of Trade*, 325–53, originally published as "The Rhapsody of Public Debt: David Hume and Voluntary State Bankruptcy," in *Political Discourse in Early Modern Britain*, ed. Nicholas Phillipson and Quentin Skinner, 321–48 (Cambridge: Cambridge University Press, 1993).

[70] Immanuel Kant, *Rechtslehre* (1797), in *Political Writings*, 189; see Sonenscher, "Nation's Debt and the Modern Republic," 322.

[71] Carl August von Struensee, *Sammlung von Aufsätzen, die grösstentheils wichtige Punkte der Staatswirthschaft betreffen*, vol. 1 (Liegnitz und Leipzig, 1776).

and others feared. On the contrary, Pinto echoed Law's basic premise that the debt could be translated into a powerful economic stimulus, generating public expenditures and stimulating a cascade of private investment. In his essay *On the means for a state to obtain money for extraordinary means, especially in times of war* (1776), Struensee rehearsed Montesquieu's and Hume's fears at length. However, he consistently defended the monetary principles underlying Law's system as well as the *assignats.* Though he acknowledged the potential for abuse and catastrophe, Struensee always defended the idea that a prudent administration supported by public opinion could use its credit to encourage growth and provide its citizens with employment.[72]

Similar arguments were also deployed in the service of much more ambitious claims about the potential of modern finance to bring about a more just and peaceful world. As Sonenscher has shown, the reasons that led Montesquieu and others to view Law as a promoter of despotism could also be seen as reasons to hope for the moral transformation of existing European societies. A monetary system like Law's would transform the propertied classes into capitalists who would invest their wealth in increasing production. It would also give the state a lever with which to mitigate the inequality of the modern division of labor without having to take the supremely contentious step of redistributing landed property through an agrarian law. A direct collision between the justice of defending property rights and the justice of providing for everyone else's livelihood could thus be averted, and the corrosive effects of inequality as Rousseau described them in his *Second Discourse* could be bypassed.[73]

Law's project was particularly attractive to admirers of Fénelon. Fénelon's *Telemachus* (1699) had outlined a comprehensive plan for revitalizing France by purging it of the luxury and militarism that had corrupted it under Louis XIV.[74] Even more, as Fénelon's Scottish Jacobite follower Andrew Michael Ramsay claimed, *Telemachus* outlined a moral vision of society that not only overturned the "injustice and irreligion" of Machiavelli and Hobbes, but also corrected the overly parsimonious and insufficiently humane justice of Grotius and Pufendorf.[75] Fénelon's classic tract inspired many imitations, including

[72] Struensee, *Wichtige Gegenstände der Staatswirthschaft,* 1:274.

[73] Sonenscher, "Nation's Debt and the Modern Republic," 74–75. It was for this reason that Bishop Berkeley, who had visited Paris during Law's experiment, described the idea of a national bank as the philosopher's stone that would show how to put a relatively backward society like Ireland on the path to realizing Plato's republic; see Istvan Hont, "The Luxury Debate in the Early Enlightenment," in *The Cambridge History of Eighteenth-Century Political Thought,* ed. M. Goldie and R. Wokler, 401–3 (Cambridge: Cambridge University Press, 2006).

[74] Montesquieu acknowledged the connection in his satire of Law's system in *Persian Letters*; see Sonenscher, *Before the Deluge,* 116–18.

[75] Andrew Michael Ramsay, "A Discourse upon Epick Poetry, and the Excellence of the Poem of Telemachus," in *The Adventures of Telemachus, the Son of Ulysses,* 12th ed. (Dublin, 1725), xiii–xiv; cited in Sonenscher, "Nation's Debt and the Modern Republic," 74.

the *Travels of Cyrus* by Ramsay (1727) and *Psammitichus* (1759–60) by J.H.G. von Justi, the premier political economist in Prussia.[76] For some enthusiastic readers of *Telemachus*, Law's system suggested how modern finance could be used to achieve Fénelon's moral vision without having to resort to the austerity of his sumptuary laws or the severity of his rural resettlement policy. Besides serving as the mild, modern equivalent of the agrarian law, a monetary system like Law's also complemented Fénelon's vision of an international order based on the spirit of commerce rather than the spirit of conquest—a vision fleshed out most fully in the abbé de Saint-Pierre's peace plan. It promised to revitalize a French economy crippled and distorted by the massive debts and monopolizing trade policies that had fueled Louis XIV's disastrous quest for military hegemony. By severing the link between public debt and interstate rivalry, it could set the stage for the creation of a peaceful system of international free trade under France's commercial hegemony.

Saint-Pierre was himself an admirer of Law; his protégé, the marquis d'Argenson, wrote a defense of Law's monetary strategy. D'Argenson also wrote a manuscript treatise on "democratic monarchy," describing the kinds of reforms that would enable the French government to administer a credit-based monetary system more responsibly than Law had. This treatise was praised by Voltaire in 1739 as the true realization of Fénelon's mythical model of a reformed France, Salentum.[77] Voltaire's praise for d'Argenson's treatise was closely linked to his support for a French foreign policy that would actively seek to impose this Fénelonian vision on the rest of Europe. Voltaire was among the French supporters of the Jacobite exiles (the same milieu out of which Law had emerged) who imagined a Stuart restoration in Britain as part of the establishment of a pacified European states system. Voltaire was also among those who envisioned France taking the lead in extending this system to Germany. In 1739,

[76] Andrew Michael Ramsay, *The Travels of Cyrus*, 2 vols. (London, 1727); Johann Heinrich Gottlob von Justi, *Die Grundfeste zu der Macht und Glückseeligkeit der Staaten, oder Ausführliche Vorstellung der gesamten Policey-Wissenschaft* (Königsberg, 1760). On Justi, see Ulrich Adam, *The Political Economy of J.H.G. Justi* (Bern: Peter Lang, 2006). Compare also Jean Terrasson, *Sethos, histoire, ou Vie tirée des monumens anecdotes de l'ancienne Égypte, traduite d'un manuscrit grec*, 3 vols. (Paris, 1731), an important source for Mozart's *Magic Flute*, which is closely examined in an unpublished paper by Mark Somos.

[77] René-Louis de Voyer de Paulmy, marquis d'Argenson, *Considérations sur le gouvernement ancien et présent de la France*, circulated in manuscript in 1739 but published (in redacted form) only in 1764. Voltaire enthusiastically claimed, "I find all my ideas in your work," and encouraged d'Argenson to publish the manuscript: "It can be said more justly of this work than of *Télémaque*, that if a book can give birth to the well-being of humankind [as the writer Jean Terrasson had said of *Télémaque*], it would be this book . . . This is not any longer the colony of Salentum where Mr de Fénelon wants there to be no pastry-chefs, and seven modes of dress. This here is something very real, which experience proves in a most striking manner" (Voltaire to d'Argenson, 8 May 1739, in Voltaire, *Correspondence and Related Documents: January–September 1739*, ed. Theodore Besterman, *Oeuvres Complètes*, vol. 90 [Geneva: Institut et Musée Voltaire, 1970], D2008).

Voltaire asked whether he could send d'Argenson's closely guarded manuscript to his royal pupil, who was still the crown prince of Prussia, but d'Argenson (who later served as minister of France in the 1750s) denied his request.[78]

A very similar spirit animated the younger Mirabeau's overture to Frederick the Great's successor upon his ascension to the throne several decades later. A wide array of strategies for implementing Fénelon's transformative vision continued to emerge throughout the latter half of the eighteenth century, which is why Benjamin Vaughan (an admirer of Adam Smith and Benjamin Franklin), writing in 1788, and Alexandre d'Hauterive, writing in 1800, could both describe Fénelon as the true founder of political economy.[79] The dream of harnessing the power of modern finance to Fénelon's moral vision was embraced by the political economist James Steuart, among many others, and taken up with great enthusiasm by Mirabeau and contemporaries like Jacques Brissot and Etienne Clavière.[80] In his 1787 letter to Frederick Wilhelm II, Mirabeau promised the same kinds of advantages for Prussia that Voltaire had sought for Frederick the Great. By adopting an ambitious program of monetary reform under Struensee's leadership, Mirabeau claimed, Prussia would become free, wealthy, and just—the first state where "all men who wish to labor shall find work."[81] Prussia could then take its place in a peaceful new international system, ideally one cemented by a commercial treaty between France and Britain.[82]

The implementation strategy detailed in Fichte's *Closed Commercial State* is another variation on the themes that Mirabeau had evoked in his letter to Frederick Wilhelm II and that had emerged among Fénelonian admirers of Law. Fichte's monetary proposal was on the radical end of the spectrum: he suggested immediately and entirely demonetizing specie and replacing it with a pure fiat currency whose value was backed solely by the credit of the state, not by land or trading-company assets, as in most eighteenth-century projects both real and imagined.[83] Nonetheless, *The Closed Commercial State* echoed the claims

[78] Voltaire to d'Argenson, 21 June 1739; and d'Argenson to Voltaire, 7 July 1739, in Voltaire, *Correspondence: January–September 1739*, 411 (letter D2035), 422 (letter D2041). See Nannerl O. Henry, "Democratic Monarchy: The Political Theory of the Marquis d'Argenson" (PhD diss., Yale University, 1968), 75.

[79] Benjamin Vaughan, *New and Old Principles of Trade Compared; or A Treatise on the Principles of Commerce Between Nations; with an Appendix* (London, 1788), vii; d'Hauterive, *State of the French Republic*, 130–31.

[80] Sonenscher, "Nation's Debt and the Modern Republic," 291–96.

[81] Comte de Mirabeau, *Lettre remise à Frédéric-Guillaume II*, 261.

[82] See Mirabeau to Calonne, 24 November 1786, in comte de Mirabeau, *Histoire secrete de la cour de Berlin*, 2:84–87 (letter 50).

[83] Several proposals for actually implementing this kind of money were broached during the debates about the assignats in 1792–93. See Seymour Edwin Harris, *The Assignats* (Cambridge, Mass.: Harvard University Press, 1930), 15; and Bruguière, "Assignats," 432. As a report to the National Convention noted, "If France did not have any foreign commercial relations, a conventional money

made by promoters of paper money since Law, and shared the ambitious hopes of Fénelon's admirers about its potential to bring about a comprehensive moral transformation of society.[84] Like them, Fichte presented his monetary strategy as a modern alternative to the forceful restoration of an agrarian economy. He claimed that the state could acquire the means of correcting the injustice of the modern division of labor by controlling the money supply. Paper money would free up specie for the purchasing of capital goods and investment in production, and the rising prosperity of the closed commercial state would enable it to secure a greater measure of justice for its citizens. Many eighteenth-century writers, including both Hume and Steuart, had speculated about how a sudden repudiation of debts might free up enough tax revenue to create an instant military advantage; Fichte claimed that his monetary strategy would generate enough hard currency to pay for the bloodless conquest of a large domestic market.[85] Perhaps Fichte's assertion that Britain and France naturally formed one political unit was a bizarre echo of the dream of a commercial treaty between France and Britain.[86]

Fichte responded to the fear that modern finance was a vehicle for despotism with an understated reference to his development of Rousseau's constitutional theory. In this respect, he was following Sieyès, who had maintained that a carefully designed government could safely manage a public debt so long as it was subordinated to the sovereign authority of the nation.[87] However, Fichte went a big step further than Sieyès in suggesting that similar constitutional mechanisms could stabilize and restrain an administration with a vastly greater responsibility: it would be tasked with managing the monetary system and regulating the entire economy in order to realize an expansive conception of justice. Fichte insisted that this ambitious approach was necessary in order to shield the state from the corrosive effects of interstate rivalry and eliminate the sources of class conflict. Only under these conditions would states be capable of participating in a legalized international order and a peaceful system of complementary trade. Only then, too, could the reforming of the state be construed as the first step toward bringing about a moral world.

---

would be sufficient for its internal and everyday exchanges; but so long as our morals are not regenerated, and the produce of our own soil is not enough for our needs, we shall be forced to resort to our neighbors to satisfy the needs which luxury invented" (Anne-Alexandre-Marie Thibault, *Rapport sur la Fabrication d'une Nouvelle Monnoie de Billon* [Paris, 1793], 2).

[84] On Tom Paine, the marquis de Condorcet, and similar thinkers of the 1790s in this context, see also Gareth Stedman Jones, *An End to Poverty? A Historical Debate* (London: Profile, 2004).

[85] Sonenscher, "Nation's Debt and the Modern Republic," 83–84.

[86] Fichte, *Der geschlossene Handelsstaat*, *Gesamtausgabe*, pt. 1, 7:118.

[87] Sonenscher, "Nation's Debt and the Modern Republic," 310–13.

Fichte's Moral Challenge Continued

The Closed Commercial State was a development of the moral critique of commercial society and power politics that had animated Fichte's early political thought. When August Wilhelm von Rehberg dismissed the "naive" principle that only those who worked could claim a right to eat, Fichte retorted in 1793 that surely it was more naive to conclude that only those who did not work could claim that right.[88] Such views were not exclusive to revolutionaries like Robespierre or Babeuf. As Michael Sonenscher has argued, and as Ramsay's preference for Fénelon over Grotius and Pufendorf illustrates, they were indicative of a much broader spectrum of eighteenth-century thought.[89] Fichte's more expansive conception of distributive justice reflects this broad dissatisfaction with the moral opacity of seventeenth-century natural-rights theories, which—so it seemed to many, including Rousseau—readily served to justify absolute sovereignty and the tremendous inequality brought about by the modern division of labor. However, as the next chapter will show, Fichte embedded his expansive conception of distributive justice in a rights theory that gave absolute priority to the independence of the individual. This was no straightforward betrayal of his youthful individualism, but the result still carries a profound ambiguity. Was Fichte a visionary moralist who couched his radical program in a deceptively skeptical juridical idiom? Or was he merely giving that idiom a much more vividly critical expression?

This ambiguity colors the theory of politics that *The Closed Commercial State* claimed to exemplify and that Fichte sketched out in his dedication to Struensee. "It would perhaps be an instructive historical investigation," Fichte wrote, "to consider the question whether more evil in the world has resulted from daring innovation, or from sluggish attachment to old rules which are no longer applicable or adequate."[90] Fichte was evidently partial to the latter conclusion. To insist on a purely empirical approach to politics was to condemn humanity to remain eternally hostage to historical contingency. At the same time, Fichte claimed that to derive metaphysical concepts like rights

[88] Fichte, *Beitrag zur Berichtigung der Urtheile über die französische Revolution*, *Gesamtausgabe*, pt. 1, 1:320; cf. 1:267.

[89] Michael Sonenscher, "Property, Community and Citizenship," in *The Cambridge History of Eighteenth-Century Political Thought*, ed. M. Goldie and R. Wokler, 465–96 (Cambridge: Cambridge University Press, 2006).

[90] Fichte, *Der geschlossene Handelsstaat*, *Gesamtausgabe*, pt. 1, 7:43. Compare John Maynard Keynes's famous remark that "the ideas of economists and political philosophers, both when they are right and when they are wrong, are more powerful than is commonly understood. Indeed the world is ruled by little else. Practical men, who believe themselves to be quite exempt from any intellectual influences, are usually the slaves of some defunct economist. Madmen in authority, who hear voices in the air, are distilling their frenzy from some academic scribbler of a few years back" (Keynes, *The General Theory of Employment, Interest, and Money* [London: Macmillan, 1936], 383).

from first principles without proceeding to show how they could be realized in the real world was to play an empty utopian game. It was not sufficient for a "speculative philosopher" to show the "practicing politician" that theory and practice could (in theory) be united. On the contrary, Fichte insisted, it was the task of the "speculative politician" to show the "practicing politician" what could (in practice) be done to bring them closer together.[91] This task employed both normative theory and historical analysis to show "what is realizable, in the given conditions, of that which conforms to right."[92] The historical analysis had to be sufficiently general to yield a general theory of politics; otherwise there could be a politics appropriate only to a particular country, or even to a particular country at a given moment: "England, France, Prussia, in fact for these states in the year 1800, in fact in the fall of the year 1800, etc." As we have seen, *The Closed Commercial State* identified "the general condition common to just about all the states of the great European republic in the era when it was established" as the relevant starting point for its analysis of modern European commerce.[93] In these conditions, Fichte claimed, the closing of the commercial state was the sole law of politics for all modern European states.[94] It was up to Struensee and his counterparts to apply this law to their own countries at the appropriate moment.

On the one hand, Fichte declared his ambition to draw a "fixed line" that would show "practicing politicians" how to proceed toward the creation of a just world, where there would no longer be any distinction between politics and rights theory.[95] On the other hand, Fichte accepted that even his theory of politics would remain nothing more than a scholarly exercise until a long-term historical process had unraveled Europe's domination over the rest of the world: it was "a link in the chain of the system," which he had to "elaborate bit by bit," and its aim was merely to give "the occasion to reflect more profoundly on these subjects."[96] The "practicing politician" to whom these remarks were addressed seems to have read them in this latter vein. It seems likely that Struensee would have been at least somewhat sympathetic to Fichte's vision of radical social transformation: after all, this was the man who reportedly declared that "in a few years there will no longer be a privileged class in Prussia."[97] In thanking Fichte for the presentation copy he had sent him, however, Struensee described the book in a more straightforwardly Kantian way, as a particularly vivid statement of a regulative ideal:

[91] Fichte, *Der geschlossene Handelsstaat*, *Gesamtausgabe*, pt. 1, 7:41–42.
[92] Ibid., 7:51.
[93] Ibid., 7:42.
[94] Ibid., 7:114.
[95] Ibid., 7:51.
[96] Ibid., 7:44.
[97] Otto to Talleyrand, 13 August 1799, in Bailleu, *Preussen und Frankreich*, 1:505.

> The book [your honor] sent me yesterday, *The Closed Commercial State*, has made me an agreeable gift. As it pleased you to dedicate this book to me publicly, so I assure you of my great gratitude for it. I reserve further discussion of the book's contents with you for the future. I have been convinced that there is a very great amount of good to be found in it, so perhaps I can now judge it to represent the ideal of a state—the ideal towards which every official who is part of the administration has the duty to strive. Whether this ideal may ever be reached is something you yourself doubt, but this does not mar the perfection of the work. In any case, I want first to finish reading your book, and then we shall take the opportunity to speak about it.[98]

Struensee made the same point in a letter to Karl Friedrich Beyme (1765–1838), the head of the royal cabinet, who later gave Fichte a prominent role in the founding of the University of Berlin. In Struensee's opinion, the politics of *The Closed Commercial State* were well suited to Prussia, but the book was hardly a guide to policy:

> The content of the book is entirely theoretical, and it can be known *a priori* that neither the state it describes nor the money it proposes will ever exist as described. But Fichte was consistent [*consequent*] nearly throughout, and therefore it is a good example of logic. Several of the ideas explained in this book even fit rather well into our system. E.g. that no foreign goods must be allowed into the country—that neither gold nor silver is necessary in order to have money—that the famous freedom of trade is nothing more and nothing less than what we call anarchy in civil society.[99]

Intriguingly, *The Closed Commercial State* did find some enthusiastic early readers who were eager to use it as a policy manual.[100] But from the perspective

[98] Struensee to Fichte, 9 November 1800, in Fichte, *Gesamtausgabe*, pt. 3, 4:353.

[99] Struensee to Beyme, 16 November 1800, in Fichte, *Gesamtausgabe*, pt. 1, 7:13. Struensee was asking Beyme to pass along a copy to the king, as Fichte had requested, should Beyme deem it appropriate. Struensee concluded: "If I can tell Prof. Fichte that you have given the King his book, and that he received it well, then I will make him very happy."

[100] The *Closed Commercial State* inspired a reform proposal sent to Czar Alexander I of Russia by a famous Russian philosophe in 1801; see Wladimir Alexejevič Abaschnik, "Das Konzept des geschlossenen Handelsstaates Fichtes in der Rezeption von Vassilij Nasarovič Karasin," *Fichte-Studien* 24 (2003): 143–54. For somewhat speculative suggestions about a similarly inclined readership in the Rhineland, see Jacques Droz, *La pensée politique et morale des cisrhénans* (Paris: Sorlot, 1940). For a discussion of the book's possible influence on the generation of reformers that re-created the Prussian state after 1807, see Frank Schuurmans, "State, Society, and the Market: Karl Sigmund Altenstein and the Languages of Reform, 1770–1807" (PhD diss., University of Wisconsin at Madison, 1995), 304–408. The book also figured in Bavarian debates about whether the remnants of

of German academic political economy, *The Closed Commercial State* was easily dismissed. In his 1807 textbook on political economy, the eminent cameralist Theodor Schmalz (later Fichte's colleague at the University of Berlin—Schmalz was the university's first rector, Fichte the second) professed great respect for Fichte as a philosopher, but wrote that it "pained him greatly" that Fichte had ever written his treatise on natural right. Likewise, Schmalz observed, *The Closed Commercial State* merely served to demonstrate Fichte's "thorough unfamiliarity in things of this sort, namely the nature of money."[101] The young Adam Müller wrote a scathing review in the *Neue Berlinische Monatsschrift*, proclaiming Fichte's complete ignorance of political economy: the review was so mean spirited that even Friedrich Gentz, Müller's patron and certainly no friend of Fichte's, strongly chastised him for his impropriety.[102] But as the next chapter shows, at least one contemporary political economist explicitly recognized both the force of Fichte's moral challenge to his discipline and the significance of the form that challenge assumed in *The Closed Commercial State.*

---

the guild system might be made compatible with a modernizing economy, as an alternative to the physiocratic model of free markets; see Kaspar von Hagens, *Philosophische und politische Untersuchung über die Rechtmässigkeit der Zünfte und Polizeytaxen und ihre Wirkungen auf die bürgerl: Gesellschaft mit besonderer Hinsicht auf Fichtes geschlossenen Handelsstaat* (München: Scherer, 1804); Franz Joseph Bern Tenzel, *Wie kann in Deutschland die Zunftverfassung am zweckmässigsten modificirt* (Landshut, Germany, 1817); Carla De Pascale, "Franz von Baader und Der Geschlossene Handelsstaat," in *Erneuerung der Transzendentalphilosophie: Im Anschluss an Kant und Fichte*, ed. Klaus Hammacher and Albert Mues, 259–73 (Stuttgart–Bad Cannstatt: Frommann-Holzboog, 1979).

[101] Theodor Schmalz, *Handbuch der Rechtsphilosophie* (Halle, 1807), v.

[102] Adam Müller, "Ueber einen philosophischen Entwurf von Hrn Fichte; betitelt: 'Der geschlossne Handelstaat,'" *Neue Berlinische Monatsschrift* 6 (December 1801): 458; Friedrich Gentz to Adam Müller, 15 December 1801, in Fuchs, Lauth, and Schieche, *Fichte im Gespräch*, 3:90–91.

Chapter 4

Fichte's Political Economy of the General Will

Hestermann's Review

Ludwig Hestermann's *Open Commercial State*, a book-length rebuttal of Fichte's work, was published in Stuttgart in 1802.[1] It was a serious and considered reply to *The Closed Commercial State*, yet it appears to be neglected by modern scholars. According to Hestermann, Fichte's book was a powerful moral challenge aimed at the discipline of political economy. *The Closed Commercial State* disputed the claim that the inequality of market society could be justified by appeal to the principle of natural liberty—a claim that Hestermann (like many others) identified closely with Adam Smith (1723–90). In Hestermann's assessment, what made *The Closed Commercial State* so remarkable was its attempt to ground this challenge in the same doctrine of individual rights expounded by partisans of natural liberty like Smith.

Developing Hestermann's insight is an important step toward clarifying the character of Fichte's property theory and the connection between this theoretical foundation and the institutions described in *The Closed Commercial State*. This chapter shows how, in the spirit of Rousseau's *Social Contract*, Fichte's *Closed Commercial State* set out to describe the civil constitution that would come closest to re-creating natural independence through artificial means in society. As we have seen, Fichte had become an especially attentive reader of Rousseau and of Kant's interpretation of Rousseau over the course of the 1790s. *The Closed Commercial State* attempted to apply Rousseau's theory of the general will to property relations in a modern economy with an extensive and expanding division of labor.

[1] Ludwig Hestermann, *Der offene Handelsstaat. Ein philosophischer Entwurf* (Stuttgart: Erhard, 1802). Hestermann's book was mentioned in the *Allgemeine Zeitung* on 9–10 June 1801; see Fuchs, Lauth, and Schieche, *Fichte im Gespräch*, 3:51. A review notice of Hestermann's book was later published in the *Neue allgemeine deutsche Bibliothek* 80, no. 1 (1803): 243–45. I have been unable to locate any further information about Hestermann. Another contemporary reader registered an (apparently unfulfilled) intention to write a response to Fichte with the same title; see Johann Jakob Wagner to Andreas Adam, 20 January 1802, in Fuchs, Lauth, and Schieche, *Fichte im Gespräch*, 3:101.

As Hestermann noticed, the foundational principle of the theory of property developed in *The Closed Commercial State* was the natural liberty of the individual. This approach reflects the stance Fichte assumed in his *Foundations of Natural Right* (1796–97): the subtitle of *The Closed Commercial State* described it as an appendix to that treatise, one that applied its principles to the particular conditions of modern Europe.[2] Chapter 1 showed how Fichte followed Rousseau in imposing only the narrowest of moral boundaries on individual activity: namely, "do your good with the least possible harm to others," or what Rousseau called the "maxim of natural goodness."[3] For Fichte as for Rousseau, this natural liberty of the individual was prior to any more extensive moral relations between people. Rousseau further claimed that the independence enjoyed by an isolated individual—the absence of interference by others—was irrevocably lost once people acquired new, nonnatural needs. Everyone became dependent on everyone else to satisfy these needs through an expanding division of labor. The result was the corruption of the passions and the onset of a Hobbesian war of all against all. Rousseau's *Social Contract* was an attempt to show how individual independence might be re-created in society through political artifice.

Like Kant, and unlike many late-eighteenth-century readers of Rousseau, Fichte took these Hobbesian elements of Rousseau's theory very seriously after 1795. This is brought out in the provocative and conspicuously Hobbesian analogy that opens *The Closed Commercial State* and clarifies its title:

> The juridical state is formed by a closed crowd [*Menge*] of men which submits to the same laws and the same supreme coercive power. This crowd of men should now be limited to mutual commerce and industry among and for themselves, and whoever has not submitted to the same legislation and the same coercive power ought to be closed off from participation in these relations. It would thus form a *commercial state*, and indeed a *closed commercial state*, as it now forms a closed juridical state.[4]

In the absence of positive laws backed by the coercive power of the state, as Hobbes had always stressed, there was nothing but a "crowd" or "multitude" of individuals.[5] These individuals were naturally free to secure their own self-

[2] Fichte, *Der geschlossene Handelsstaat*, *Gesamtausgabe*, pt. 1, 7:42.

[3] Rousseau, "Discourse on the Origin of Inequality," in *Discourses*, 154.

[4] Fichte, *Der geschlossene Handelsstaat*, *Gesamtausgabe*, pt. 1, 7:38.

[5] See Hobbes, *On the Citizen*, 75–77 (chap. 6, art. 1, and the note by Hobbes) as well as the editor's discussion, xl–xli. A discussion of the importance of the distinction between "*Volk*" and "*Menge*" in Hobbes's political theory can be found in Ludwig Feuerbach, *Geschichte der neuern Philosophie: Von Bacon von Verulam bis Benedikt Spinoza* (1833), ed. Wolfgang Harich (Berlin: Akademie-Verlag, 1969), 133.

preservation as they saw fit. In the Hobbesian account, this natural liberty necessarily precluded sustainable social relations, which could be achieved only if all bound themselves to one another by submitting to the authority of a common judge. Fichte's analogy suggested that commercial anarchy was just as untenable as political anarchy. As we saw in chapter 2, *The Closed Commercial State* developed a historical account of modern European market relations as a Hobbesian war of all against all. Fichte was far from alone in drawing this conclusion in the aftermath of the French Revolutionary wars. *The Closed Commercial State* was one of several contemporary books to dispute the claim that the rise of commerce was gradually emancipating European societies from their feudal fetters and that it promised to realize the natural liberty of their citizens. On the contrary, Fichte argued that European history since the fall of Rome reflected the increasing distortion of market relations because of the intensifying geopolitical competition between states. Fichte followed Rousseau in insisting that the conditions of modern European civilization were no longer conducive to the preservation of natural liberty. What some called natural liberty was actually a corruption of natural liberty: "People want to be thoroughly free to destroy each other."[6]

Fichte completed his Hobbesian analogy in the "philosophical" investigation of "What is rightful in the rational state with regard to commercial relations," which constitutes the first third of *The Closed Commercial State*. Hobbes had claimed that individuals could not coexist unless they gave up their natural liberty and submitted themselves to a common sovereign. Fichte's claim was that individuals could not retain their natural liberty in the economic sphere either. In Rousseau's terms, *The Closed Commercial State* was a call to apply the theory of the general will to the economies as well as the political institutions of existing European societies. Rousseau's general will was the will that all citizens had to have if they were to coexist as independent individuals, and it mandated equality. As we saw in chapter 1, Fichte had grappled with the constitutional problem of the general will in his *Foundations of Natural Right*. Like Sieyès and Kant, he claimed that representative institutions were necessary if citizens of large societies were to be dependent only on the disembodied laws, of which they were both subjects and coauthors. In *The Closed Commercial State*, Fichte's focus was specifically on determining the kind of property regime that was necessary to prevent citizens of such societies from sliding into increasingly oppressive forms of dependence. His answer was that the state had to guarantee all its citizens a right to work by adopting the policies and institutions described in chapter 3.

As Hestermann's review suggested, Fichte's answer represents a significant but hardly straightforward divergence from Smith—as well as from Rousseau,

[6] Fichte, *Der geschlossene Handelsstaat*, *Gesamtausgabe*, pt. 1, 7:99.

Sieyès, and Kant. Fichte is sometimes supposed to have arrived at this answer under the influence of Gracchus Babeuf (1760–97) and the "Conspiracy of Equals" that failed to overthrow the French government in 1796 but later became a major source of inspiration for many nineteenth-century revolutionaries.[7] Fichte's demand for a right to work, and the kinds of extensive state interventions in economic life that he claimed were necessary to realize it, went well beyond anything either Sieyès or Kant ever said, and certainly did bring him very close to the ideas of egalitarian thinkers like Babeuf.[8] This convergence helps explain why Fichte came to be known as an intellectual progenitor of socialism.[9] However, while Fichte shared a great deal of Babeuf's moral outrage, *The Closed Commercial State* was an attempt to define a right to work on the basis of very different foundational principles. What set Fichte apart as a reader of Rousseau, and linked him to Sieyès and Kant, was a commitment to the primacy of the individual: he insisted on the principle that all social relations had to be constructed voluntarily, and took seriously Rousseau's declaration that "all the rules of natural right" could be derived without invoking the principle of "sociability" or postulating any more substantial preexisting and involuntary qualifications to the natural liberty of the individual.[10] Georg Wilhelm Friedrich von Hegel (1770–1831), who later succeeded Fichte as professor of philosophy at the University of Berlin, once described both Kant and Fichte as the true heirs to what he called "the anti-socialistic systems of natural right," which "posit the being of the individual as the first and highest thing."[11] The task

[7] Fleischacker, *Distributive Justice*, 161; Reiss, *Political Thought of the German Romantics*, 16; Léon, *Fichte et son temps*, 2:101–20.

[8] See David James, "Applying the Concept of Right: Fichte and Babeuf," *History of Political Thought* 30, no. 4 (Winter 2009): 647–77. On redistribution and the diminishing of international trade to a complementary exchange of superfluities, see Buonarroti, *Conspiration pour l'égalité*, 160–63.

[9] See, e.g., Denis, *Histoire de la Pensée Économique*, 254–86. Interestingly, a French translation of one of Fichte's 1813 lectures, "Ueber den Begriff der wahrhaften Krieges," was published in 1831 by Babeuf's grandson, Louis-Pierre Babeuf: Fichte, *De l'idée d'une guerre legitime*, ed. Louis Babeuf, trans. M. Lortet (Lyon, 1831). As Jean-Christophe Goddard has observed, one noteworthy feature of the translation is that it used the term "*prolétaires*" for Fichte's term "*Nichteigenthümer*," so Fichte's observation, "Die Menschheit zerfällt in zwei Grundstämme: die *Eigenthümer*, und die *Nichteigenthümer*," became "L'humanité se devise en deux classes principales: les *propriétaires* et les *prolétaires*," anticipating *The Communist Manifesto*'s famous description of "two great classes directly facing one another: Bourgeoisie and Proletariat"; see Goddard, "Fichte est-il réactionnaire ou révolutionnaire," in *Fichte et la politique*, 484–86; and cf. Karl Marx and Friedrich Engels, *The Communist Manifesto* (1848), ed. Gareth Stedman Jones (London: Penguin, 2002), 220.

[10] Rousseau, "Discourse on the Origin of Inequality," in *Discourses*, 127.

[11] G.W.F. von Hegel, "On the Scientific Ways of Treating Natural Law" (1802–3), in *Political Writings*, ed. L. Dickey and H. B. Nisbet, trans. Nisbet, 118 (Cambridge: Cambridge University Press, 1999). On Hegel's remark, see Wolfgang Schieder, "Sozialismus," in *Geschichtliche Grundbegriffe: Historisches Lexikon zur politisch-sozialen Sprache in Deutschland*, ed. Otto Brunner, Werner Conze, and Reinhart Koselleck, 5:931 (Stuttgart: Klett-Cotta, 1984).

of this chapter is to show how Fichte attempted to arrive at the institutions of the closed commercial state from an "anti-socialistic" starting point.

The Closed Commercial State reflects a careful reworking of Rousseau's complex engagement with the central premises of the modern natural-law tradition regarding the nature of community and the character of individual rights. For members of society to coexist freely, according to Rousseau, they all had to limit their own activity so that others were also able to act without interference. This assignation of rights could not be determined by reference to the natural character of social relations. However, Rousseau also refused to follow Hobbes in concluding that the scope of individual rights could be determined only arbitrarily by the will of an absolute sovereign power: this was to sanction the predation and depravity exhibited by existing European regimes. *The Closed Commercial State* sought to repair the grave defects that Fichte attributed to Rousseau's approach to this problem (which may have had as much to do with readers of Rousseau like Babeuf as with Rousseau himself). Fichte claimed that Rousseau had linked the restoration of independence in society to the contraction of human needs. This was to restore independence by permanently constricting autonomy, for to limit the expansion and diversification of needs was to limit the nature of the activity that could be undertaken to meet them. *The Closed Commercial State* proposed to substitute a new political economy in place of this kind of austerity regime. Fichte sought to show how the state should regulate the expansion of needs so that this process could take place in a manner compatible with every citizen's independence. Examining Fichte's attempt to navigate this quintessential problem of Rousseau's is the best way to assess the political theory of *The Closed Commercial State* and its character as a development of the social-contract tradition.

Open Commercial State versus *Closed Commercial State*

Ludwig Hestermann read *The Closed Commercial State* as a moral challenge to the discipline of political economy. He declared himself "not a little surprised . . . to see a constitution of the commercial state derived from principles of justice," and he introduced Fichte's book as the only recent work of political economy (*Staatswirtschaft*) that had attempted to develop "the principles of property and industry from the perspective of justice [*in rechtlicher Hinsicht*]."[12] Hestermann welcomed *The Closed Commercial State* as an ally against what he described as the two major schools of political economy in his day. The oldest and most powerful was that of the cabinet advisors who had dazzled "money-

[12] Hestermann, *Der offene Handelsstaat*, iii, 3. All translations from *Der offene Handelsstaat* are my own.

grubbing princes and governments" with their seemingly clever techniques for increasing revenue. The second had "sprung from the heads of speculative philosophers." Its "simplicity and seeming naturalness" gave it "the mark of a higher perfection," evoked "the beautiful prospect of a fortunate future that must be created," and had earned it the allegiance of "fanatical supporters" (*schwärmenden Beförderer*). For all their fundamental differences, both schools served "financial interests, and the increase of state power." Neither paid any attention to "the rightfulness of the relations of individual members of the state."[13] *The Closed Commercial State* had blindsided all these cameralists and Physiocrats.[14] It had undermined their notions of the general good or the good of the state by insisting that this good could be understood only in terms of individual right.

Hestermann claimed that Fichte's approach also presented an important challenge to a third school of political economy, which he hinted was linked to Adam Smith. This school had not yet gained much influence outside the academy, but Hestermann noted that it had been growing steadily since its birth twenty-five years earlier—namely, in 1776, the year the *Wealth of Nations* was published.[15] Hestermann was not the only early reader of Fichte's *Closed Commercial State* to cast it in opposition to Adam Smith: Adam Müller's review in the *Neue Berlinische Monatsschrift* ended by recommending that readers simply turn to Smith in order to avoid the pitfalls that he attributed to Fichte's complete ignorance of political economy.[16] However, Hestermann judged that the Smithian school had not been prepared for Fichte's challenge to the justice of its principles.[17] He proposed to meet this challenge on the same terrain where it was made, by figuring out how Fichte had managed to arrive at a system of property right so far removed from the conclusions of the Smithian school. His own work, *The Open Commercial State*, aimed to start with the same principles that Fichte had declared in *The Closed Commercial State* and show where they

[13] Ibid., 4–6.

[14] For an overview of late-eighteenth-century German political economy, see Tribe, *Governing Economy*.

[15] Hestermann, *Der offene Handelsstaat*, 6–7. A similar tripartite division (mercantilism, Physiocracy, and Smith) was already becoming a standard typology of political economy; see Theodor Schmalz, *Encyclopädie der Cameralwissenschaften: Zum Gebrauch academischer Vorlesungen* (Königsberg, 1797), pt. 2.

[16] Müller, "Ueber einen philosophischen Entwurf," 458. As Richard Gray has pointed out, Müller's defense of Smith is noteworthy, given that he later became an outspoken opponent of Smith and a communitarian critic of property rights ("Economic Romanticism: Monetary Nationalism in Johann Gottlieb Fichte and Adam Müller," *Eighteenth-Century Studies* 36, no. 4 [2003]: 548). For another comparison of Smith and Fichte, one that attributes the former's defense of free trade to English reasons of state, see I. H. Fichte's note in Fichte's *Sämmtliche Werke*, 3:lx–lxi.

[17] Hestermann, *Der offene Handelsstaat*, 7.

ought to have led.[18] In comparing the two books, Hestermann observed, "it ought to be striking that entirely different results, such as those which are established in both works, could be derived from the same principles."[19]

The shared foundation of both theories of property, as Hestermann saw it, was natural liberty, or the principle that all possessed a natural right to secure their own self-preservation as they saw fit.[20] Everyone had an equal right to live and therefore an equal claim to acquire the raw products of nature. As Fichte put it in *The Closed Commercial State*, "The end of all human activity is to be able to live; and all whom nature has given life have an equal claim on this possibility of living."[21] An individual could not extinguish everyone else's equal claim to the products of nature merely through prior occupation or labor. An exclusive right to property—without which individual industry could not be secured from interference—could be established only through everyone else's consent. The only way to make the transition from living off the natural bounty of the earth to living from human industry was through a mutual renunciation of the natural right to acquisition. All had to renounce their original claims to acquire other people's property. Since this promise of mutual noninterference had to be universally binding in order to be valid, it had to take the form of a contract of all with all—in other words, the property contract had to be instituted by the state, the only agency capable of acting on everyone's behalf. Both Hestermann and Fichte were therefore opponents of the claim that there was a natural right to property that was prior to the political community, and both denied that the state's function was restricted to protecting this property. In their view, the eclipse of natural equality and the introduction of exclusive property required the consent of all, and the necessary condition of this consent was that everyone's natural right to self-preservation would continue to be secured. In Fichte's words, "The division must be made so that all are able to exist within it. Live and let live!"[22]

Hestermann and Fichte were in agreement that a limit on natural liberty had to be introduced for society to make the transition from living off the natural bounty of the earth to living off the fruits of its own industry. A society that lived solely off the natural bounty of the earth would satisfy its members' right to live by dividing these natural resources equally among them. But such a communal society could not expand beyond a small population at an indi-

[18] Another early response to *The Closed Commercial State* that set itself the same task was Hagens, *Philosophische und politische Untersuchung*. Hagens took his epigraph from Smith's *Wealth of Nations*.

[19] Hestermann, *Der offene Handelsstaat*, 287.

[20] Ibid., 13–15.

[21] Fichte, *Der geschlossene Handelsstaat*, *Gesamtausgabe*, pt. 1, 7:55.

[22] Ibid.

gent level of subsistence, because exclusive property rights were a condition for unleashing human industry. To secure this industry, there had to be property rights; and for an individual to possess something, everyone else's natural right to acquire that thing had to be renounced. The right to live now manifested itself as the right to enjoy the fruits of one's labor. This right to live from one's own labor was constrained in that it was no longer permissible to exercise it on another person's property without consent.

Hestermann claimed that all the considerable differences between the Smithian school and *The Closed Commercial State* stemmed from Fichte's imposition of additional limitations on this right. Hestermann maintained that within the constraints established by this pact of mutual noninterference, natural liberty was to remain as undiminished as possible. Fichte parted ways by requiring an additional limit to natural liberty as a condition of the property contract. He claimed that it was not sufficient for all to renounce their claims to acquire the property of others. In addition to this negative duty of noninterference, all also had to agree to curtail their natural liberty in commerce by assuming a positive obligation to exchange the fruits of their industry with one another. To introduce private property, it was not sufficient "that one merely *may* exchange," Fichte insisted; it had to be the case "that one *must* do so."[23]

Fichte and Hestermann parted ways over a vexed question that grew out of the natural-jurisprudence tradition and figured centrally in Smith's *Wealth of Nations*. The natural history of society as developed by the natural jurists and taken over by Smith described a progression from a hunting-and-gathering stage to shepherding and finally to agriculture.[24] As human industry continues to develop, Smith claimed, everyone "becomes in some measure a merchant, and the society itself grows to be what is properly a commercial society."[25] In such a society, it was no longer the case that all members of society could work directly on the land. Human needs, and the division of the labor undertaken to meet them, had expanded to the point that a significant part of the population earned its livelihood by exchanging its labor or manufactured products for the agricultural surplus of the landowners. The key question was how a theory of property grounded in the right to self-preservation could accommodate the rights of this class of workers, who lacked property in land.[26]

As Istvan Hont and Michael Ignatieff argued in their essay "Needs and Justice in the Wealth of Nations," Smith's approach to this question was a development of the natural-law theories promulgated by Hugo Grotius and his

[23] Ibid., 7:57.

[24] See Hont, *Jealousy of Trade*, 159–84.

[25] Smith, *Wealth of Nations*, bk. 1, chap. 4, para. 1.

[26] See Ursula Vogel, "When the Earth Belonged to All: The Land Question in Eighteenth-Century Justifications of Private Property," *Political Studies* 36, no. 1 (March 1988): 102–22.

followers, especially the German jurist Samuel Pufendorf (1632–94).[27] In the traditional Thomist account, private property was legitimated as an extension or implementation of natural law because humanity was charged with taking good care of God's property. At the same time, however, private property was qualified by the principle that God had given the earth to humanity in common. This principle of an original commonality of goods implied that property rights could be overridden if the needs of the community required it, even permitting theft during a famine. Grotius and his followers transformed this traditional account by redefining the original commonality of goods in radically narrower terms: in their view, the original community of humanity extended only to the recognition of every individual's natural liberty to make use of God's earth. Their starting point was a theory of "negative" community rather than "positive" community: in other words, the earth was nobody's exclusive possession and was available for everybody's use, rather than for anybody's or everybody's collective possession.[28] The import of this redefinition was a "radically thinned down" vision of social life as it had been understood in Aristotelian terms.[29] It excluded questions of desert or merit from "strict justice" and demoted them to the domain of equity or humanity.[30] Justice "consists wholly in abstaining from that which is another Man's," Grotius wrote, and "the very Nature of Injustice consists in nothing, else, but in the Violation of another's Rights."[31] In this view, nobody's needs or merits could trump another's property right unless sheer survival were at stake or more extensive social arrangements had been instituted. As Hont and Ignatieff put it succinctly, "A man had a right only to what was his own. He had no right to what was his due."[32]

To varying degrees, Grotius and his followers introduced important qualifications to this minimalist vision of social life. Nonetheless, as Hont and Ig-

[27] Istvan Hont and Michael Ignatieff, "Needs and Justice in the Wealth of Nations," in Hont and Ignatieff, eds., *Wealth and Virtue: The Shaping of Political Economy in the Scottish Enlightenment*, 1–44 (Cambridge: Cambridge University Press, 1983), reprinted in Hont, *Jealousy of Trade*, 389–443.

[28] Samuel Pufendorf, *De jure naturae et gentium* (1672), trans. *Of the Law of Nature and Nations*, ed. Basil Kennet (Oxford, 1703), bk. 4, chap. 4, sect. 5. See also the seminal statement of the sea as an open commons in Grotius, *The Free Sea*, chap. 5. The extent to which this characterization applies to Locke's theory of property—the extent to which he was a theorist of negative rather than positive community—remains contested. See James Tully, *A Discourse on Property: John Locke and His Adversaries* (Cambridge: Cambridge University Press, 1980); and Richard Boyd, "The Calvinist Origins of Lockean Political Economy," *History of Political Thought* 23, no. 1 (Spring 2002): 30–60.

[29] Tuck, *Philosophy and Government*, 175.

[30] Pufendorf, *Law of Nature and Nations*, bk. 3, chap. 4, sect. 1.

[31] Hugo Grotius, *De jure belli ac pacis* (1625), trans. in 1738 from the 1715 French edition of Jean Barbeyrac by John Morrice et al. as *The Rights of War and Peace*, ed. Richard Tuck (Indianapolis, Ind.: Liberty Fund, 2005), 1:120–21 (prolegomena, sect. 45).

[32] Hont and Ignatieff, "Needs and Justice," in *Jealousy of Trade*, 425; cf. Richard Tuck, *Natural Rights Theories: Their Origin and Development* (Cambridge: Cambridge University Press, 1979), 60–61.

natieff argued, these theories ultimately created the space for the argument that despite (or because of) the unprecedented inequality generated by private property, the right of those who did not have any could be secured through increased productivity and commerce rather than redistribution. Communal property regimes were associated with a remote historical past: they belonged to an earlier stage of society whose simplicity had long since been overwritten by the development of needs and the division of labor. Smith's *Wealth of Nations* transposed this jurisprudential claim into the language of political economy and deployed it in the grain-trade debates of the 1770s. Philosophes across Europe debated whether there should be free trade in subsistence goods, or whether states should curtail property rights and provide for the needs of the poor by continuing to maintain a "just price" regime. Smith used the standard of natural liberty to critique these laws and to explain how the needs of the poor could best be met by removing these fetters on commerce. A commercial society without these artificial constraints would be strikingly unequal but it would meet a minimal standard of justice because its tremendous productivity could ensure that nobody starved (and, as Smith stressed, nobody would be driven to commit infanticide).[33]

Fichte rejected this justification of material inequality in a commercial society. Such a society did not do enough to ensure the survival of those who were without property in land: "It is not proper [*anständig*] for a constitution completely conforming to right to say, 'all that will just arrange itself, everyone will always find work and bread, and let good fortune take care of it.'" Fichte used the appropriately agricultural metaphor of threshing grain to make his point that increasing agricultural productivity by giving landed property to some was not enough to secure the basic rights of the rest of society: "Are we talking about some sparrow that is free to find some kernels of grain so long as it evades the net? But this is not at all counted upon, and we would much rather that it did not find its kernels. If the state abandons these classes of the people to chance, it gives them absolutely nothing."[34]

The premise of the property contract was that all consented to relinquish their natural liberty to acquire the means of subsistence in exchange for a right to live from their own labor. Fichte refused to regard the disparity between the labor of the landowner and the labor of the landless as the outcome of legitimate consent.

> I very readily see that the associated crowd [*verbundene Menge*] of landowners could use force to prevent the weak individual from voicing his

[33] Hont and Ignatieff, "Needs and Justice," in *Jealousy of Trade*, 419. See especially Adam Smith's discussion of infanticide in *The Theory of Moral Sentiments*, ed. A. L. Macfie and D. D. Raphael (Indianapolis, Ind.: Liberty Classics, 1982), 209–11, and in the introduction to *Wealth of Nations*.

[34] Fichte, *Der geschlossene Handelsstaat*, *Gesamtausgabe*, pt. 1, 7:90.

> rightful claim, or from asserting it. However, here I am not asking about force, but about right; and I find that this crowd has no right, because they could only have acquired it through a contract which this individual did not conclude [*geschlossen*] with them, and which therefore does not bind him.[35]

This passage calls to mind Hobbes's stricture that it was prideful pretense—a violation of natural law—not to "allow equal rights to equals."[36] Those who claimed that their property rights were prior to the community were, Hobbes charged, "speaking as if they were still in a disorganized crowd [*dissoluta multitudo*] and no commonwealth were yet formed."[37] Fichte took the next step in the Hobbesian argument. If the landowners' state denied that a commonwealth had been formed, then the individuals it had subjugated were not bound by it and still retained their full natural liberty:

> They have therefore not at all renounced their right to the property of others. No right permits the state to impose laws on their industry and determine their relations with the other classes of the people [*Volksklassen*]. They are free in every respect, deprived of laws as well as right, without rules or guarantees; they are half savages in the bosom of society. Because of the complete insecurity in which they find themselves, they cheat and steal—it is true that it is not called theft, but profit—they cheat and steal, as long and as well as they can, from those who cheat and steal from them in turn, as soon as they are the stronger. They go on doing this as long as possible, and set aside as much as they can in case of the necessity from which nothing secures them. And in all of this they do nothing beyond their most perfect right.[38]

For the contract establishing property to be valid, the state had to secure everybody's right to the fruits of his or her industry to the same degree that it secured the farmer's right to work his land. "It is thus clear," Fichte claimed, "that not only the farmer, but every inhabitant in the state must have an exclusive property, because without that he cannot be bound to recognize the property right of the farmer, nor can he rightfully be prevented from driving him from his field and robbing him of his fruits."[39] The problem that Fichte then faced was how to ensure that every member of society could have an exclusive property right. An agrarian law redistributing land to all was out of the question because, like Hestermann, Fichte scoffed at the suggestion that society

[35] Ibid., 7:89.
[36] Hobbes, *On the Citizen*, 50 (chap. 3, art. 14).
[37] Ibid., 136–37 (chap. 12, art. 7).
[38] Fichte, *Der geschlossene Handelsstaat*, *Gesamtausgabe*, pt. 1, 7:90.
[39] Ibid., 7:89.

should return to a precommercial stage. A society without a nonagricultural sector was necessarily "a miserable nation, still half left behind in barbarism."[40] "What, then," Fichte asked, "might this exclusive property of the non-farmer (the manufacturer and the merchant) be, in return for which they might have ceded the property right over the land to the farmer?"[41] The worker's labor and knowledge could not be considered his possession in the same way that the farmer possessed his land. A merchant did not owe his abilities or his labor to the state, but to nature—he would still have them even if he washed up "naked on the shore"—whereas a farmer could not have an exclusive right to property in land unless the state gave it to him.

The way to eliminate this disparity, Fichte announced with great fanfare, was easy to see if property was conceived of as a right to exclude others from a certain activity rather than dominion over an object. To define a property claim to a certain object, one simply had to ask whether others had renounced their claim to act upon it. Metaphysical notions of "intelligible possession" of an object (the thorny question of how to explain possession beyond actual physical contact) were beside the point, Fichte argued, since conflict over property arose only when one person's activity interfered with another's.[42] On the contrary, there could be an exclusive right to engage in a certain kind of activity without any question of possessing an object. This redefinition enabled Fichte to demand that the state also secure the labor of nonagricultural workers as a property right. The state would have to go to greater lengths to protect their rights than it did for landowners, since starvation was more a threat to merchants and manufacturers than to landowners (in other words, a grower of wheat could sooner go without watches than a watchmaker could go without bread).[43] The state would have to guarantee them work, the natural resources required to practice their trade, and a market for their products. "Only through this protection [*Versicherung*] does the state bind them to itself," Fichte claimed.[44] Fichte derived the economic institutions of the closed commercial state—the withdrawal from foreign trade, the introduction of a national currency, the system of price controls, the balancing of production and consumption, and the regulation of the workforce—as means of securing the industry of all its citizens, including those who did not own land, as a property right.

Hestermann concluded that Fichte had both sacrificed natural liberty and lost sight of it as a foundational principle. Fichte's aim was no longer to describe

[40] Ibid., 7:71.

[41] Ibid., 7:89.

[42] Ibid., 7:87–89. On "intelligible possession," see Kant, *Rechtslehre*, trans. Mary Gregor in *The Metaphysics of Morals* (Cambridge: Cambridge University Press, 1996), 54–56 (sect. 17).

[43] Fichte, *Der geschlossene Handelsstaat*, *Gesamtausgabe*, pt. 1, 7:57.

[44] Ibid., 7:89.

how everybody's survival could best be secured, he charged, but to ensure that all had an equal right to the fruits of their industry:

> The conflict therefore lies solely here: what is the condition of the general validity of the property contract. Is the condition that an exclusive sphere of activity be allocated to each, or rather that life be secured for each?[45]

Hestermann hewed more closely to the kind of justification of commercial society that Smith had embedded in the *Wealth of Nations*. For Hestermann, the right to live was the sole condition of the rightfulness of the property contract. It was permissible for property to be distributed unequally so long as this system satisfied everyone's right to self-preservation and gave everyone enough to eat:

> The claims that everyone brought to the property contract were not to have property, but to be able to live. The property contract was accepted only because the possibility of living could best be secured through property and the labor applied to it. Thus the security of life was the single condition that each had to reserve for himself in this contract, whether he received property or not.[46]

Hestermann ruled out any redistribution of property because this would constitute theft and undermine the basis of human industry. He did suggest, however, that the property contract would have to provide for those excluded from the initial distribution by guaranteeing them an income to live on. Workers would earn this income by selling their labor to the landowners. If necessary, the state would provide employment or supplement wages in order to make them a "living wage"—this was not a redistribution of property, Hestermann claimed, since everyone's ability to work for a living was a condition for having property in the first place.[47] Hestermann was perfectly candid about how inequitable the results of this system would nonetheless be. Some people's labor would be chosen less freely and rewarded less than other people's labor. The natural liberty of those who possessed only an income would be greatly circumscribed since they would be dependent on the utility of their labor to the property owners. They would not share equally in their society's wealth. But he claimed that the self-preservation of all would be equally protected.[48] The true vocation of political economy, he concluded, was to discover how best to mitigate the unavoidable inequities of a market society.[49]

[45] Hestermann, *Der offene Handelsstaat*, 293.
[46] Ibid., 290.
[47] Ibid., 33, 93–94, 105.
[48] Ibid., 30–36.
[49] Ibid., 129ff., 294.

Hestermann dismissed the institutions of the closed commercial state as an unworkable system and denied that Fichte's demand for equality was a correct application of the principle of natural liberty. It was not necessary to interpose the state into every commercial transaction in order to secure everyone's right to life. Hestermann charged Fichte with distorting the principle of natural liberty in order to pursue a more extensive vision of justice—one that was fundamentally flawed because it misattributed surplus value to the laborer alone.[50] Such distortions and excesses, Hestermann commented, led to the specter of ancient demagogues agitating for an agrarian law. They also inspired latter-day egalitarians who argued for a redistribution of land. The continuing popularity of their "balance of power system," Hestermann warned, "which would like to expand over all property with a dreadful consequence," could be attributed to this distorted sense of the principle of natural liberty.[51] In Hestermann's final judgment, then, Fichte's *Closed Commercial State* was an attempt to justify the extension of republicanism to a postagrarian commercial society by a distorted application of the principle of natural liberty. As we shall see, Hestermann was not alone in characterizing the book's ambitions in this way. But a full evaluation of Fichte's application of his theoretical foundations requires a closer look at his derivation of a right to work.

Needs and Rights in Fichte's Theory of Property

The key moment in Fichte's derivation of a right to work is the elision in *The Closed Commercial State* between an equal right to live and an equal right to live "agreeably." Initially, Fichte asserted that "the end of all human activity is to be able to live."[52] Yet he went on to claim that "within the scope of the doctrine of right, the end of all free activity is the possibility and agreeableness of life."[53] This elision is produced by a complex set of claims about human needs and how they become rights—claims that Fichte presented in compressed form in *The Closed Commercial State* but had developed more fully in his *Foundations of Natural Right*. Fichte's earlier treatise claimed to derive the concept of right from the conditions of personality, or what it meant to be a human being. As we saw in chapter 1, Fichte held that to be a human being was to engage in "an ongoing reciprocal interaction, dependent only on the person's own will, be-

[50] "The closed commercial state believes that it gives equal wages to equal work, but it calculates the quantity of work according to the product that consists of work and profit from capital, and calculates falsely" (ibid., 296).

[51] Ibid., 41. On eighteenth century attempts to find a modern equivalent to an agrarian law, see Sonenscher, "Property, Community and Citizenship."

[52] Fichte, *Der geschlossene Handelsstaat*, *Gesamtausgabe*, pt. 1, 7:55.

[53] Ibid., 7:65.

tween the person and the sensible world outside of him."[54] In other words, an autonomous relationship between the individual will and the natural world was the primary constituent of personhood. "This is what constitutes the person's individual character," Fichte wrote, "through this determination, the person is *the one* that he is, this or that person, called by this or that name."[55] Crucially, for Fichte, rights had to do only with what it meant to be a natural being, not a moral being.[56] Fichte distinguished between right and morality just as strictly as the natural jurists did. To be a moral being was to determine one's own ends rationally in accordance with the universal moral law, whereas the human being as a natural being was distinguished by the fact that, unlike plants and animals, it had no determinate ends.[57] For Fichte, then, the natural liberty of the individual consisted in the absence of any inherent limits to his or her relation with nature—a relation that Fichte depicted as an eternal striving to eliminate all natural obstacles to human activity and bring the entire natural world under human command.

Since the individual relation with nature was not inherently social, it was not necessarily mediated by rights. Rights were necessary only in order to mediate conflict between people.[58] They described the limitations people had to impose on their activity if they were to coexist without interfering with one another's activity. As we saw in chapter 1, Fichte described a certain relationship between people as the second condition for becoming a human being: to achieve personhood, one had to be perceived as a person by another, or to be "summoned" to self-consciousness. However, Fichte was adamant that this indispensable moment of mutual recognition could not serve as the basis for permanent social relations. Any continuation or deepening of social relations beyond this initial moment of recognition had to proceed on a purely voluntary basis.[59] The only natural right was the right to be recognized as a potential participant in a contractual relationship, or what Fichte called "the one true human right . . . the right to be able to acquire rights."[60] Since a voluntary relationship of mutual self-limitation was contingent on its reciprocity, Fichte held that it could be achieved only through the state. There were no natural rights, and there could not be an exclusive right to property without the state.

[54] Fichte, *Foundations of Natural Right*, 183.

[55] Ibid., 53.

[56] See Neuhouser, "Right and Morality."

[57] Fichte, *Foundations of Natural Right*, 74.

[58] Ibid., 51.

[59] "In the doctrine of right there is no talk of moral obligation; each is bound only by the free, arbitrary [*willkürlichen*] decision to live in community with others, and if someone does not at all want to limit his free choice [*Willkür*], then within the field of the doctrine of right, one can say nothing further against him, other than that he must then remove himself from all human community" (Fichte, *Foundations of Natural Right*, 11–12; see also 80–81).

[60] Ibid., 333.

The strength of Fichte's commitment to the priority of the individual's natural liberty over all social relations is particularly evident in his bid to eliminate the venerable juridical category of a right of necessity. For Grotius and his followers, the condition of necessity remained an exceptional case, namely, when someone could claim a right to another's property on the basis of need—the basic need of survival. In other words, it was a right to one's due rather than to one's own. The classical example of this case was what Fichte referred to as "that famous and wonderful plank, talked about in the schools, which is too small to carry both of the shipwreck survivors clinging to it."[61] Fichte argued that neither survivor could claim a right to wrest away the plank and save himself at the other's expense. At the same time, Fichte insisted that someone who did save himself at the other's expense could not be described as having violated the other's rights. In Fichte's terms, the concept of right was simply inapplicable to a situation in which coexistence through mutual self-limitation was impossible. The outcome of the interaction would be determined by physical strength and individual choices. These choices certainly ought to be guided by morality—each individual had an unconditional duty to do nothing and to leave his fate in God's hands—but they could not be guided by considerations of right. By constructing his solution to the problem of necessity in this elaborate way, Fichte ensured that needs could never harden into rights without consent. Needs could become rights only through a contractual relationship, or in other words, through the state.

The Closed Commercial State began with a terse, epigrammatic account of this theoretical foundation. Initially, Fichte wrote, each individual independently looked after his or her own needs: "A crowd [*Haufen*] of men live together in the same sphere of action. Each moves about and goes freely after his own nourishment and his own pleasure [*Vergnügen*]."[62] There was no such thing as property so long as individual activity was free from interference by other people's activity. An isolated individual on a remote island would have no property rights, Fichte explained, because the concept simply could not be applied: "He may take for himself as much as he wants and is able."[63] Rights had no bearing on the individual relationship to nature, since, as Fichte stated, echoing Pufendorf, "neither the ground which was trampled nor the tree whose fruits are plucked enters into a contestation of right with the man who did it." On the other hand, "on what grounds can one man claim a right to do this that another does not possess?"[64] When one individual's activity came into conflict

[61] Ibid., 220–21. See Marcus Tullius Cicero, *On the Commonwealth*, ed. James Zetzel (Cambridge: Cambridge University Press, 1999), 68.

[62] Fichte, *Der geschlossene Handelsstaat, Gesamtausgabe*, pt. 1, 7:53.

[63] Ibid., 7:86; cf. Fichte, *Foundations of Natural Right*, 51.

[64] Fichte, *Der geschlossene Handelsstaat, Gesamtausgabe*, pt. 1, 7:54; see Pufendorf, *Law of Nature and Nations*, bk. 3, chap. 5, sect. 3.

with another's, one would destroy or use the other's goods for himself, "and so, all against all." "It is not necessary here to speak of morality, of equity and of things of this sort," Fichte continued, "because we find ourselves on the terrain of the doctrine of right. However, the concept of right cannot be applied in the conditions which have been described."[65] Mutual interference prevented individuals in these conditions from engaging in an autonomous relationship with nature: "In these conditions nobody is free; because all are unlimited, nobody can carry anything out purposefully or count on it to last a moment into the future." The only way of resolving this "conflict of free powers" was to consent to a reciprocal self-limitation of activity by creating a state. This agreement was the sole basis of property rights, for "only now does each have something of his *own*, his alone and not at all the other's; a right, and an exclusive right." "It is the state alone," Fichte concluded, "which unites an indeterminate crowd of men into a *closed whole*, into a *unity*."[66]

Fichte denied that there were any natural rights and described the social contract as an unconditional submission to the will of the community. However, as the *Foundations of Natural Right* made clear, Fichte's exacting definition of rights imposed an important boundary on the state's authority to impose moral constraints on its citizens. In Fichte's terms, rights served only to demarcate spheres of independence. They were concerned with how people interfered in one another's activity, but not with the nature of that activity.[67] The conditions of personality can become rights "only insofar as they appear in the sensible world and can be violated by other free beings (as forces in the sensible world)," Fichte wrote. "Thus there can be, for example, a right to self-preservation in the sensible world, to the preservation of my body as such, but by no means a right to *think* or to *will* freely."[68] In protecting the rights of its citizens, then, the state was charged only with protecting their independence—that is, with preventing them from interfering with one another's relationship to the natural world. Fichte insisted that the state had no authority to make them act more autonomously, rationally, or morally.

At the same time, Fichte's refusal to acknowledge any inherent limits to individual activity produced a correspondingly expansive account of what might constitute interference. "The body must neither be set into motion nor restricted in its motion by any external cause," Fichte wrote; "there must be absolutely nothing that immediately exercises an effect upon it." Moreover, any

[65] Fichte, *Der geschlossene Handelsstaat*, *Gesamtausgabe*, pt. 1, 7:54.

[66] Ibid.

[67] "Insofar as the person is the absolute and final ground of the concept of his own efficacy, of his own concept of an end, the freedom that is expressed therein lies beyond the bounds of the present investigation, for that kind of freedom never enters the sensible world and cannot be restricted by anything within it" (Fichte, *Foundations of Natural Right*, 103).

[68] Ibid., 102.

realistically possible effect of the body's motion in the world had to take place without any potential for disruption from other human agents.[69] As Fichte pointed out in a striking example, an individual's purposive activity with respect to the natural world could very well take the form of refraining from changing it:

> Think, for example, of an isolated inhabitant of a desert island who sustains himself by hunting in the island's woods. He has allowed the woods to grow as they might, but he knows them and all the conveniences they afford for his hunting. One cannot displace or level the trees in his woods without rendering useless all the knowledge he has acquired (thus robbing him of it), without impeding his path as he pursues game (thus making it more difficult or impossible for him to acquire his sustenance), that is, without disturbing the freedom of his efficacy.[70]

Fichte's example is a telling one because it begins to reveal the implications he drew from pairing a limitless conception of natural liberty with a theory of rights as boundaries against mutual interference. Fichte's theory of property did not privilege certain historically conditioned forms of activity (such as intensive European-style agriculture) over others (like hunting). This was a major divergence from earlier property theories grounded in the principle of natural liberty, like those of Grotius or Locke, which did draw distinctions in the property status of different stages of productive activity.[71] Significantly, the latter were as heavily implicated in justifications of European imperialism as Fichte was outspoken in his condemnations.[72] Fichte's more open-ended conception of natural liberty created a platform for his demand that the structure of property relations continue to keep pace with the changing character of economic activity in increasingly postagrarian European societies.

Fichte's theory of property can be described as a development of Hobbes's approach to natural law as amended by Rousseau. As Leo Strauss once observed, this is what Hegel meant when he described Fichte's philosophy as the

[69] Ibid., 104; cf. 108.

[70] Ibid., 106.

[71] See Hugo Grotius, "Defense of Chapter V of the Mare Liberum" (ca. 1615, discovered in 1864), in *The Free Sea*, 87, 116. Locke's theory of property distinguishes between the nature of property rights before and after the introduction of a money-based economy (Locke, *Two Treatises of Government*, 293ff).

[72] See, among many recent discussions, Barbara Arneil, "John Locke, Natural Law, and Colonialism," *History of Political Thought* 13, no. 4 (Winter 1992): 587–603; Tuck, *Rights of War and Peace*; and David Armitage, "John Locke, Carolina, and the Two Treatises of Government," *Political Theory* 32, no. 5 (2004): 602–27.

apotheosis of an "anti-socialistic" theory of natural liberty.[73] As Strauss put it, Hobbes had located natural liberty in the individual's complete independence in judging the means necessary for self-preservation, but had ultimately given precedence to self-preservation over independence. Rousseau unambiguously gave precedence to the independence of the individual, but identified this independence in the first instance with the brute physical survival of a solitary animal. Re-creating this independence on a human level was Rousseau's great concern.[74] Taking up Rousseau's formulation of this problem, Fichte followed Rousseau in giving precedence to individual independence. In the *Foundations of Natural Right*, Fichte refused to confine natural liberty to a right to self-preservation:

> There is no separate right to self-preservation; for it is merely contingent that, in a particular instance, we happen to be using our body as a tool, or things as a means, for the end of securing the continued existence of our body as such. Even if our end were more modest than self-preservation, other persons would still not be permitted to disturb our freedom, for they are not permitted to disturb it at all.[75]

At the same time, Fichte recognized that all of the ends a human being might choose were contingent on the most basic of ends, which was physical survival. In the first instance, then, natural liberty could be taken to consist in securing whatever was necessary for one's self-preservation, and the state's duty to protect individual independence had to take the form of securing each citizen's right to live from his own labor, or a right to work:

> We find that the need for nourishment alone is the original impetus—and its satisfaction the ultimate end—of the state and of all human life and conduct. This is true, obviously, only so long as the human being remains entirely under the direction of nature, and does not elevate himself through freedom to a higher existence: thus the need for nourishment alone is the highest synthesis, which unites all contradictions. Accordingly, the highest and universal end of all free activity is to be able to live. Everyone has this end; therefore, just as freedom in general is guaranteed, so too is this end. If this end were not attained, freedom and the person's continued existence would be completely impossible.

[73] "Rousseau may be said to have originated 'the philosophy of freedom,'" Leo Strauss wrote. "The connection between the developed form of 'the philosophy of freedom,' i.e., German idealism, and Rousseau, and hence Hobbes, was realized by no one more clearly than by Hegel" (Strauss, *Natural Right and History* [Chicago: University of Chicago Press, 1953], 279).

[74] Ibid., 282.

[75] Fichte, *Foundations of Natural Right*, 108.

> And so we arrive at a more detailed description of the exclusive use of freedom that is granted to each individual in the property contract. To be able to live is the absolute, inalienable property of all human beings. We have seen that a certain sphere of objects is granted to the individual solely for a certain use. But the final end of this use is to be able to live. The attainment of this end is guaranteed; this is the spirit of the property contract. A principle of all rational state constitutions is that everyone ought to be able to live from his labor.[76]

As we have already seen, Fichte did not confine himself to demanding a right to work on this basis. Instead, he went on to insist that protecting individual independence in society had to take the form of an equal right to live "as agreeably as possible" from one's labor. According to Fichte, anything less would represent a failure to solve Rousseau's problem, a failure to restore individual independence within the realm of social life rather than in conjectural subhuman solitude.

The difference between the isolated natural man and the citizen, Fichte explained in the *Foundations of Natural Right*, was that the latter's needs could be satisfied only through the division of labor.

> The former acts merely in order to satisfy his needs [*Bedürfnisse*], and none of his needs are satisfied except through his own actions; he is what he is externally only by virtue of himself. The citizen, by contrast, has various things to do and leave undone, not for his own sake, but for the sake of others; his highest needs are satisfied by the actions of others, without any contribution from himself.[77]

In the historical section of *The Closed Commercial State*, as we saw in chapter 2, Fichte showed in detail how the expansion of European trade had made this dependence on others intolerable: "What transpires without great injustice or oppression among nations with a simple way of life is transformed with increased needs into the most fearsome injustice and the source of great misery."[78] The resulting war of all against all "becomes more and more violent, unjust, and dangerous in its consequences as the world becomes more populous, as the commercial state expands through adventitious acquisitions, as production and the arts increase, and as the quantity of goods that come into circulation increases and diversifies together with everyone's needs."[79] Like Rousseau, Fichte claimed that the state's legitimacy hinged on its ability to restore the independence of all its citizens. *The Closed Commercial State* was a "political economy of the general

[76] Ibid., 185.
[77] Ibid., 181.
[78] Fichte, *Der geschlossene Handelsstaat, Gesamtausgabe*, pt. 1, 7:98.
[79] Ibid.

will" for postagrarian societies in that it sought to define the kind of economy such a society had to have in order for its citizens to become dependent on the law alone. Fichte concluded that in a society with an advanced division of labor, protecting individual independence had to take the form of guaranteeing each citizen's right to live "as agreeably as possible" from his or her labor. "Everyone wants to live as agreeably [*angenehm*] as possible," Fichte wrote,

> and since each demands this as a human being, and nobody is more or less of a human being than another, there is equal right in everyone's demand. According to this equality of right the division must be made so that each and everyone can live as agreeably as possible given the number of men who coexist in the available sphere of action; that is, so that all can live with approximately equal agreeableness [*ohngefähr gleich angenehm*].[80]

Fichte's theory of property explicitly adhered to Rousseau's principles in establishing the priority of natural liberty to all social relations and insisting on the potentially limitless character of human activity—the quality Rousseau had termed "perfectibility." But Fichte claimed he had significantly modified Rousseau's evaluation of the needs generated by the development of the arts and sciences. "Agreeableness" had been used by many eighteenth-century writers as a nonpejorative equivalent for what was often called "luxury."[81] But Rousseau himself was famous for his outspoken condemnation of this continual multiplication and refinement of needs as the corruption of nature. According to Rousseau, the arts and sciences were spawned by this process and propelled it onward in turn. Their flourishing was a symptom of humanity's loss of independence: they were "garlands of flowers over the iron chains with which they are laden."[82] Rousseau claimed that individual independence could be restored in society only if, through a combination of exceptional circumstance and legislative feat, this runaway expansion of human needs could be brought under control. To address the deformity of humanity in society, Rousseau had explained in his 1762 masterpiece *Emile*, it was necessary to eliminate "the disproportion between our desires and faculties." Restoring harmony psychologically as well as socially meant finding a way to re-create the natural equilibrium between need and ability:

> In what, then, consists human wisdom or the road of true happiness? It is not precisely in diminishing our desires, for if they were beneath

[80] Ibid., 7:55.

[81] See, e.g., Vattel, "Dialogue entre le Prince de *** & son Confident, sur quelques parties essentielles de l'Administration publique," in *Mélanges de littérature, de morale et de politique* (Neuchâtel: Chez les Edit. du Journal Helvetique, 1760)," 31–32. On the eighteenth-century debate about luxury and its significance, see Hont, "Luxury Debate."

[82] Rousseau, "Discourse on the Sciences and Arts" (1751), in *Discourses*, 6.

> our power, a part of our faculties would remain idle, and we would not enjoy our whole being. Neither is it in extending our faculties, for if, proportionate to them, our desires were more extended, we would as a result only become unhappier. But it is in diminishing the excess of the desires over the faculties and putting power and will in perfect equality. It is only then that, with all the powers in action, the soul will nevertheless remain peaceful and that man will be well ordered.[83]

Rousseau went on to stress the impossibility of restoring this equilibrium through the expansion of human faculties alone. Rather, restoring an individual's harmony meant keeping him as close as possible to the "natural condition" of having "only the desires necessary to his preservation and the faculties sufficient to satisfy them." Once the imagination was awakened, the more stimulation it received, the more it produced an insatiable stream of new desires. "Therefore, do not fancy that in extending your faculties you extend your strength," Rousseau warned. "The real world has its limits; the imaginary world is infinite. Unable to enlarge the one, let us restrict the other, for it is from the difference between the two alone that are born all the pains which make us truly unhappy."[84]

Fichte addressed Rousseau's treatment of this problem directly in a public lecture he gave while still a professor at Jena in 1794.[85] The fifth installment of his famous lecture series "Morality for Scholars," subsequently published as the final part of *Some Lectures on the Vocation of the Scholar*, was devoted to an "examination of Rousseau's claims about the influence of the arts and sciences on the good of humanity." In his lecture, Fichte celebrated Rousseau as an eloquent and perceptive critic of social inequality and of hypocritical philosophes. As Rousseau had seen, the proliferation of needs had transformed humans into debased creatures untroubled by morality and willing to sacrifice everything in order to satisfy their desires—and those who claimed to know best were often the worst offenders. However, Fichte went on to claim, Rousseau had drawn the wrong conclusions from the lamentable state of affairs that he had so eloquently described. The heart of his argument was that Rousseau had gone astray by blaming the onset of increasing needs for causing the deformity of humanity in society, rather than attributing it to the fact that humanity retained its natural tendency to indolence even after it had begun acquiring many unnatural needs.

[83] Rousseau, *Emile*, 80.

[84] Ibid., 80–81.

[85] The fifth lecture in Fichte's *Some Lectures on the Vocation of the Scholar* (1794), entitled "Examination of Rousseau's claims about the influence of the arts and sciences on the well-being of mankind," in Fichte, *Gesamtausgabe*, pt. 1, 3:59–68. An English translation of the lectures can be found in Fichte, *Early Philosophical Writings*, 137–84.

Like Rousseau's *Emile*, Fichte's lecture indicated two potential alternatives to this mismatch between needs and the degree of activity undertaken to satisfy them. The first was to eliminate unnatural needs and return to a natural state of desire; the other was to retain unnatural desires but eliminate natural indolence. Fichte claimed that Rousseau had fallen for the idea of ataraxia, the restoration of humanity to a natural state of desire, and had revived the poetic dream of a return to a lost golden age. Returning to this state would indeed eliminate the deformities that Rousseau had detected. Relieved of the burden of needs that could neither be satisfied nor left unsatisfied without suffering, human beings would be left at peace with themselves and with one another. However, eliminating unnatural needs would also mean returning to a bestial condition, and it was wrong to imagine otherwise. "The specifically human predispositions [*Anlagen*] would not yet be cultivated; they would not even be apparent," Fichte wrote. "Man would have no needs other than those of his animal nature; he would live like the beast beside him in the pasture." This was no longer a human being, Fichte concluded, but "a new kind of animal."[86] Fichte recognized that of course "Rousseau did not want to return humanity to the state of nature with regard to its spiritual cultivation, but simply with regard to their physical needs."[87] But Fichte claimed that the two were inseparable, and that Rousseau had ruled out his own account of perfectibility, for to arrest the multiplication of physical needs was to forfeit the development of the activity undertaken to meet them and therefore to foreclose on the human potential for cultivating nonmaterial needs:

> Rousseau forgot that humanity can and ought to approach nearer to this state only through care, toil, and labor. Nature is rude and savage without the hand of man, and ought to be so, in order to force man to leave his inactive natural state, and work; in order to make man, a mere product of nature, become a free rational being.—He certainly leaves this natural state; he risks plucking the apple of knowledge, for the drive to be like God is indelibly implanted within him. The first step out of this state leads him to misery and toil: his needs are developed, and penetratingly demand to be satisfied; but man is naturally idle and sluggish, like the matter of which he is composed. Thus arises the hard struggle between need and indolence; the first triumphs, but the latter complains bitterly. Now he sows the field with the sweat of his brow, and is annoyed that it also contains thorns and thistles which he must uproot.—It is not need that is the source of vice; need is the stimulus to activity and virtue; idleness is the source of all vice. *How to enjoy as much as possible, and how to do as little as possible?*—this is the mis-

[86] Fichte, *Bestimmung des Gelehrten,* in *Gesamtausgabe*, pt. 1, 3:63–64.
[87] Ibid., 3:65.

> sion of corrupted nature, and the various attempts made to answer this question are its vices. There is no salvation for man until this natural indolence has been combated successfully, and until man finds all his joys and pleasures in activity, and activity alone.[88]

According to Fichte, the role of need was to spur activity, which is why the feeling of need was providentially associated with pain. In various writings, Fichte applied this principle to a variety of empirical cases. The *Foundations of Natural Right* dwelled on a description of hunger as "the original impetus" of all activity; a decade later, the *Addresses to the German Nation* deployed the same model with respect to the pain of seeing one's country occupied by a foreign army, and the activity of doing something about it.[89] In his lecture on Rousseau, Fichte recast Rousseau's account of pity in this way, as a spur to action. Rousseau's chief failing in Fichte's eyes was that his own great pity for the plight of mankind had not spurred him to make productive use of his eloquence by exhorting his readers to strive to overcome their vestigial natural indolence. "This is where Rousseau erred," Fichte wrote. "He felt strongly the misery of men, but he felt much less strongly his own power to remedy this . . . He took into account the suffering, but not that strength to help themselves which men possess within themselves."[90] Fichte claimed to discern the same flaw in Rousseau's novels. Rousseau's lovers managed to become virtuous without revealing "the most interesting and instructive thing of all: the struggle between reason and passion and the gradual, slow victory which the former achieves by means of exertion, effort, and labor."[91] Likewise, Rousseau's famous pupil Emile flourished because the obstacles of nature had been removed for him, not by him. By contrast, Fichte's own lecture concluded with his famous exhortation: "Act! Act!"[92]

The ideal of a restored balance between need and ability, the poetic golden age that Rousseau had identified with the state of nature, was located in humanity's future, not in its past.[93] Matched by expanding human activity, the spiral

[88] Ibid., 3:66. Fichte went on to develop these themes in his 1798 treatise on ethics, in which he similarly concluded that "the true, inborn radical evil lying in human nature itself is therefore inertia or *laziness*" (Fichte, *System of Ethics*, 191).

[89] Fichte, *Foundations of Natural Right*, 185; Fichte, *Addresses to the German Nation*, 11–12. This moral psychology is reminiscent of Hobbes's description of the passions, since Hobbes also classified the passions according to whether they issued in productive endeavor (Hobbes, *The Elements of Law Natural and Politic* [1640], ed. J.C.A. Gaskin [Oxford: Oxford University Press, 1994], 50 [pt. 1, chap. 8, sect. 8]); see Susan James, *Passion and Action: The Emotions in Seventeenth-Century Philosophy* (Oxford: Oxford University Press, 1997), 132–33.

[90] Fichte, *Bestimmung des Gelehrten*, in *Gesamtausgabe*, pt. 1, 3:66.

[91] Ibid., 3:67.

[92] Ibid.

[93] Ibid., 3:65. Compare Saint-Simon: "The imagination of the poets placed the Golden Age at the cradle of mankind, amidst the ignorance and rudeness of early times: it is rather the Age of Iron that ought to be relegated there. The Age of Gold of humankind is not behind us, it is before us,

of increasing unnatural needs was potentially the route to re-creating natural liberty in society and raising it into moral virtue. As long as their many desires got them to work, having many desires would compel members of society to lift themselves out of their natural indolence as well as their natural indigence. Work would make desires easier to satisfy and render life increasingly "agreeable," but most importantly it would also awaken the workers' awareness of themselves as efficacious rational actors. Ultimately, it would also put them in a position to make moral choices about their needs: "It is certainly true, that the closer man comes to his highest goal, the easier it will become to satisfy his physical needs . . . as the rule of reason spreads, man will always need less—not, as in the rude state of nature, because he does not know of agreeableness [*Annehmlichkeit*]—but because he can do without it; indeed, he will always be ready to enjoy the best tastefully, when he can have it without violating his duties, and to do without everything which he cannot have honorably."[94]

Fichte's account of human needs is the source of the elision in *The Closed Commercial State* between the right to live, and the right to live agreeably, and the foundation of the state's duty to guarantee everyone's right to work for a living. Only through the parallel expansion of need and activity, Fichte claimed, was it possible to end up acting like an independent human being rather than an independent beast by choosing and realizing all the ends more elevated than bare physical survival. This is why Fichte, though he refused to join Grotius and Locke in identifying natural property rights with the agricultural stage of history, demanded that "wilderness" always give way to "civilization" within civil societies.[95] It was a demand of right that society continue to develop beyond a purely agrarian stage, and that the division of labor continue expanding to include the production of the means for living ever more agreeably. As Fichte stressed in *The Closed Commercial State*, all his complex provisions to protect the property of merchants and manufacturers could not be dismissed as "merely affairs of interest and ability, and thus entirely arbitrary and not at all the object of strict right":

> It is not merely a pious wish, but an indispensable demand of human right and human destiny, that humanity live on earth as easily, as freely, with as much command over nature, and in as genuinely *human* a man-

it is in the perfection of the social order" (Claude-Henri de Rouvroy, comte de Saint-Simon, and Augustin Thierry, *De la Réorganisation de la Société Européenne* [Paris: Égron, 1814], 111–12).

[94] Fichte, *Bestimmung des Gelehrten,* in *Gesamtausgbe*, pt. 1, 3:65.

[95] Fichte, *Foundations of Natural Right*, 200; cf. 192: "Whatever grows wild must always give way to the cultivation of the land, since more sustenance can be gained from the latter than from the former. Thus uncultivated lands must be divided up as soon as the needs of individuals make it necessary; and if someone wants to possess something as his own field, it may not be left uncultivated." This was not to say that forests must all be cut down, Fichte specified, but that woodlands must also be subjected to "a kind of agriculture."

> ner, as nature will permit. Man should work; but not like a beast of burden, which falls asleep under its load, and is roused to carry the same burden after the briefest restoration of its spent power. He should work without fear, with pleasure and joy, and he should have time left to elevate his spirit and his gaze to the heavens which he was born to contemplate.[96]

The "political economy of the general will" that Fichte developed in *The Closed Commercial State* sought to ensure that everyone's pursuit of the greatest possible agreeableness could continue in a manner that remained consistent with everybody else's independence. The only way to protect the independence of nonagricultural workers, whose labor produced this agreeableness, was to ensure that they also had an exclusive right to the fruits of their labor. To secure the property of these laborers, as we saw in chapter 3, the state had to regulate their numbers, because these industries could be allowed to expand only at the pace set by agricultural productivity. Provision for everyone's survival had to take precedence over the development of industries that were concerned with living more and more agreeably; necessary manufactures had to take precedence over relative luxuries. A state whose agriculture was undeveloped and that still lacked basic tools could not indulge the "needs of luxury" (*Bedürfnisse des Luxus*). "Everyone should have enough to eat and a place to live before someone ornaments his home," Fichte demanded; "everyone should be dressed warmly and comfortably before someone dresses splendidly."[97] The only needs that Fichte absolutely ruled out were pure status goods, "which are merely and solely intended for opinion."[98] To put these principles into practice, Fichte proposed that the state establish a nationally appropriate but essentially arbitrary standard for basic subsistence. The "agreeableness" of all other goods would be calculated in terms of how much of the national staple could have been produced in their place. Then the labor needed to meet all of these needs could be divided equally among the population. Inequality was permissible only within these constraints. Scholars in their studies could eat foods more delicate than the heartier fair of the peasants in the fields, but all had to have access to "an absolutely human experience" to the extent that their society was able to achieve it.[99] A state that failed to follow these principles, Fichte claimed, was failing to protect the independence of its citizens.

The liberal thinker Benjamin Constant overstated the case, then, when he dismissed *The Closed Commercial State* as a rejection of commercial modernity

[96] Fichte, *Der geschlossene Handelsstaat*, in *Gesamtausgabe*, pt. 1, 7:70–71.

[97] Ibid., 7:60–61.

[98] Ibid., 7:116.

[99] Ibid., 7:65–68.

and a call to restore the frugal mores of ancient Sparta.[100] A more insightful rendering was produced by Ferdinand d'Eckstein, a German Catholic émigré living in France in the 1820s.[101] In an 1827 article on "industrialism" (a fancy new word, he observed, for what had once been called luxury), Eckstein described Fichte's philosophy as a more profound version of Saint-Simonianism.[102] The "vulgar industrialism" preached by Saint-Simon was to be condemned because it sought to enshrine petty self-interest and "transform the social order into a republic of beavers, ants, or bees."[103] By contrast, Eckstein described *The Closed Commercial State* as a "theory of transcendental industrialism," an intriguing effort (though ultimately unconvincing to a Catholic writer) to emancipate the individual through labor: "In this theory man works, lives from work, but for him work is not the goal of life. This goal is freedom of individual spirit, emancipated from the bonds of matter. Transformed into an instrument of the social existence of man, matter attests to the first triumph of human will; its second triumph is to make spirit rule over work itself, to render industrial man free and philosophical."[104] The English romantic poet Samuel Taylor Coleridge (1772–1834) likewise denied that Fichte's *Closed Commercial State* had actually discovered a way to heal the corrosive ugliness of commercial society without sacrificing its unprecedented dynamism and emancipatory potential.[105] This was, indeed, a challenge that continued to confound Karl Marx as well as later generations of Marxists.[106] But these early-nineteenth-century responses to Fichte's reworking of Rousseau enable us to pinpoint the character of his attempted solution.

[100] Benjamin Constant, "Journaux Intimes," 27 May 1804, in *Oeuvres*, ed. Alfred Roulin (Paris: Gallimard, 1979), 277.

[101] Ferdinand, baron d'Eckstein, "De l'Industrialisme," *Le Catholique* 5 (1827): 233–63, cited in Sonenscher, introduction to Sieyès, *Political Writings*, xii.

[102] D'Eckstein, "De l'Industrialisme," 233.

[103] Ibid., 234.

[104] Ibid., 241.

[105] Reacting to Fichte's demand that the necessary be given priority over the superfluous, Coleridge scribbled in the margin of his copy of *The Closed Commercial State*: "Nonsense! Where no one dare purchase the ornaments & dispensable comforts of Life, what motive exists for the increased Industry & Talents of the Rest? Is it for the comforts' sake or for the rank designated by it, that men wish & toil for fine furniture, fine clothes, foreign wines, &c? – Assuredly, for the latter. Fichte's Vanity strangely misled him in this Essay. The style excepted, it possesses no characteristic of his metaphysical Works: it is always shallow, & most often grossly erroneous" (*Marginalia*, 2:617).

[106] On Marx's criticism of Proudhon's failure in this regard, and on his own subsequent inability and that of twentieth-century communist regimes to avoid the same result, see Stedman Jones, introduction to Marx and Engels, *Communist Manifesto*, 182–83.

The Transcendental Industrialism of *The Closed Commercial State*

The Closed Commercial State claimed to show how natural liberty could be re-created artificially in the circumstances of modern European societies. Its premise was that the natural independence of the individual had been irrevocably lost in the distant past. The modern global economy was a remnant from that simpler time that had been thoroughly corrupted by the rising level of industry and the intensifying competition between states. Fichte followed Rousseau in probing Hobbes's explanation why a juridical state of nature between sovereign states could be tolerated: "Because they uphold thereby the industry of their subjects, there does not follow from it that misery which accompanies the liberty of particular men."[107] Fichte claimed that a world of open commercial states could not fulfill this condition. Even states that were successful on the global market would eventually face decline, and the consequences of a state's decline for the industry of its citizens were potentially catastrophic. Only by closing the commercial state, Fichte concluded, could the state secure their independence.

The political theory of *The Closed Commercial State* is neither socialist nor totalitarian in any straightforward sense. Fichte certainly shared his radical critique of the existing European order with Gracchus Babeuf and many other contemporaries. Yet Fichte added a significant twist to their vision of a communal regime based on the natural social concord that would emerge after the corrupt edifice of European power politics had been torn down. Fichte's aim was to show that the jurisprudential foundation of this edifice—the theory of the state as an artificial political union of individuals—would remain unfinished until all citizens' right to work was established on the same basis as property rights. Fichte was indeed a socialist in the original, eighteenth-century sense of that term: he aspired to a fuller notion of community than the one that had been articulated by Hobbes's doctrine of natural law and eventually came to dominate the discipline of political economy.[108] What makes Fichte's socialism noteworthy, and sets it apart from that of contemporaries like Babeuf, is the depth and sophistication of his effort to build this more complete account of social life on a theoretical foundation that remained—in Hegel's phrase—"anti-socialistic."

[107] Hobbes, *Leviathan*, 90. Rousseau's rejection of Hobbes's claim is most apparent in his manuscript fragment on war, which would not have been available to Fichte and his contemporaries, but can also be discerned in the *Second Discourse* and in book 5 of *Emile*; see "Discourse on the Origin of Inequality," in *Discourses*, 174; "State of War," in *Social Contract*, 162–176; and *Emile*, 466.

[108] Hont, *Jealousy of Trade*, 159–60; and Gregory Claeys, "'Individualism,' 'Socialism,' and 'Social Science': Further Notes on a Process of Conceptual Formation, 1800–1850," *Journal of the History of Ideas* 47, no. 1 (March 1986): 81–93.

The Closed Commercial State demanded that the state exert a vast degree of control over the economic activity of its citizens, but this demand did not issue from a philosophy that was somehow profoundly and ineluctably totalitarian. Isaiah Berlin famously worried that any theory of liberty that extended beyond the "negative liberty" of the absence of interference was a recipe for a moral dictatorship of philosopher-kings.[109] He also singled out Fichte as the clearest example of this danger. However, the philosopher-kings who ran Fichte's closed commercial state were not charged with forcing producers to master themselves, to internalize their autonomy and become rational moral beings, or anything of that nature. Indeed, they were expressly forbidden from doing so. Rather, they were charged with reversing the loss of independence that Fichte attributed to the expansion of the division of labor in modern European societies.

As Fichte contended at the beginning of *The Closed Commercial State*, meeting this responsibility in modern conditions required a reexamination of what it meant for the state to protect the property rights of its citizens:

> In our time we have sufficiently refuted the opinion that the state is, without restriction, the tutor of humanity in all its affairs; that it should make humanity happy, rich, healthy, orthodox, virtuous, and, God willing, eternally blessed. On the other hand, it seems to me that the duties and rights of the state have in turn been too narrowly constricted. It is not exactly incorrect, and it even admits of good sense, to say that the state has nothing more to do than maintain and protect everyone in his individual rights and property: but often it is tacitly implied that property exists independently of the state, that the state has only to consider the condition of its citizen's goods as it encounters them, and not to ask about the juridical principle of their acquisition. Contrary to this opinion I would say that it is the purpose of the state first *to give* to each his own, first to *establish* him in his property, and then to *protect* him in it.[110]

This formula for the state's role in securing property rights, which Fichte repeated later in the book, first appeared in Fichte's discussion of Rousseau's general will in the *Foundations of Natural Right*, where it has proved perplexing to commentators.[111] In the *Social Contract*, Rousseau maintained that indepen-

[109] Isaiah Berlin, "Two Concepts of Liberty," in *Four Essays on Liberty* (London: Oxford University Press, 1969), 118–72; on Fichte, see especially 145, 149–52. See also Berlin, *Freedom and Its Betrayal: Six Enemies of Human Liberty*, ed. Henry Hardy (London: Chatto and Windus, 2002), 50–73.

[110] Fichte, *Der geschlossene Handelsstaat*, *Gesamtausgabe*, pt. 1, 7:53. For a discussion of this key passage in relation to Fichte's exchanges with Wilhelm von Humboldt and Karl von Dalberg in Jena, see Moggach, "Freedom and Perfection." As Moggach explains, Fichte aligned himself with Humboldt in a Kantian critique of Dalberg's Wolffian paternalism, but was in turn critical of the extent to which Humboldt sought to curtail state interventions aimed at preserving freedom.

[111] "In modern Europe there were hardly any states for a considerable time. We are presently still among the attempts to form them. Until now, moreover, the mission of the state has only been half

dent individuals could assert a natural right to acquire whatever was necessary to meet their needs, but that any such claim had to be subordinated to the community in order to become "a genuine right."[112] In his 1797 treatise on rights, Kant developed this position into an account of "provisional rights."[113] The stance Fichte took in the *Foundations of Natural Right* ruled out this approach: "According to our theory, no individual can bring anything with him to the civil contract, for prior to this contract he has nothing. The first condition of giving something up is that one already have received something. Therefore, this contract—far from starting with giving—ought to begin with receiving."[114] Fichte's obsessive insistence on ruling out a provisional property right recalls his similarly strenuous effort to eliminate the idea of a right of necessity. Fichte was absolutely determined to close every loophole that might conceivably compromise the principle that all social relations had to be constructed voluntarily. Otherwise, given the indefinite time horizon of conclusive constitutional reform, provisional rights could easily allow the limitations of existing social relations to ossify. In an increasingly postagrarian society, allowing a provisional right to exclude others from using certain objects potentially served to perpetuate the dominance of the landowning elite over the growing industrial workforce. Kant himself matched Fichte's refusal to accord exclusive property status to certain forms of labor over others: just as Fichte insisted on an absolute equivalence between the indigenous hunter's knowledge of the terrain and the European settler's efforts to clear it for planting, Kant scoffed at the idea that only particular forms of labor could serve as evidence of natural acquisition, rather than "many other signs that cost less effort."[115] But where Fichte decried how an expanding division of labor was producing dependent "metics," Kant joined Sieyès in defending a distinction between active and passive citizens and included all workers who lacked an independent source of livelihood among those who "lack civil personality."[116] Fichte's claim was that so long as this kind

---

grasped, only from one side, as an institution for maintaining the citizen in the state of property where he was found, by means of the law. The more profound duty of the state, which is first to establish each in the possession due to him, has been overlooked" (Fichte, *Der geschlossene Handelsstaat, Gesamtausgabe*, pt. 1, 7:95). For an example of the perplexity this formulation has caused, see Philonenko, *Théorie et praxis*, 183–85.

[112] Rousseau, *Social Contract*, 56.

[113] Kant, *Metaphysics of Morals*, 51–53 (sects. 14–15). Given the eventual inevitability of contact between even the most far-flung communities, Kant stressed that even property determinations within a community had to remain provisional "unless this contract extends to the entire human race."

[114] Fichte, *Foundations of Natural Right*, 177/11.

[115] Kant, *Metaphysics of Morals*, 52 (sect. 15).

[116] Ibid., 92 (sect. 46). Sieyès also accepted this distinction (Sonenscher, introduction to Sieyès, *Political Writings*, xxxi).

of dependence persisted, it would prevent societies from fully extracting themselves from intensifying social conflict and progressing toward perpetual peace.

The central concern of *The Closed Commercial State* was to show not only how to restore independence within modern European societies, but also how this could be done without turning existing property relations into a permanent ceiling on the nature of human activity.[117] Kant, as well as Fichte, had described this very problem as one that had been posed most powerfully by Rousseau.[118] Fichte's highly technical reworking of Rousseau's theory of property is a crucial aspect of his approach to this problem. But what ultimately sets Fichte apart from Rousseau and Kant is his aspiration to set out a more proactive political strategy for achieving a social order that is peaceful both internally and externally, yet not stagnant. Kant's writings seemed to suggest that the pathologies of interdependence that Rousseau described would be cured only through a long-term historical process propelled forward by those very pathologies. Like Adam Smith, Kant described an invisible hand orchestrating insatiable desires into a social equilibrium that was at least minimally and outwardly just. Only when this process reached its violent climax—unsustainable warfare between states—could a genuinely peaceful and legal social order begin to emerge. Only within this order, Kant concluded in his "Idea for a Universal History with a Cosmopolitan Purpose," could humanity finally turn the corner and begin to realize its ultimate moral potential:

> This state of affairs is not completely free from *danger*, lest human energies should lapse into inactivity, but it is also not without a principle of

[117] See Fichte, *Foundations of Natural Right*, 176–177. On this concern, see Raymond Geuss, "Freedom as an Ideal, I," *Proceedings of the Aristotelian Society* (supplement) 69 (1995): 87–100.

[118] See especially Kant's "Conjectures on the Beginning of Human History" (1786):

> In this way, it is possible to reconcile with each other and with reason the often misunderstood and apparently contradictory pronouncements of the celebrated *J.J. Rousseau*. In his essays *On the Influence of the Sciences* and *On the Inequality of Man*, he shows quite correctly that there is an inevitable conflict between culture and the nature of the human race as a *physical* species each of whose members is meant to fulfill his destiny completely. But in his *Émile*, his *Social Contract*, and other writings, he attempts in turn to solve the more difficult problem of what course culture should take in order to ensure the proper development, in keeping with their destiny, of man's capacities as a *moral* species, so that this [moral] destiny will no longer conflict with his character as a natural species. Since culture has perhaps not yet really begun—let alone completed—its development in accordance with the true principles of man's *education* as a human being and citizen, the above conflict is the source of all the genuine evils which oppress human life, and of all the vices which dishonour it. At the same time, the very impulses which are blamed as the causes of vice are good in themselves, fulfilling their function as abilities implanted by nature. But since these abilities are adapted to the state of nature, they are undermined by the advance of culture and themselves undermine the latter in turn, until art, when it reaches perfection, once more becomes nature—and this is the ultimate goal of man's moral destiny. (*Political Writings*, 227–28)

> *equality* governing the *actions and counter-actions* of these energies, lest they should destroy one another. When it is little beyond the half-way mark in its development, human nature has to endure the hardest of evils under the guise of outward prosperity before this final step (i.e. the union of states) is taken; and Rousseau's preference for the state of savagery does not appear so very mistaken if only we leave out of consideration this last stage which our species still has to surmount.[119]

In a similar vein, Fichte asserted that *The Closed Commercial State* would remain nothing more than a scholarly exercise until a long-term historical process finally put an end to Europe's domination over the rest of the world. But the main thrust of the book was that states had to take immediate and decisive action or else they would indeed be destroyed by the intensifying forms of conflict that so many eighteenth-century writers had discerned. Fichte claimed that the monetary strategy he outlined could serve as an alternative to commerce. It would provide the stimulus necessary to avoid a permanently stagnant peace without engendering all the conflicts endemic to commercial interdependence. Only among closed commercial states, Fichte concluded, could a strictly noncompetitive form of international trade safely resume, alongside other noncommercial forms of cultural engagement, without unleashing these self-destructive dynamics.

Early readers of *The Closed Commercial State* were virtually unanimous in rejecting Fichte's claim that a substitute for global commerce could be created. They shared the conviction that the continuing expansion of global commerce was the indispensable engine propelling humanity toward the fulfillment of its infinite potential and concluded that Fichte's proposal to eliminate it was a recipe for eternal stagnation. This criticism was conveyed particularly effectively by the theologian Friedrich Schleiermacher (1768–1834), who was in Berlin when Fichte arrived there from Jena and became quite close to him at the time. Schleiermacher never realized his intention to publish a review of *The Closed Commercial State* when it first appeared, but was still discussing it in lectures he delivered several decades later.[120] According to Schleiermacher, the expansion of the division of labor inevitably made the industry of individuals less secure, and this insecurity could be addressed only by the state. This intervention could take many forms, the "most severe" of which was illustrated in principle by Fichte's *Closed Commercial State*. Schleiermacher identified its closest historical analogues as the caste systems of ancient Egypt or contemporary India. Such

[119] Kant, "Idea for a Universal History with a Cosmopolitan Purpose," in *Political Writings*, 49.

[120] Friedrich Daniel Ernst Schleiermacher to August Wilhelm Schlegel, 14 October 1800, and Schleiermacher to Friedrich Schlegel, 20 October 1800, in Schleiermacher, *Briefwechsel und biographische Dokumente, 1800*, ed. Andreas Arndt and Wolfgang Virmond, pt. 5, vol. 4, of *Kritische Gesamtausgabe*, ed. Hans-Joachim Birkner, Hermann Fischer, et al. (Berlin: de Gruyter, 1980), 4:289–92, 299–303.

a system would dramatically constrict needs, Fichte's denial notwithstanding, because every time a new need was allowed, an entire new class of producers would have to be created to supply it.[121] Schleiermacher denied that the stimulating effects of global commerce could be equaled by an expanded domestic market coupled with noncommercial forms of cultural exchange among nations, "for the ideal communication which is necessary for progress cannot be separated from material communication." Closing the commercial state, he concluded, represented "a step backward toward the original condition of isolation which is in contradiction with the general ethical tendency."[122]

As we have seen, this conclusion was shared by readers of *The Closed Commercial State* as widely divergent as Benjamin Constant and Friedrich Gentz. The polemical cast of much of this criticism tends to obscure the fact that this was an outcome that Fichte had been trying to avoid and that Fichte himself had criticized Rousseau for failing to avoid it. Unlike Kant and Fichte, Constant no longer identified peace without stagnation as a problem that Rousseau had posed: he portrayed Rousseau as an austere moralist whose preference for republican antiquity over commercial modernity had led to the Terror, and lamented the fact that the well-intentioned philosophers he encountered in Germany were repeating the same mistakes.[123] Like Constant, Hegel flattened the differences between Rousseau and Fichte; like Gentz, he denied that peace without stagnation was a problem that could be solved. In his view, the only perpetual peace was a stagnant and materialistic one; the only vision of social life that Rousseau, Kant, and Fichte could produce from their property-based contractual theories of the state was one that throttled the "ethical life" of the community (and possibly guillotined some of its members in the process).[124]

[121] "Kolleg 1817 Nachschrift Varnhagen," in Schleiermacher, *Vorlesungen über die Lehre vom Staat*, ed. Walter Jaeschke, pt. 2, vol. 8, of *Kritische Gesamtausgabe*, ed. Birkner, Fischer, et al. (Berlin: de Gruyter, 1998), 340.

[122] Schleiermacher, "Lehre vom Staat" (1829–33), in *Vorlesungen*, 8:122–23.

[123] Constant, *Oeuvres*, 277. Richard Whatmore has suggested that Constant's strong distinction between ancients and moderns ought to be understood in the context of intraliberal debates during the Restoration period with Jean-Baptiste Say over whether France ought to emulate the English model of economy and politics or revive the Fénelonian effort to achieve a more "social" modern economy (Whatmore, "Democrats and Republicans in Restoration France," *European Journal of Political Theory* 3, no. 1 [2004]: 37–51; and "The Politics of Political Economy from Rousseau to Constant," in *Markets in Historical Contexts: Ideas and Politics in the Modern World*, ed. Mark Bevir and Frank Trentmann, 46–49 [Cambridge: Cambridge University Press, 2004]). See also Helena Rosenblatt, "Re-evaluating Benjamin Constant's Liberalism: Industrialism, Saint-Simonianism and the Restoration Years," *History of European Ideas* 30 (2004): 23–37.

[124] Hegel on the stagnancy of perpetual peace: "War preserves the ethical health of peoples in their indifference to determinate things; it prevents the latter from hardening, and the people from becoming habituated to them, just as the movement of the winds preserves the seas from that stagnation which a permanent calm would produce, and which a permanent (or indeed 'perpetual') peace would produce among peoples" ("Scientific Ways of Treating Natural Law," 141). For the view that the social life envisioned by Rousseau, Kant, and Fichte would throttle the "ethical life" of

Nonetheless, as we have seen, in the 1790s the debate over the economic conditions for a peaceful yet dynamic social order was one that could and did unfold within the conceptual space created by Rousseau. This was further confirmed by Joseph Görres's 1798 essay on perpetual peace. Two years before Fichte published *The Closed Commercial State*, Görres had employed a version of the same theoretical idiom to survey the ways of applying the principles of a republican constitution to commerce. Görres defined a "commercial nation" (*Handelsnation*) as a "crowd [*Menge*] of individuals" who recognized the same "laws" of trade, or prices.[125] As in constitutional matters, every individual was subject to the general will of the "nation" (*Nation*), which could exercise its legislative power collectively or through representation. In the former case, prices would be set through the market mechanism and the government would limit itself to investigating and correcting abuses. In the latter case, the government would legislate prices. Görres concluded that the benefits of a "representative" commercial state were far outweighed by the difficulty of preventing the kinds of economic abuses that France had suffered under Robespierre, such as excessive restrictions on trade and uncontrollable expansion of the money supply. The separation of powers and other techniques might help control the behavior of political representatives, Görres allowed, but there was no way to apply them to "representatives of the mercantile will."[126]

Seeing *The Closed Commercial State* as a contribution to this debate yields a more incisive comparison between Smith and Fichte than the one suggested by Hestermann. It also helps illuminate the ambiguity over the scope of Fichte's ambition, which was discussed at the end of the previous chapter. In the *Wealth of Nations*, Smith claimed that modern Europe had not followed the natural progression described by the property theory of the natural jurists, that is, by proceeding from simpler to more complex forms of industry and meeting progressively more refined needs. Like Fichte, Smith viewed contemporary Europe as an "unnatural and retrograde order," rife with growing inequalities and mired in mercantilism. But Smith sought to show how the very pathologies of this retrograde order had unintentionally produced the civil liberties enjoyed by Europeans and that a dogmatically systematic attempt to revert to a natural order would destroy these mitigating features of the modern world.[127]

---

the community, see Hegel, *Elements of the Philosophy of Right*, ed. Allen Wood, trans. H. B. Nisbet (Cambridge: Cambridge University Press, 1991), 37–38, 58, 106, 277 (sects. 5–6, 29, 75, 258).

[125] Görres, "Der Allgemeine Frieden, Ein Ideal," in *Ausgewählte Werke*, 1:61. Even in modern Europe, Görres observed, there were hardly any large unified markets: even large political states still comprised many small and disconnected "commercial states" (*Handelsstaaten*).

[126] Ibid., 1:62–63.

[127] See Hont, *Jealousy of Trade*, 354–88, originally published as "Adam Smith and the Political Economy of the 'Unnatural and Retrograde' Order," in *Französische Revolution und Politische Ökonomie*, Schriften aus dem Karl-Marx-Haus 41 (Trier: Friedrich-Ebert-Stiftung, 1989), 122–49.

The Closed Commercial State was read as a statement in this Smithian spirit of resigned mitigation by no less a reader than Rahel Varnhagen (1771–1833), the daughter of a Jewish merchant who long presided over one of the most celebrated and distinguished salons of Berlin, which Fichte frequented.[128] Varnhagen compared *The Closed Commercial State* to Rousseau's *Emile* and claimed that Fichte had sought to do in political economy what Rousseau had done in education:

> Through Rousseau's *Emile* we learn how an entire world would have to be arranged in order to raise a child into a man who is healthy in every sense; but he also shows us how far away we are from this condition and that we can only aim for very small incremental steps in education. Fichte shows us in his *Closed Commercial State*, likewise through a condition that must not be fulfilled, what would have to be done for a state if one could close off all others or arrange them too. . . . It is wrong not to thank the authors, but to think that one is refuting them merely by demonstrating what is impossible, which they themselves have made clear.[129]

In Varnhagen's reading, Fichte had used a hypothetical account of healthy natural development, in isolation from the distortions caused by external pressures, to develop a critical standard for those who had already traveled a great distance down an unnatural path.

Varnhagen was right that *The Closed Commercial State* is most profitably read as the radical rearticulation of a critical standard. As we have seen, Carl August von Struensee, the Prussian minister to whom the work was dedicated, also chose to receive it in this spirit. However, it is the Baron d'Eckstein's description that gauges the scope of Fichte's own ambition more convincingly. *The Closed Commercial State* was an ambitious strategy for extending liberty to all members of society. It sought to secure the rights of every citizen, not by restoring nature, but by eliminating its corrupt vestiges. This was precisely the kind of systematizing politics of liberty that Smith had warned would destroy the mitigating features of a pathologically unjust world. In a chapter Smith added to the *Theory of Moral Sentiments* in 1789, just before his death, he issued an eloquent warning against the "man of system" who imagined that rearranging

[128] See Petra Wilhelmy, *Der Berliner Salon im 19. Jahrhundert, 1780–1914* (Berlin: de Gruyter, 1989). Hannah Arendt, who considered Rahel Levin to be a kindred spirit, wrote her biography: *Rahel Varnhagen: The Life of a Jewess*, ed. Liliane Weissberg, trans. R. and C. Winston (Baltimore: Johns Hopkins University Press, 1997).

[129] H.E.G. Paulus, *Conversations-Saal und Geister Revüe: Ein Panorama interessanter Personen, Gedanken und Zeitmaterien, für Menschenkenntniss und Wissenschaft* (Stuttgart: Schweizerbart, 1837), 913–14; cited in Fichte, *Gesamtausgabe*, pt. 1, 7:19.

human society to perfection was like moving inert pieces on a chessboard.[130] *The Closed Commercial State* is shot through with this spirit of system.[131]

From this perspective, then, *The Closed Commercial State* stands as testament to the dangers of an excessively dogmatic approach to politics. Yet it remains vital not to conflate a dogmatic politics with a dogmatic system of liberty. *The Closed Commercial State* is the product of both.

[130] Smith, *Theory of Moral Sentiments*, 234 (pt. 6, sect. 2, ch. 2, para. 17).

[131] Fichte's riposte to Smithian caution was to suggest that "daring innovation" was still less of a problem than "sluggish attachment to old rules which are no longer applicable or adequate" (Fichte, *Der geschlossene Handelsstaat*, *Gesamtausgabe*, pt. 1, 7:43). He further attributed the dogma of natural liberty to the prevalence of "the gambling urge" (*Spieltrieb*), the debased form of individualism that was pervading contemporary culture and led people to "transform life into a game": "Such are those who incessantly call for freedom, for freedom of trade and acquisition, freedom from supervision and administration, freedom from all order and customs. To these people, everything demanded by strict rightfulness, and a solidly ordered and thoroughly uniform course of things, implies an encroachment of their natural liberty. To them, the thought of organizing public commerce so that there will no longer be any deceitful speculation, windfall profit, or sudden riches, can only be revolting" (140–41).

Conclusion

Eighteenth-century discussions of perpetual peace examined the possibility of a social world no longer dominated by the imperatives of survival: a world in which those imperatives had been disentangled from the dynamics of interstate rivalry. In Fichte's eyes, Rousseau and Kant were powerfully critical proponents of this ideal: critics whose skepticism had ultimately prevented them from providing meaningful strategic guidance to those who sought to bring this vision of the future closer to reality. Fichte claimed he had found the way through this impasse by developing a more thoroughly constructivist theory of society than his predecessors had possessed. *The Closed Commercial State* took up the challenge of extending Rousseau and Kant's critique into a strategy for extracting modern European states from their self-destructive trajectory. Fichte concluded that in the absence of a genuinely borderless cosmopolitan community, the only way to insulate property relations from the pressures of international power politics and expose them to greater considerations of justice was to construct a largely self-sufficient national economy. He further claimed that modern finance gave states the capacity to construct such an economy without forfeiting the quest to release humanity from the bondage of nature.

The attraction of national self-sufficiency has continued to ebb and flow along with the tides of globalization, and efforts to achieve it have taken a great variety of forms. They have encompassed strategies for becoming globally competitive as well as strategies for escaping a competitive world—aggressive bids for imperial hegemony as well as pacifist urgings to avoid foreign entanglements. Fichte's *Closed Commercial State* has figured in many debates about all these strategies ever since the Napoleonic wars.[1] It resurfaced repeatedly during the revolutions of 1848 and was still being invoked before, during, and after

[1] E.T.A. Hoffmann's tale "Ritter Gluck: A Recollection from the Year 1809," which begins by evoking the atmosphere in Berlin cafés during the Napoleonic blockades, notes that the idea of the closed commercial state was a subject of conversation. The reference was added by Hoffmann's editor, Friedrich Rochlitz, in a bid to make him seem topical (*Tales of E.T.A. Hoffmann*, ed. Leonard J. Kent and Elizabeth C. Knight [Chicago: University of Chicago Press, 1972], 3). The association of Fichte's *Closed Commercial State* with Napoleon's "continental system" became commonplace. See also Lotz, *Handbuch der Staatswirthschaftslehre*, 1:146.

the world wars of the twentieth century.[2] This book has shown that *The Closed Commercial State* was an intensive investigation into the prospects of Europe's transformation into the kind of international federation envisioned by Kant. Fichte's analysis was not the product of an alien ideology. Rather, it represented a notable attempt to join the constitutionalism of Rousseau, Sieyès, and Kant to widespread and fairly mainstream eighteenth-century views of commerce, finance, and the European states system.

Fichte's aspiration was to preserve the idealism of his political thought while keeping it grounded in the historical realities he had identified in his account of state formation and the impact of global trade in modern Europe. To some of his critics, Fichte's politics—like his philosophy more generally[3]—was a failure because it retained too much of Kant's scepticism; to others, it failed to retain enough. From the former perspective, *The Closed Commercial State* was a particularly grotesque statement of a Kantian regulative ideal that was forever beyond reach: in Fichte's hands, the emancipatory ideals of the social contract and perpetual peace had receded so far as to become pretexts for intensifying the despotism of the state while exacerbating the solipsistic tendencies of an increasingly materialistic culture. From the latter perspective, the idea of a closed commercial state was the irresponsible product of a feverishly utopian imagination. In its zeal to establish heaven on earth, it ran roughshod over the political constraints imposed by a corrupt commercial age, and promised to destroy whatever hope of redemption that age might continue to entertain.

Both criticisms certainly retain their force. The story of *The Closed Commercial State* and its reception offers a glimpse at the formative stages of the rival ideologies that, as Albert Hirschman described, have long disputed whether commercial society creates or dissolves the moral foundations necessary for its

[2] Fichte was proclaimed the philosopher of the times in 1848 by Wilhelm Busse in his *J. G. Fichte und seine Beziehung zur Gegenwart des deutschen Volkes*. One political economist, writing in 1847, described *The Closed Commercial State* as a not-so-distant precursor to the mercantilism of Friedrich List and the communism of Pierre-Joseph Proudhon, warning that a revival of Fichte's monetary plan would utterly destroy modern civilization (Alexander Schneer, "Ueber Fichte's Handelsstaat," in *Uebersicht der Arbeiten und Veränderungen der Schlesische Gesellschaft für vaterländische Kultur im Jahre 1847* [Breslau: 1848], 312–19). *The Closed Commercial State* also figured in Italian polemics against Giuseppe Mazzini over the failures of 1848 and the question of the right to work; see, for example, Claudio Cesa, "G. B. Passerini und die erste italienische Übersetzung von 'Der geschlossene Handelsstaat,'" in *Erneuerung der Transzendentalphilosophie: Im Anschluss an Kant und Fichte*, ed. Klaus Hammacher and Albert Mues (Stuttgart–Bad Cannstatt: Frommann-Holzboog, 1979), 84–95. Notable instances of the book's recurring presence in later debates about globalization include Weber, *Fichte's Sozialismus*; Albert Hirschman, *National Power and the Structure of Foreign Trade* (Berkeley and Los Angeles: University of California Press, 1945); and Heilperin, *Studies in Economic Nationalism*.

[3] Frederick C. Beiser, "The Enlightenment and Idealism," in *The Cambridge Companion to German Idealism*, ed. Karl Ameriks, 31–32 (Cambridge: Cambridge University Press, 2000).

own operation.[4] But Fichte's book also cast itself as a dispassionate attempt to see past these recurring cycles of debate. As we have seen, notable readers like Rahel Varnhagen took it seriously as an attempt to produce a genuinely critical perspective on the political economy of a pacified Europe. So long as we continue to ask ourselves whether we may (or already do) inhabit the "perpetual peace" of the eighteenth-century imagination, we would do well to keep Fichte's efforts in full view.

Like Kant's *Perpetual Peace*, Fichte's *Closed Commercial State* was written in anticipation of a potentially transformative peace settlement. In both cases, the anticipated moment of opportunity faded almost instantly. Prussia remained stubbornly submerged in a toxic international environment, and was overrun by Napoleon in 1806. Though many have claimed that the fundamental orientation of Fichte's politics changed quite dramatically in response to these developments, the great nineteenth-century historian Otto von Gierke's sense that he "never broke away altogether from his previous system of ideas" still seems the more plausible view.[5] The problems that preoccupied Fichte in *The Closed Commercial State* were neither a fleeting concern nor a peripheral dimension of his political thought. Indeed, Fichte never abandoned the proposals he made in *The Closed Commercial State*, and even continued reworking his monetary ideas in unpublished manuscripts and lectures until his death in 1814—despite the fact that, as Fichte put it in 1805, "on this point there is a veil over the eyes of the age which is impossible to pull away; and it is in vain to waste words about this."[6]

Fichte's *Addresses to the German Nation*, delivered in occupied Berlin in the winter of 1808–9, have achieved much greater notoriety than *The Closed Commercial State* as a supposed transmission of ancien régime power politics into the age of nationalism. In fact, they represent a further effort to extend Fichte's constitutional theory into a strategic response to immensely constricting historical circumstances. Like many of his contemporaries throughout Europe, Fichte saw Napoleon's triumph as confirmation that modern civilization was reliving the decline and fall of classical antiquity and that the onset of a second dark age—a future foretold by generations of anxious eighteenth-century

[4] Hirschman, *Rival Views of Market Society*.

[5] Gierke, *Natural Law and Society*, 133–34. "In his later writings Fichte considerably changed his original theory, and advanced towards a really organic view of society," Gierke wrote, but "the 'higher view of the State,' which he preached in his later days, never reached the stage of a definite expression in terms of juristic ideas." See also Douglas Moggach, "Fichte's Engagement with Machiavelli," *History of Political Thought* 14, no. 4 (1993): 573–89.

[6] Fichte, *Die Grundzüge des gegenwärtigen Zeitalters*, *Gesamtausgabe*, pt. 1, 8:359. On the reworked political economy that Fichte presented in his 1812 lectures, see Isabel Thomas-Fogiel, "Sens et statut de la theorie des échanges commerciaux dans le système de Fichte," *Astérion*, no. 5 (July 2007): 33–55.

writers—had actually come to pass.[7] In his *Addresses*, Fichte blamed Germany's participation in this fate on its failure to follow the advice he had given in *The Closed Commercial State*:

> Almost a decade ago, before anyone could foresee what has since come to pass, the Germans were counseled to make themselves independent of world trade and to establish a closed commercial state. This proposal ran contrary to our habits, but particularly to our idolatrous worship of coined metal, and was passionately attacked and pushed aside. Since that time we are learning, in dishonour and under the compulsion of an external power, to do without that, and much else besides, which once we insisted we could not do without, though then we might have done so freely and with the greatest honour to ourselves. May we take this opportunity, when enjoyment of these things at least no longer corrupts us, to correct our notions forever! May we see at last that, although all those swindling theories of international trade and manufacture are fit for the foreigner and part of the arsenal with which he has waged war on us since time immemorial, they have no application for the Germans; that, besides the unity of the Germans among themselves, their internal self-sufficiency and commercial independence are the second means to their salvation and thereby the salvation of Europe.[8]

In 1800, Prussia and the other German states had still enjoyed their own political independence as well as the tremendous opportunity created by the revolution in France. A powerful republic had appeared that was prepared to serve as what the marquis de Mirabeau had called the "friend of mankind": a republic whose own interest was closely aligned with the general interest of humanity and that was in a position to become the lynchpin of a future republican federation.[9] Prussia and its neighbors had failed to take advantage of this opportunity, Fichte charged, and since then, France had abandoned the principles of its own revolution. The republican friend of mankind had itself become an imperial military machine, even more aggressive than its rivals because it was fueled by nationalist passions that threatened to ignite the rest of Europe. Clear-sighted Germans had long appreciated that no amount of national glory would heal individual wounds, but "if no higher view of life is brought before us," Fichte

[7] Fichte, *Addresses to the German Nation*, 195–96. For another contemporary example of these expectations (dating from 1811), see J. R. Seeley, *Life and Times of Stein, or, Germany and Prussia in the Napoleonic Age* (Cambridge: Cambridge University Press, 1878), 2:392.

[8] Fichte, *Addresses to the German Nation*, 171. *The Closed Commercial State*, as we have seen, was written for multiple German states. It is not at all obvious that the *Addresses* imagine a unified and centralized state rather than a federation.

[9] Marquis de Mirabeau, *L'ami des hommes*.

warned in his first address, Germans themselves might very well become "dangerous preachers of this very understandable and attractive doctrine."[10]

Fichte's *Addresses* sought to show how Germany could still avoid the path that commercial modernity had taken in France. France's pursuit of England's hegemony had ended in a turn to despotism and a race for empire. Fichte claimed that Germany's divergent historical development since the fall of Rome, and the unique cultural endowments that development had bestowed, made it possible to imagine an alternative to a future German replay of modern French history. Napoleon's conquests had deprived German states of their political agency, and Russian pretensions notwithstanding, they no longer had recourse to any other potential friends of mankind. But Fichte claimed that French occupation had also created a new opportunity to lay the groundwork for the establishment of a republic in Germany. While foreign occupation ruled out most forms of political agency, it still permitted—and could serve as powerful motivation for—the development of a new system of universal public education.[11] Eighteenth-century refinements on the Renaissance arts of princely education had ultimately failed to produce "patriot kings" or enlightened despots capable of delivering their subjects from the return of the dark ages. However, Fichte claimed, the scientifically designed patriotic education of the entire nation would create a solid foundation for moderate and limited government.[12] The patriotic national identity constructed through this education would become the site of consensus on the legitimacy of the state. Internally, it would demand conformity to the rule of law; externally, it would restrict the exertion of state power to cases of true necessity. As Friedrich Meinecke suspected, Fichte's proposal for a new system of universal public education was not an abandonment of his idealism: it was another mechanism to set in motion the kinds of comprehensive transformations that would insulate society from the Machiavellian imperatives of international relations as much as possible.[13]

German history, of course, took a different turn. Twentieth-century Germany did attempt a military challenge to the economic hegemony of the English-

[10] Fichte, *Reden an die deutsche Nation*, *Gesamtausgabe*, pt. 1, 10:115.

[11] Fichte, *Addresses to the German Nation*, 144.

[12] Ibid., 88–90.

[13] Friedrich Meinecke, *Weltbürgertum und Nationalstaat* (1908), trans. Robert B. Kimber as *Cosmopolitanism and the National State* (Princeton, N.J.: Princeton University Press, 1970), 83. It is worth noting that upon close examination, the actual schools Fichte proposed turn out to be closed commercial states in miniature: they would be economically self-sufficient communities, each resembling a "little state," a "little economic state" (*kleinen Wirthschaftsstaates*); the principles of his educational system described the "fundamental principles" of a "constitution" for a "commonwealth of pupils" (Fichte, *Reden an die deutsche Nation*, *Gesamtausgabe*, pt. 1, 10:129, 237).

speaking world.[14] In the case of Nazi Germany, this challenge was animated by a depraved ideology that distorted Great Power rivalry into a crusade for racial survival in the face of a global Jewish conspiracy. Along the way to its ultimate defeat, it unleashed barbarism, death, and destruction on a scale that truly did return parts of Europe to the dark ages. Yet the problem of disengaging the state's capacity to secure the economic welfare of its population from Great Power rivalry had been present long before the cataclysm of the twentieth century, and it continued to confront those who set out to plan Europe's postwar future. Fichte's hopes of inoculating Germany from the diseases of commercial modernity—and the efforts of the early-nineteenth-century Prussian reformers with whom those hopes resonated most sympathetically—were ultimately dashed in the most spectacular fashion.[15] But in a broad sense, Fichte's prognosis of the European states system was corroborated by some of the witnesses to its ultimate demise who began to re-imagine its reincarnation as a future European Union. William Beveridge, the author of the famous 1942 report that laid the groundwork for Britain's postwar welfare state, was far from alone in imagining that the postwar international economy might have to be confined—much as Fichte had projected—to a series of bilateral trade agreements among almost entirely autarkic welfare states.[16]

Such assessments were easily dismissed as contagion from a debased "German idea of the state"—as Michael Heilperin, an associate of the libertarian economist Ludwig von Mises, subsequently did when he accused Beveridge, along with John Maynard Keynes and Gunnar Myrdal, of unwittingly reinventing Fichte's *Closed Commercial State*.[17] But the affinities between Fichte and these prominent theorists of the postwar welfare state take on a different significance when Fichte is reassessed as a contributor to long-running pan-European debates about how to tame the fiscal-military machines that had emerged through centuries of escalating international competition. In the 1920s, Keynes began to think that the levels of international integration achieved in the nineteenth century reflected a unique set of historical circumstances that had since disappeared. "The transition from economic anarchy to a regime which deliberately aims at controlling and directing economic forces in the interests of social justice and social stability, will present enormous difficulties both technical and

[14] These remarks are shaped by the insightful new account in Adam Tooze, *The Wages of Destruction: The Making and Breaking of the Nazi Economy* (London: Allen Lane, 2006).

[15] See Schuurmans, "State, Society, and Market," 304–408.

[16] William Beveridge, *Full Employment in a Free Society* (London: George Allen and Unwin, 1944), 240–41.

[17] Heilperin, *Studies in Economic Nationalism*, 88, 97, 109, 113, 117, 138, 144–47, 149, 174. On the "German idea of state" (whose progenitors included Fichte), see Friedrich Hayek, *The Road to Serfdom* (London: Routledge, 1944), 125–26.

political," Keynes wrote in 1925. "I suggest, nevertheless, that the true destiny of New Liberalism is to seek their solution."[18] Keynes's quest to save the West from fascism by finding a middle ground between laissez-faire orthodoxy and doctrinaire socialism eventually took him quite close indeed to Fichte's *Closed Commercial State*. "A gradual trend in the direction of economic self-sufficiency may be more conducive to peace than economic internationalism," Keynes famously opined in his 1933 article "National Self-Sufficiency": "I sympathize, therefore, with those who would minimize, rather than with those who would maximize, economic entanglement among nations. Ideas, knowledge, science, hospitality, travel—these are the things which should of their nature be international. But let goods be homespun whenever it is reasonably and conveniently possible and, above all, let finance be primarily national."[19] Keynes's article—much more credibly, perhaps, than Fichte's *Closed Commercial State*—tempered this claim by placing great emphasis on the degree of political prudence that would be necessary if the cure were not to become a far greater scourge than the disease itself. "Words ought to be a little wild—for they are the assault of thoughts upon the unthinking," Keynes allowed. "But when the seats of power and authority have been attained, there should be no more poetic license." Above all, Keynes cautioned, "those who seek to disembarrass a country of its entanglements should be very slow and wary. It should not be a matter of tearing up roots but of slowly training a plant to grow in a different direction."[20]

Keynes foresaw great tragedy awaiting "experiments" like those underway in the 1930s in Italy, Germany, and Russia, because of the violent haste, dogmatic rigidity, and stultifying intolerance with which they were being conducted. Nonetheless, "National Self-Sufficiency" has often been regarded as a rapprochement with fascism. It was immediately cited by the founder of the British Union of Fascists, Oswald Mosley, as an endorsement of his cause (Keynes retorted that he had written it "not to embrace you, but to save the country from you") and has remained a source of some discomfort to many of Keynes's latter-day admirers.[21] Yet Keynes's article is better regarded not as a foray into fascism, but as part of an independently evolving response to the much more generic problem of how best to keep reasons of state from intruding violently into economic life.

[18] Keynes, "Am I a Liberal?" (1925), in *The Collected Works of John Maynard Keynes*, vol. 9, *Essays in Persuasion* (London: Macmillan, 1972), 305.

[19] Keynes, "National Self-Sufficiency," 758. For context, see Donald Markwell, *John Maynard Keynes and International Relations: Economic Paths to War and Peace* (Oxford: Oxford University Press, 2006), 162ff.; and Robert Skidelsky, *John Maynard Keynes* (London: Macmillan, 1992–2001), 2:476–79.

[20] Keynes, "National Self-Sufficiency," 767, 758.

[21] Oswald Mosley, "Economic Nationalism and World Peace," *Age of Plenty* 2 (April–June 1934): 8–9. Keynes's response is cited in Skidelsky, *John Maynard Keynes*, 2:478. "It was the nearest he ever came to endorsing communist, or fascist, economics," Skidelsky wrote of Keynes's 1933 article.

Keynes hoped that solving this problem would not necessarily be incompatible with restoring and maintaining international economic ties. His treatise *The General Theory of Employment, Interest and Money* (1936) concluded with a discussion of the special economic conditions in modern Europe that had left "no means open to a government whereby to mitigate economic distress at home except through the competitive struggle for markets." Keynes claimed that a less rigid monetary policy and a better understanding of the kinds of economic interventions available to governments opened up the possibility of eliminating those conditions without sacrificing international trade.

> If nations can learn to provide themselves with full employment by their domestic policy (and, we must add, if they can also attain equilibrium in the trend of their population), there need be no important economic forces calculated to set the interest of one country against that of its neighbours. . . . International trade would cease to be what it is, namely, a desperate expedient to maintain employment at home by forcing sales on foreign markets and restricting purchases, which, if successful, will merely shift the problem of unemployment to the neighbour which is worsted in the struggle, but a willing and unimpeded exchange of goods and services in conditions of mutual advantage.[22]

In the early 1940s, Keynes, like Beveridge and many other Britons, feared that the overwhelming dominance of the American economy would ultimately limit postwar international trade to highly restrictive bilateral exchanges among regional blocs. But toward the end of the war, and toward the end of his life, Keynes eventually became more confident that Anglo-American negotiations, in which he played a major role, might result in the establishment of a new multilateral system with sufficient safeguards to accommodate the needs of each nation's economic security.[23]

The challenges of disentangling economic life from power politics remained vivid to Gunnar Myrdal (1898–1987) well after the Second World War. An architect of the Swedish welfare state who spent the decade after the war leading the United Nations Economic Commission for Europe, Myrdal became frustrated with the slow progress of economic reintegration. In Myrdal's view, European states had finally acquired the capacity to secure the economic welfare of their citizens, but only at the cost of "international disintegration," and this dilemma did not disappear after the war. "The main trend towards economic nationalism is unbroken," he announced in his Storrs Lectures at Yale University in 1958. "The fact is that the setting in which the modern Welfare State has been developing in the Western world has been one of progressive international

[22] Keynes, *General Theory*, 382–83.

[23] Markwell, *Keynes and International Relations*, 210–67.

disintegration."[24] Increasingly successful "strivings in individual countries" to realize the ideals of liberty, equality, and fraternity were compromising those very ideals on a global level. However, Myrdal insisted that the cosmopolitanism of the "world of 1913" could not be re-created without undoing mass suffrage, reopening the social question, and reversing decolonization. The only way to rescue a "vision of a world in perfect integration" was to "find the means by which national and international ideals can be reconciled in a new and wider 'created harmony.'" The common good of humanity could be furthered only indirectly, by finding effective ways to pacify economic nationalism and make it conducive to the progressive liberalization of international relations: a process he imagined as the "economic disarmament" of the democratic welfare state and the creation of a "welfare world."[25]

Myrdal's exhortation to "economic disarmament" evokes what the economic historian Alan Milward later called the "European rescue of the nation-state" after its near extinction through German conquest in the 1940s.[26] The legitimacy of postwar European states depended on their capacity to ensure the economic security of a greatly expanded domestic coalition. Given the unresolved problem of Germany's preponderance, Milward claimed, doing so required these states to create new mechanisms for fulfilling their functions without reengaging military interests in economic relations.[27] The "economic disarmament" imagined by Myrdal and the "further stage in the reassertion of the role of the nation state" described by Milward belong to a different world from the one whose strategic options Fichte sought to probe in 1800.[28] Nonetheless, they remain within the spirit of his vision of perpetual peace as the ultimate reunification of a humanity successfully divided into closed commercial states.[29]

[24] Gunnar Myrdal, *Beyond the Welfare State: Economic Planning and Its International Implications* (London: Duckworth, 1960), 115, 118.

[25] Myrdal, *Beyond the Welfare State*, 121, 126; see also his *International Economy: Problems and Prospects* (London: Routledge, 1956). The actual content of economic nationalism, as Eric Helleiner has argued, does indeed vary from very liberal and internationalist to very protectionist and isolationist (Helleiner, "The Meaning and Contemporary Significance of Economic Nationalism," in *Economic Nationalism in a Globalizing World*, ed. E. Helleiner and A. Pickel, 220–34 [Ithaca, N.Y.: Cornell University Press, 2005]); see also Helleiner, "Economic Nationalism as a Challenge to Economic Liberalism? Lessons from the 19th Century," *International Studies Quarterly* 46 (2002): 307–29.

[26] Alan S. Milward, *The European Rescue of the Nation-State*, 2nd ed. (London: Routledge, 2000).

[27] The external pressures of the Cold War should also be stressed.

[28] Milward, *European Rescue of the Nation-State*, 44.

[29] "In the state," Fichte wrote in 1796, "nature re-unites what she had previously separated when she produced several individuals. Reason is one, and it is exhibited in the sensible world also as one; humanity is a single organized and organizing whole of reason. Humanity was divided into several independent members; the natural institution of the state already cancels this independence pro-

From this perspective, it is striking that the challenges of transition that remained so vivid to Myrdal and his generation have largely disappeared from view among many more recent efforts to elaborate a Kantian approach to global politics. John Rawls's famous *Theory of Justice* (1971) remained implicitly on Myrdal's wavelength in that it was "conceived for the time being as a closed system isolated from other societies."[30] In his 2004 Storrs Lectures—delivered nearly half a century after Myrdal's—Thomas Nagel declined to explore the ideal of global socioeconomic justice as an attribute of human universality in a theoretically stateless world and elaborated an approach more akin to Myrdal's vision of tamed nation-states.[31] For the most part, however, recent attempts to apply the ideals of the social contract to modern economic life and international relations have sidelined the challenges that preoccupied previous generations. They have tended to proceed from normative foundations that are conspicuously deemed unavailable in Rousseau's, Kant's, and Fichte's discussions of perpetual peace.

For all the many important differences among them, recent discussions of the "Kantian peace" tend to draw their inspiration almost exclusively from a rather narrow band of historical experience; much less attention is devoted to the antecedent conditions necessary for the emergence of the "Kantian triangle"—democracy, commercial interdependence, and international law and organizations—which is said to form "the structure of a peaceful world."[32] This neglect leaves them rather ill equipped to grapple with the prospect of reliving the rise and fall of the old European states system on a global scale. A "refu-

---

visionally and molds individual groups into a whole, until morality re-creates the entire species as one" (*Foundations of Natural Right*, 176). Like *The Closed Commerical State*, Fichte's popular work *The Vocation of Man* (also published in 1800) concluded its account of perpetual peace with a vision of humanity reunited into a cosmopolitan community:

> Until the existing culture of every age has spread over the whole populated globe and our species is capable of the most unrestricted communication with itself, one nation must await the other and one continent the other on the common path, and each must bring its centuries of apparent standstill or retreat as a sacrifice to the common bond for the sake of which alone they exist. Once this first goal has been reached, once everything useful which has been found at one end of the earth will immediately be communicated and known to all, then mankind will without interruption, without standstill and retreat, with common strength, and in a single stride elevate itself to a culture which is at present beyond our conception. (86)

30 John Rawls, *A Theory of Justice* (1971), rev. ed. (Cambridge, Mass.: Harvard University Press, 1999), 7.

31 Thomas Nagel, "The Problem of Global Justice," *Philosophy and Public Affairs* 33, no. 2 (2005): 113–47;cf. the responses by Joshua Cohen and Charles Sabel, "Extra Rempublicam Nulla Justitia?" *Philosophy and Public Affairs* 34, no. 2 (2006): 147–75; and A. J. Julius, "Nagel's Atlas," *Philosophy and Public Affairs* 34, no. 2 (2006): 176–92.

32 Bruce M. Russett and John R. Oneal, *Triangulating Peace: Democracy, Interdependence, and International Organizations* (New York: Norton, 2001), 10.

gee from the eighteenth century," as the political theorist Judith Shklar once called herself, would certainly recognize that many of the structural dilemmas that confronted Rousseau, Kant, and Fichte have, at least in certain parts of the world, been greatly alleviated.[33] But current discussions of how to perpetuate and extend that condition ought to reflect a much fuller understanding of the long intellectual history of European union and the pacification of the West. Rediscovering Fichte's *Closed Commercial State* is a good place to start.

[33] Judith N. Shklar, "The Liberalism of Fear," in *Liberalism and the Moral Life*, ed. Nancy L. Rosenblum, 37 (Cambridge, Mass.: Harvard University Press, 1989).

Bibliography

Primary Sources

Audouin, François-Xavier. *Du commerce maritime, de son influence sur la richesse et la force des états, démontrée par l'histoire des nations anciennes et modernes; situation actuelle des puissances de l'Europe, considérées dans leurs rapports avec la France et l'Angleterre; réflexions sur l'armament en course, sa législation et ses avantages.* 2 vols. Paris, 1800.

Bailleu, Paul, ed. *Preussen und Frankreich von 1795 bis 1807: Diplomatische Correspondenzen, Publikationen aus den K. Preussischen Staatsarchiven.* 2 vols. Leipzig: Hirzel, 1881.

Buonarroti, Philippe. *Conspiration pour l'égalité dite de Babeuf.* 1828. Paris: Éditions sociales, 1957.

Burke, Edmund. *Select Works of Edmund Burke.* Edited by Francis Canavan. 4 vols. Indianapolis, Ind.: Liberty Fund, 1999.

Buss, Franz Joseph von. *Geschichte und System der Staatswissenschaft.* 3 vols. Freiburg, 1839.

Busse, Wilhelm. *J. G. Fichte und seine Beziehung zur Gegenwart des deutschen Volkes.* 2 vols. Halle: Heynemann, 1848.

Chastellux, François-Jean de. *De la félicité publique, ou considérations sur le sort des hommes dans les differentes époques de l'histoire.* 2 vols. Amsterdam, 1772.

Cicero, Marcus Tullius. *On the Commonwealth.* Edited by James Zetzel. Cambridge: Cambridge University Press, 1999.

Coleridge, Samuel Taylor. *Marginalia.* Edited by George Whalley. Vol. 12, parts 1–6, *The Collected Works of Samuel Taylor Coleridge*, edited by Kathleen Coburn and Bart Winer. Princeton, N.J.: Princeton University Press, 1980–2001.

Clarke, Thomas Brooke. *A survey of the strength and opulence of Great Britain: wherein it is shewn, the progress of its commerce, agriculture, population, &c.* London: Cadell and Davies, 1801.

———. *An Historical and Political View of the Disorganization of Europe Wherein the Laws and Characters of Nations, and the Maritime and Commercial System of Great Britain and Other States, Are Vindicated Against the Imputations and Revolutionary Proposals of M. Talleyrand and M. Hauterive, Secretaries of State to the French Republic.* London: Cadell and Davies, 1803.

Constant, Benjamin. *Oeuvres.* Edited by Alfred Roulin. Paris: Gallimard, 1979.

Dietze, A., and W. Dietze, eds. *Ewige Friede? Dokumente einer deutschen Diskussion um 1800.* Munich: Beck, 1989.

Eckstein, Ferdinand d'. "De l'Industrialisme." *Le Catholique* 5 (1827): 233–63.

Fénelon, François de Salignac de La Mothe-. *Telemachus, son of Ulysses*. 1699. Edited and translated by Patrick Riley. Cambridge: Cambridge University Press, 1994.

Ferrari, Jean, and Simone Goyard-Fabre, eds. *L'année 1796: Sur la paix perpétuelle de Leibniz aux héritiers de Kant*. Paris: Vrin, 1998.

Feuerbach, Ludwig. *Geschichte der neuern Philosophie: Von Bacon von Verulam bis Benedikt Spinoza*. 1833. Edited by Wolfgang Harich. Berlin: Akademie-Verlag, 1969.

Feuerbach, Paul Johann Anselm. *Anti-Hobbes, oder ueber die Grenzen der höchsten Gewalt und das Zwangsrecht der Bürger gegen den Oberherrn*. Erfurt, 1798.

Fichte, Johann Gottlieb. *Addresses to the German Nation*. 1808–9. Translated by Gregory Moore. Cambridge: Cambridge University Press, 2008.

———. *Early Philosophical Writings*. Edited by Daniel Breazeale. Ithaca, N.Y.: Cornell University Press, 1988.

———. *L'état commercial fermé*. Edited by J. Gibelin. Paris: Librairie generale de droit et de jurisprudence, 1940.

———. *L'état commercial fermé*. Edited by Daniel Schulthess. Lausanne: L'Age d'homme, 1980.

———. *Foundations of Natural Right: According to the Principles of the Wissenschaftslehre* [*Grundlage des Naturrechts nach der Principien der Wissenschaftslehre*, 1796–97]. Edited by Frederick Neuhouser. Translated by Michael Baur. Cambridge: Cambridge University Press, 2000.

———. *Gesamtausgabe der Bayerischen Akademie der Wissenschaften*. Edited by R. Lauth, H. Jacob, and H. Gliwitzky. 41 vols. in 4 parts. Stuttgart–Bad Cannstatt: Frommann, 1962–.

———. *Der geschlossene Handelsstaat: Ein philosophischer Entwurf als Anhang zur Rechtslehre und Probe einer künftig zu liefernden Politik*. Tübingen: Cotta, 1800. The version cited in the text is that included in Fichte, *Gesamtausgabe der Bayerischen Akademie der Wissenschaften*, part 1, vol. 7, edited by R. Lauth and H. Gliwitzky, 1–141. Stuttgart–Bad Cannstatt: Frommann, 1988.

———. *De l'idée d'une guerre legitime*. Edited by Louis Babeuf. Translated by M. Lortet. Lyon, 1831.

———. *Introductions to the Wissenschaftslehre, and Other Writings, 1797–1800*. Edited by Daniel Breazeale. Indianapolis, Ind.: Hackett, 1994.

———. *Lettres et Témoinages sur la Révolution française*. Edited by Ives Radrizzani. Paris: Vrin, 2002.

———. "On the Linguistic Capacity and the Origin of Language." 1795. In *Language and German Idealism: Fichte's Linguistic Philosophy*, translated by Jere Paul Surber, 117–45. Atlantic Highlands, N.J.: Humanities Press, 1996.

———. "Review of Immanuel Kant, Perpetual Peace: A Philosophical Sketch." 1796. Translated by Daniel Breazeale. *Philosophical Forum* 32, no. 4 (Winter 2001): 311–21.

———. "Rezension." In Kant, *Zum ewigen Frieden*, 93–101.

———. *Sämmtliche Werke*. Edited by Immanuel Hermann Fichte. 8 vols. Berlin: Veit, 1845–46. Reprint, de Gruyter, 1965.

———. *The System of Ethics: According to the Principles of the Wissenschaftslehre*. 1798. Edited by Daniel Breazeale and Günter Zöller. Cambridge: Cambridge University Press, 2005.

———. *The Vocation of Man*. 1800. Translated by Peter Preuss. Indianapolis, Ind.: Hackett, 1987.

Frederick II of Prussia. *The Refutation of Machiavelli's Prince: Or, Anti-Machiavel*. Edited and translated by Paul Sonnino. Athens: Ohio University Press, 1981.

Fuchs, Erich, Reinhard Lauth, and Walter Schieche, eds. *J. G. Fichte im Gespräch: Berichte der Zeitgenossen*. 6 vols. Stuttgart–Bad Cannstatt: Frommann-Holzboog, 1978–92.

Gentz, Friedrich von. *On the state of Europe before and after the French Revolution: Being an answer to the work entitled De l'état de la France à la fin de l'an VIII*. 5th ed. London: Printed for J. Hatchard, 1804.

———. "Über den ewigen Frieden." 1800. In Kant, *Zum ewigen Frieden*, 250–91.

Görres, Joseph von. *Ausgewählte Werke*. Edited by Wolfgang Frühwald. 2 vols. Freiburg: Herder, 1978.

Grotius, Hugo. *De jure belli ac pacis*. 1625. Translated in 1738 from the 1715 French edition of Jean Barbeyrac by John Morrice et al. as *The Rights of War and Peace*. Edited by Richard Tuck. 3 vols. Indianapolis, Ind.: Liberty Fund, 2005.

———. *Mare liberum*. 1609. Translated by Richard Hakluyt as *The Free Sea*. Edited by David Armitage. Indianapolis, Ind.: Liberty Fund, 2004.

Hagens, Kaspar von. *Philosophische und politische Untersuchung über die Rechtmässigkeit der Zünfte und Polizeytaxen und ihre Wirkungen auf die bürgerl: Gesellschaft mit besonderer Hinsicht auf Fichtes geschlossenen Handelsstaat*. Munich: Scherer, 1804.

Hamilton, Alexander, John Jay, and James Madison. *The Federalist Papers*. Edited by Clinton Rossiter. New York: New American Library, 1961.

Hauterive, Alexandre-Maurice Blanc de Lanautte, comte d'. *De l'état de la France, à la fin de l'an VIII*. Paris, 1800.

———. *State of the French Republic at the End of the Year VIII*. Translated by Lewis Goldsmith. London: Jordan, 1801.

Hegel, Georg Wilhelm Friedrich. *Elements of the Philosophy of Right*. Edited by Allen Wood. Translated by H. B. Nisbet. Cambridge: Cambridge University Press, 1991.

———. "On the Scientific Ways of Treating Natural Law." 1802–3. In *Political Writings*, edited by L. Dickey and H. B. Nisbet, translated by H. B. Nisbet, 102–80. Cambridge: Cambridge University Press, 1999.

Heine, Heinrich. *Historisch-kritische Gesamtausgabe*. Edited by Manfred Windfuhr. 16 vols. Hamburg: Hoffmann und Campe, 1973.

Herder, Johann Gottfried. *Another Philosophy of History, and Selected Political Writings*. Edited by Ioannis Evrigenis and Daniel Pellerin. Indianapolis, Ind.: Hackett, 2004.

———. *Briefe zu Beförderung der Humanität*. 1793–97. Edited by Hans Dietrich Irmscher. Vol. 7, *Werke*, edited by Martin Bollacher. Frankfurt am Main: Deutscher Klassiker Verlag, 1991.

———. *Ideen zur Philosophie der Geschichte der Menschheit*. 1784–91. Edited by Heinz Stolpe. 2 vols. Berlin: Aufbau-Verlag, 1965.

———. *Philosophical Writings*. Edited by Michael N. Forster. Cambridge: Cambridge University Press, 2002.

Hestermann, Ludwig. *Der offene Handelsstaat: Ein philosophischer Entwurf*. Stuttgart: Erhard, 1802.

Hobbes, Thomas. *The Elements of Law Natural and Politic*. 1640. Edited by J.C.A. Gaskin. Oxford: Oxford University Press, 1994.

———. *Leviathan*. 1651. Edited by Richard Tuck. Cambridge: Cambridge University Press, 1996.

———. *On the Citizen*. 1642. Edited by Richard Tuck. Translated by Michael Silverthorne. Cambridge: Cambridge University Press, 1998.

Hoffmann, Ernst Theodor Amadeus. *Tales of E.T.A. Hoffmann*. Edited by Leonard J. Kent and Elizabeth C. Knight. Chicago: University of Chicago Press, 1972.

Hume, David. *Essays: Moral, Political, and Literary*. Rev. ed. Edited by Eugene Miller. Indianapolis, Ind.: Liberty Classics, 1987.

Jakob, Ludwig Heinrich von. *Antimachiavel, oder über die Grenzen des bürgerlichen Gehorsams: Auf Veranlassung zweyer Aufsätze in der Berl. Monatsschrift, Sept. und Dec. 1793, von den Herren Kant und Genz*. Halle, 1794.

Justi, Johann Heinrich Gottlob von. *Die Grundfeste zu der Macht und Glückseeligkeit der Staaten; oder Ausführliche Vorstellung der gesamten Policey-Wissenschaft*. Königsberg, 1760.

———. *Die Wirkungen und Folgen sowohl der wahren, als der falschen Staatskunst in der Geschichte des Psammitichus Königes von Egypten und der damaligen Zeiten*. 2 vols. Frankfurt, 1759.

Kaempfer, Engelbert. *The history of Japan, giving an account of the ancient and present state and government of that empire; of its temples, palaces, castles and other buildings; of its metals, minerals, trees, plants, animals, birds and fishes; of the chronology and succession of the emperors, ecclesiastical and secular; of the original descent, religions, customs, and manufactures of the natives, and of their trade and commerce with the Dutch and Chinese. Together with a description of the Kingdom of Siam*. Translated by J. G. Scheuchzer. 2 vols. London, 1727.

Kant, Immanuel. *The Metaphysics of Morals*. Edited by Mary Gregor. Cambridge: Cambridge University Press, 1996.

———. *Perpetual Peace: A Philosophical Sketch*. Translated by H. B. Nisbet. In *Political Writings*, 2nd ed., edited by Hans Reiss, 93–130. Cambridge: Cambridge University Press, 1991.

———. *Political Writings*. 2nd ed. Edited by H. S. Reiss. Translated by H. B. Nisbet. Cambridge: Cambridge University Press, 1991.

———. *Zum ewigen Frieden: Ein philosophischer Entwurf; Texte zur Rezeption, 1796–1800*. Edited by Manfred Buhr and Steffen Dietzsch. Leipzig: Reclam, 1984.

Krug, Wilhelm Traugott. *Allgemeines Handwörterbuch der philosophischen Wissenschaften nebst ihrer Literatur und Geschichte*. 5 vols. Leipzig, 1827.

Locke, John. *Two Treatises of Government*. Edited by Peter Laslett. Cambridge: Cambridge University Press, 1988.

Lotz, Johann Friedrich Eusebius. *Handbuch der Staatswirthschaftslehre*. 3 vols. Erlangen: Palm und Enke, 1821.

Marwitz, Friedrich August von der. *Lebenschreibung*. Edited by Friedrich Meusel. 2 vols. Berlin, 1908.

Marx, Karl, and Friedrich Engels. *The Communist Manifesto*. 1848. Edited by Gareth Stedman Jones. London: Penguin, 2002.

Mirabeau, Honoré-Gabriel de Riqueti, comte de. *De la monarchie prussienne, sous Frédéric le Grand; avec un appendice contenant des recherches sur la situation actuelle des principales contrées de l'Allemagne.* 7 vols. London, 1788.

———. *Histoire secrete de la cour de Berlin, ou correspondance d'un voyageur françois, depuis le mois de juillet 1786 jusqu'au 19 janvier 1787.* 2 vols. London, 1789.

———. *Lettre remise à Frédéric-Guillaume II, Roi Regnant de Prusse, le jour de son Avénement au Trône.* Berlin, 1787.

Mirabeau, Victor Riqueti, marquis de. *L'ami des hommes, ou traité de la population.* 1756. Paris: Guillaumin, 1883.

Montesquieu, Charles-Louis de Secondat, baron de. *The Spirit of the Laws.* 1748. Edited by Anne M. Cohler, Basia C. Miller, and Harold S. Stone. Cambridge: Cambridge University Press, 1989.

Müller, Adam. "Ueber einen philosophischen Entwurf von Hrn Fichte; Betitelt: 'Der geschlossne Handelstaat.'" *Neue Berlinische Monatsschrift* 6 (December 1801): 436–58.

Oelsner, Konrad Engelbert. *An account of the life of Sieyes, member of the first National Assembly, and of the Convention.* London, 1795.

Paine, Thomas. *Pacte Maritime, adressée aux Nations neutres, Par un Neutre.* Paris: Imprimerie-Librairie du Cercle-Social, 1800.

Paulus, H.E.G. *Conversations Saal und Geister Revüe: Ein Panorama interessanter Personen, Gedanken und Zeitmaterien, für Menschenkenntniss und Wissenschaft.* Stuttgart: Schweizerbart, 1837.

Pufendorf, Samuel. *Of the Law of Nature and Nations.* Translation of *De jure naturae et gentium* (1672). Edited by Basil Kennet. 8 vols. Oxford, 1703.

Ramsay, Andrew Michael. "A Discourse upon Epick Poetry, and the Excellence of the Poem of Telemachus." In *The Adventures of Telemachus, the Son of Ulysses,* 12th ed., i–xxvii. Dublin, 1725.

———. *The Travels of Cyrus.* 2 vols. London, 1727.

Rayneval, Joseph-Mathias-Gérard de. *De la liberté des mers.* 2 vols. Paris, 1811.

Reiss, Hans, ed. *The Political Thought of the German Romantics, 1793–1815.* Oxford: Blackwell, 1955.

Rousseau, Jean-Jacques. *The Collected Writings of Rousseau.* Edited by Christopher Kelly. 13 vols. Hanover, N.H.: University Press of New England, 1990–2009.

———. *The Discourses, and Other Early Political Writings.* Edited by Victor Gourevitch. Cambridge: Cambridge University Press, 1997.

———. *Emile, or On Education.* 1762. Edited by Alan Bloom. New York: Basic Books, 1979.

———. *Oeuvres Complètes.* Edited by Bernard Gagnebin and Marcel Raymond. 4 vols. Bibliothèque de la Pléiade. Paris: Gallimard, 1964.

———. *Principes du droit de la guerre: Ecrits sur le* Projet de Paix Perpétuelle de l'Abbé de *Saint-Pierre.* Edited by B. Bachofen and C. Spector. Paris: Vrin, 2008.

———. *The Social Contract, and Other Later Political Writings.* Edited by Victor Gourevitch. Cambridge: Cambridge University Press, 1997.

———. *Vom gesellschaftlichen Vertrage oder über die Grundsätze der Staatslehre-Neu übersetzt.* Frankfurt am Main, 1800.

Saint-Just, Louis-Antoine-Léon-Flozelle de. *Oeuvres complètes.* Edited by Michèle Duval. Paris: Lebovici, 1984.

Saint-Pierre, Charles-Irénée de Castel, abbé de. *Projet pour rendre la paix perpétuelle en Europe*. 3 vols. Utrecht: Schouten, 1713–17.
Saint-Simon, Claude-Henri de Rouvroy, comte de, and Augustin Thierry. *De la Réorganisation de la Société Européenne*. Paris: Égron, 1814.
Schlegel, Friedrich. "Essay on the Concept of Republicanism Occasioned by the Kantian Tract 'Perpetual Peace.'" 1796. In *Early Political Writings of the German Romantics,* edited by Frederick C. Beiser, 93–112. Cambridge: Cambridge University Press, 1996.
———. "Versuch über den Begriff des Republikanismus." 1796. In Kant, *Zum ewigen Frieden*, 104–20.
Schleiermacher, Friedrich Daniel Ernst. *Briefwechsel und biographische Dokumente*. Part 5, vols. 1–8, *Kritische Gesamtausgabe*, edited by Hans-Joachim Birkner, Hermann Fischer, et al. Berlin: de Gruyter, 1980.
———. *Vorlesungen über die Lehre vom Staat*. Edited by Walter Jaeschke. Part 2, vol. 8, *Kritische Gesamtausgabe*, edited by Hans-Joachim Birkner, Hermann Fischer, et al. Berlin: de Gruyter, 1998.
Schmalz, Theodor. *Encyclopädie der Cameralwissenschaften: Zum Gebrauch academischer Vorlesungen*. Königsberg, 1797.
———. *Handbuch der Rechtsphilosophie*. Halle, 1807.
Schmidt-Phiseldek, Conrad Georg Friedrich Elias von. *Europe and America: Or, the Relative State of the Civilized World at a Future Period* [*Europa und Amerika: Oder, die Künftigen Verhältnisse der Civilisirten Welt*, 1820]. Translated by Joseph Owen. Copenhagen: RHODOS, 1976.
Schneer, Alexander. "Ueber Fichte's Handelsstaat." In *Uebersicht der Arbeiten und Veränderungen der Schlesische Gesellschaft für vaterländische Kultur im Jahre 1847*, 312–19. Breslau, 1848.
Selden, John. *Mare Clausam*. 1635. Translated by Marchamont Nedham as *Of the Dominion or Ownership of the Sea*. London: Du-Gard, 1652.
Sieyès, Emmanuel Joseph. *Political Writings: Including the Debate between Sieyès and Tom Paine in 1791*. Edited by Michael Sonenscher. Indianapolis, Ind.: Hackett, 2003.
———. *Politische Schriften, 1788–1790: Vollständig gesammelt von dem deutschen Uebersezer nebst zwei Vorreden über Sieyes Lebensgeschichte, seine politische Rolle, seinen Charakter, seine Schriften*. Edited by Konrad Engelbert Oelsner. 2 vols. 1796.
Smith, Adam. *An Inquiry into the Nature and Causes of the Wealth of Nations*. Edited by R. H. Campbell, A. S. Skinner, and W. B. Todd. 2 vols. Oxford: Clarendon Press, 1979. Reprint, Indianapolis, Ind.: Liberty Classics, 1981.
———. *The Theory of Moral Sentiments*. Edited by A. L. Macfie and D. D. Raphael. Oxford: Clarendon Press, 1976. Reprint, Indianapolis, Ind.: Liberty Classics, 1982.
Staël, Anne-Louise-Germaine de. *De l'Allemagne*. 1810. Edited by Simone Balayé. 2 vols. Paris: Garnier-Flammarion, 1967.
Struensee, Carl August von. *Abhandlungen über wichtige Gegenstände der Staatswirthschaft*. 3 vols. Berlin: Unger, 1800.
———. *Sammlung von Aufsätzen, die grösstentheils wichtige Punkte der Staatswirthschaft betreffen*. Liegnitz und Leipzig, 1776.
Tenzel, Franz Joseph Bern. *Wie kann in Deutschland die Zunftverfassung am zweckmässigsten modificirt*. Landshut, Germany, 1817.

Terrasson, Jean. *Sethos, histoire, ou Vie tirée des monumens anecdotes de l'ancienne Égypte, traduite d'un manuscrit grec.* 3 vols. Paris, 1731.

Thibault, Anne-Alexandre-Marie. *Rapport sur la Fabrication d'une Nouvelle Monnoie de Billon.* Paris, 1793.

Usteri, Paul, ed. *Beyträge zur Geschichte der französischen Revolution.* 1795–96. 7 vols. Nendeln, Liechtenstein: Kraus Reprint, 1972.

Vattel, Emer de. "Dialogue entre le Prince de *** & son Confident, sur quelques parties essentielles de l'Administration publique." In *Mélanges de littérature, de morale et de politique*, 20–48. Neuchâtel: Chez les Edit. du Journal Helvetique, 1760.

———. *The Law of Nations, or, principles of the law of nature, Applied to the Conduct and Affairs of Nations and Sovereigns.* 1758. London: Robinson, 1797.

Vaughan, Benjamin. *New and Old Principles of Trade Compared; or A Treatise on the Principles of Commerce Between Nations; with an Appendix.* London, 1788.

Voltaire, François-Marie Arouet de. *Anti-Machiavel.* Edited by Werner Bahner and Helga Bergmann. Vol. 19, *Oeuvres Complètes.* Oxford: Voltaire Foundation, 1996.

———. *Correspondence and Related Documents: January–September 1739.* Edited by Theodore Besterman. Vol. 90, *Oeuvres Complètes.* Geneva: Institut et Musée Voltaire, 1970.

———. *Le Siècle de Louis XIV.* 1751. 2 vols. London, 1752.

Secondary Sources

Abaschnik, Wladimir Alexejevič. "Das Konzept des geschlossenen Handelsstaates Fichtes in der Rezeption von Vassilij Nasarovič Karasin." *Fichte-Studien* 24 (2003): 143–54.

Adam, Ulrich. *The Political Economy of J.H.G. Justi.* Bern: Peter Lang, 2006.

Adler-Bresse, Marcelle. *Sieyès et le Monde Allemand.* 2 vols. Lille: Atelier Reproduction des thèses, Université de Lille III, 1977.

Arendt, Hannah. *Rahel Varnhagen: The Life of a Jewess.* Edited by Liliane Weissberg. Translated by R. and C. Winston. Baltimore: Johns Hopkins University Press, 1997.

Armitage, David. "Edmund Burke and Reason of State." *Journal of the History of Ideas* 61, no. 4 (2000): 617–34.

———. "John Locke, Carolina, and the Two Treatises of Government." *Political Theory* 32, no. 5 (2004): 602–27.

Arneil, Barbara. "John Locke, Natural Law, and Colonialism." *History of Political Thought* 13, no. 4 (Winter 1992): 587–603.

Artaud de Montor, Alexis-François. *Histoire de la vie et des travaux politiques du comte d'Hauterive, comprenant une partie des actes de la diplomatie française, depuis 1784 jusqu'en 1830.* 2nd ed. Paris: Le Clere, 1839.

Azouvi, F., and D. Bourel. *De Königsberg à Paris: La réception de Kant en France, 1788–1804.* Paris: Vrin, 1991.

Baumgartner, Hans, ed. *Schriften zu J .G. Fichtes Sozialphilosophie.* Hildesheim: Olms, 1987.

Baumgold, Deborah. "Hobbes's and Locke's Contract Theories: Political not Metaphysical." *Critical Review of International Social and Political Philosophy* 8, no. 3 (2005): 289–308.

Behrens, C.B.A. *Society, Government and the Enlightenment: The Experiences of Eighteenth-Century France and Prussia*. London: Thames and Hudson, 1985.

Beiser, Frederick C. "The Enlightenment and Idealism." In *The Cambridge Companion to German Idealism*, edited by Karl Ameriks, 18–36. Cambridge: Cambridge University Press, 2000.

———. *Enlightenment, Revolution, and Romanticism: The Genesis of Modern German Political Thought, 1790–1800*. Cambridge, Mass.: Harvard University Press, 1992.

Bell, David A. *The First Total War: Napoleon's Europe and the Birth of Modern Warfare*. London: Bloomsbury, 2007.

Berlin, Isaiah. *Freedom and Its Betrayal: Six Enemies of Human Liberty*. Edited by Henry Hardy. London: Chatto and Windus, 2002.

———. "Two Concepts of Liberty." In *Four Essays on Liberty*, 118–72. London: Oxford University Press, 1969.

Bernstein, Edward. *Ferdinand Lassalle as a Social Reformer*. Translated by Eleanor Marx Aveling. London: Swan Sonnenschein, 1893.

Beveridge, William. *Full Employment in a Free Society*. London: George Allen and Unwin, 1944.

Biro, Sydney Seymour. *The German Policy of Revolutionary France: A Study in French Diplomacy during the War of the First Coalition, 1792–1797*. 2 vols. Cambridge, Mass.: Harvard University Press, 1957.

Blanning, T.C.W. *The French Revolutionary Wars, 1787–1802*. London: Arnold, 1996.

Bohman, J., and M. Lutz-Bachmann, eds. *Perpetual Peace: Essays on Kant's Cosmopolitan Ideal*. Cambridge, Mass.: MIT Press, 1997.

Bourel, Dominique. "Un regicide ambassadeur à la cour des Hohenzollern." In *Contribution à l'histoire de la Revolution et de l'Empire*, edited by Hervé Brouillet, 277–86. Paris: Atelier d'Impression de l'Armée de Terre 3, 1989.

Boyd, Richard. "The Calvinist Origins of Lockean Political Economy." *History of Political Thought* 23, no. 1 (Spring 2002): 30–60.

Breazeale, Daniel. "'More than a Pious Wish': Fichte on Kant on Perpetual Peace." In *Proceedings of the Eighth International Kant Congress, Memphis, 1995*, edited by Hoke Robinson, 1:943–59. Milwaukee, Wis.: Marquette University Press, 1995.

Bruguière, Michel. "Assignats." In *A Critical Dictionary of the French Revolution*, edited by François Furet and Mona Ozouf, translated by Arthur Goldhammer, 426–36. Cambridge, Mass.: Harvard University Press, 1989.

Burtscher, Michael. "Die Fichte-Rezeption im Kaiserreich: Ideenpolitische Aspekte." Master's thesis, Ludwig-Maximilians-Universität München, 1991.

Busch, Otto. *Militärsystem und Sozialleben im alten Preussen, 1713–1807: Die Anfänge der sozialen Militarisierung der preussisch-deutschen Gesellschaft*. Berlin: de Gruyter, 1962.

Cesa, Claudio. "G. B. Passerini und die erste italienische Übersetzung von 'Der geschlossene Handelsstaat.'" In *Erneuerung der Transzendentalphilosophie: Im Anschluss an Kant und Fichte*, edited by Klaus Hammacher and Albert Mues, 84–95. Stuttgart–Bad Cannstatt: Frommann-Holzboog, 1979.

Charvet, John. *The Social Problem in the Philosophy of Rousseau*. Cambridge: Cambridge University Press, 1974.

Claeys, Gregory. "'Individualism,' 'Socialism,' and 'Social Science': Further Notes on a Process of Conceptual Formation, 1800–1850." *Journal of the History of Ideas* 47, no. 1 (March 1986): 81–93.

Clark, Christopher M. *Iron Kingdom: The Rise and Downfall of Prussia, 1600–1947*. London: Allen Lane, 2006.

Cohen, Joshua, and Charles Sabel. "Extra Rempublicam Nulla Justitia?" *Philosophy and Public Affairs* 34, no. 2 (2006): 147–75.

Coves, Faustino Oncina. "De l'antimachiavéllisme de Kant au machiavélisme de Fichte." In *Fichte lecteur de Machiavel: Un nouveau Prince contre l'occupation napoléonienne*, edited by Ives Radrizzani, 26–54. Basel: Schwabe, 2006.

Dagger, Richard. "Understanding the General Will." *Western Political Quarterly* 34, no. 3 (1981): 359–71.

Darwall, Stephen. "Fichte and the Second-Person Standpoint." *International Yearbook of German Idealism* 3 (2005): 91–113.

De Madariaga, Isabel. *Britain, Russia, and the Armed Neutrality of 1780: Sir James Harris's Mission to St. Petersburg during the American Revolution*. London: Hollis and Carter, 1962.

Denis, Henri. *Histoire de la Pensée Économique*. Paris: Presses universitaires de France, 1966.

De Pascale, Carla. "Franz von Baader und Der Geschlossene Handelsstaat." In *Erneuerung der Transzendentalphilosophie: Im Anschluss an Kant und Fichte*, edited by Klaus Hammacher and Albert Mues, 259–73. Stuttgart–Bad Cannstatt: Frommann-Holzboog, 1979.

Dewey, John. *German Philosophy and Politics*. New York: Holt, 1915.

Droz, Jacques. *L'Allemagne et la Révolution française*. Paris: Presses universitaires de France, 1949.

. *La pensée politique et morale des cisrhénans*. Paris: Sorlot, 1940.

Dunn, John. "Capitalist Democracy: Elective Affinity or Beguiling Illusion?" *Daedalus* 136, no. 3 (Summer 2007): 5–13.

———. *Democracy: A History*. New York: Atlantic Monthly Press, 2005.

———. "The Identity of the Bourgeois Liberal Republic." In *The Invention of the Modern Republic*, edited by Biancamaria Fontana, 206–25. Cambridge: Cambridge University Press, 1994.

———. *Setting the People Free: The Story of Democracy*. London: Atlantic, 2005.

Dwyer, Philip. "The Politics of Prussian Neutrality, 1795–1806." *German History* 12 (1994): 351–74.

———. "Prussia and the Armed Neutrality: The Invasion of Hanover in 1801." *International History Review* 15 (1993): 661–87.

Easley, Eric S. *The War over Perpetual Peace: An Exploration into the History of a Foundational International Relations Text*. New York: Palgrave Macmillan, 2004.

Echeverria, Durand. *Mirage in the West: A History of the French Image of American Society to 1815*. Princeton, N.J.: Princeton University Press, 1968.

Edmondson, Nelson. "The Fichte Society: A Chapter in Germany's Conservative Revolution." *Journal of Modern History* 38, no. 2 (June 1966): 161–80.

Elliot, J. H. "A Europe of Composite Monarchies." *Past and Present* 137 (November 1992): 48–71.
Engelbrecht, Helmuth C. *Johann Gottlieb Fichte: A Study of His Political Writings with Special Reference to his Nationalism.* New York: Columbia University Press, 1933.
Espagne, Michel. "Die Rezeption der Philosophie Fichtes in Frankreich." *Fichte-Studien* 2 (1990): 193-222.
Ferry, Luc. "The Distinction between Law and Ethics in the Early Philosophy of Fichte." *Philosophical Forum* 19, nos. 2–3 (1987): 182–96.
Fleischacker, Samuel. *A Short History of Distributive Justice.* Cambridge, Mass.: Harvard University Press, 2004.
———. "Values Behind the Market: Kant's Response to the *Wealth of Nations.*" *History of Political Thought* 17, no. 3 (1996): 379–407.
Fontana, Biancamaria, editor. *The Invention of the Modern Republic.* Cambridge: Cambridge University Press, 1994.
Forsyth, Murray. "The Old European States-System: Gentz vs. Hauterive." *Historical Journal* 23, no. 3 (1980): 521–38.
———. "Thomas Hobbes and the Constituent Power of the People." *Political Studies* 29, no. 2 (1981): 191–203.
Geuss, Raymond. "Freedom as an Ideal, I." *Proceedings of the Aristotelian Society* (supplement) 69 (1995): 87–100.
———. "Kultur, Bildung, Geist." *History and Theory* 35, no. 2 (1996): 151–64.
Gierke, Otto Friedrich von. *Natural Law and the Theory of Society, 1500 to 1800.* 1913. Edited and translated by Ernest Barker. Cambridge: Cambridge University Press, 1934.
Goddard, Jean-Christophe, and Jacinto Rivera de Rosales, eds. *Fichte et la politique.* Milan: Polimetrica, 2008. http://www.polimetrica.com/
Gray, Richard. "Economic Romanticism: Monetary Nationalism in Johann Gottlieb Fichte and Adam Müller." *Eighteenth-Century Studies* 36, no. 4 (2003): 535–57.
Guilhaumou, Jacques. "Sieyès, Fichte et la liberté humaine (1774–1794)." *Chroniques Allemandes* 2 (1993): 113–30.
Hampsher-Monk, Iain. "Edmund Burke's Changing Justification for Intervention." *Historical Journal* 48, no. 1 (2005): 65–100.
Harris, Seymour Edwin. *The Assignats.* Cambridge, Mass.: Harvard University Press, 1930.
Hayek, Friedrich. *The Road to Serfdom.* London: Routledge, 1944.
Heilperin, Michael. *Studies in Economic Nationalism.* Geneva: Droz, 1960.
Helleiner, Eric. "Economic Nationalism as a Challenge to Economic Liberalism? Lessons from the 19th Century." *International Studies Quarterly* 46 (2002): 307–29.
———. "The Meaning and Contemporary Significance of Economic Nationalism." In *Economic Nationalism in a Globalizing World*, edited by E. Helleiner and A. Pickel, 220–34. Ithaca, N.Y.: Cornell University Press, 2005.
Henry, Nannerl O. "Democratic Monarchy: The Political Theory of the Marquis d'Argenson." PhD diss., Yale University, 1968.
Hinsley, F. H. *Power and the Pursuit of Peace: Theory and Practice in the History of Relations between States.* Cambridge: Cambridge University Press, 1963.

Hintze, Otto. "Prussian Reform Movements before 1806." 1896. In *The Historical Essays of Otto Hintze*, edited by Felix Gilbert, 64–87. New York: Oxford University Press, 1975.

Hirsch, Hans. "Fichtes Beitrag zur Theorie der Planwirtschaft und dessen Verhältnis zu seiner praktischen Philosophie." In *Der Transzendentale Gedanke: Die gegenwärtige Darstellung der Philosophie Fichtes*, edited by Klaus Hammacher, 215–30. Hamburg: Meiner, 1981.

———. "Fichtes Planwirtschaftsmodell als Dokument der Geistesgeschichte und als Bleibender Denkanstoß." *Fichte-Studien* 24 (2003): 165–77.

Hirschman, Albert. *National Power and the Structure of Foreign Trade*. Berkeley and Los Angeles: University of California Press, 1945.

———. *Rival Views of Market Society, and Other Recent Essays*. New York: Viking, 1986.

Hont, Istvan. *Jealousy of Trade: International Competition and the Nation-State in Historical Perspective*. Cambridge, Mass.: Harvard University Press, 2005.

———. "The Luxury Debate in the Early Enlightenment." In *The Cambridge History of Eighteenth-Century Political Thought*, edited by M. Goldie and R. Wokler, 379–418. Cambridge: Cambridge University Press, 2006.

———. "The 'Rich Country–Poor Country' Debate Revisited: The Irish Origins and French Reception of the Hume Paradox." In *David Hume's Political Economy*, edited by Carl Wennerlind and Margaret Schabas, 243–322. London: Routledge, 2008.

Hont, Istvan, and Michael Ignatieff. "Needs and Justice in the Wealth of Nations." In Istvan Hont and Michael Ignatieff, eds., *Wealth and Virtue: The Shaping of Political Economy in the Scottish Enlightenment*, 1–44. Cambridge: Cambridge University Press, 1983; reprinted in Istvan Hont, *Jealousy of Trade*, 389–443.

James, David. "Applying the Concept of Right: Fichte and Babeuf." *History of Political Thought* 30, no. 4 (Winter 2009): 647–77.

James, Susan. *Passion and Action: The Emotions in Seventeenth-Century Philosophy*. Oxford: Oxford University Press, 1997.

Jaurès, Auguste-Marie-Joseph Jean. *Les Origines du Socialisme Allemande*. Translated by Adrien Veber. Paris, 1927.

Johnson, Neal. *Louis XIV and the Age of the Enlightenment: The Myth of the Sun King from 1715 to 1789*. Studies on Voltaire and the Eighteenth Century 172. Oxford: Voltaire Foundation, 1978.

Julius, A. J. "Nagel's Atlas." *Philosophy and Public Affairs* 34, no. 2 (2006): 176–92.

Kaplan, Steven. *Bread, Politics and Political Economy in the Reign of Louis XV*. The Hague: Nijhoff, 1976.

Kapossy, Béla. *Iselin contra Rousseau: Sociable Patriotism and the History of Mankind*. Basel: Schwabe, 2006.

Kaufman, Alexander. *Welfare in the Kantian State*. Oxford: Oxford University Press, 1999.

Kaufmann, F. W. "Fichte and National Socialism." *American Political Science Review* 36, no. 3 (June 1942): 460–70.

Kazui, Tashiro. "Foreign Relations during the Edo Period: Sakoku Reexamined." *Journal of Japanese Studies* 8, no. 2 (1982): 283–306.

Keohane, Nannerl O. "'Masterpiece of Policy in Our Century': Rousseau on the Morality of the Enlightenment." *Political Theory* 6, no. 4 (1978): 457–84.

Keynes, John Maynard. "Am I a Liberal?" 1925. In *The Collected Works of John Maynard Keynes*, vol. 9, *Essays in Persuasion*, 295–306. London: Macmillan, 1972.

———. *The General Theory of Employment, Interest, and Money*. London: Macmillan, 1936.

———. "National Self-Sufficiency." *Yale Review* 22, no. 4 (June 1933): 755–69.

Kleingeld, Pauline. "Kant's Theory of Peace." In *The Cambridge Companion to Kant and Modern Philosophy*, edited by Paul Guyer, 477–504. Cambridge: Cambridge University Press, 2006.

———. "Six Varieties of Cosmopolitanism in Late Eighteenth-Century Germany." *Journal of the History of Ideas* 60, no. 3 (July 1999): 505–24.

Krause, Werner. "Fichtes ökonomische Anschauungen im Geschlossenen Handelsstaat." In *Wissen und Gewissen: Beiträge zum 200. Geburtstag Johann Gottlieb Fichtes, 1762–1814*, edited by Manfred Buhr, 224–40. Berlin: Akademie Verlag, 1962.

Labbé, François. "La rêve irénique du marquis de la Tierce: Franc-Maçonnerie, lumières, et projets de paix perpétuelle dans le cadre du Saint-Empire sous le règne de Charles VII (1741–1745)." *Francia* 18, no. 2 (1991): 47–69.

La Vopa, Anthony J. *Fichte: The Self and the Calling of Philosophy, 1762–1799*. Cambridge: Cambridge University Press, 2001.

———. "The Revelatory Moment: Fichte and the French Revolution." *Central European History* 22 (1989): 130–59.

Léon, Xavier. *Fichte et son temps*. 2 vols. Paris: Colin, 1922.

Losurdo, Domenico. "Fichte, die Französische Revolution und das Ideal vom ewigen Frieden." In *Fichte—die Französische Revolution und das Ideal vom ewigen Frieden*, edited by Manfred Buhr and Domenico Losurdo, 74–136. Berlin: Akademie Verlag, 1991.

Mager, Wolfgang. "Republik." In *Geschichtliche Grundbegriffe: Historisches Lexikon zur Politisch-Sozialen Sprache in Deutschland*, edited by Otto Brunner, Werner Conze, and Reinhart Koselleck, 5:549–651. Stuttgart: Klett-Cotta, 1984.

Manin, Bernard. *The Principles of Representative Government*. Cambridge: Cambridge University Press, 1997.

Markwell, Donald. *John Maynard Keynes and International Relations: Economic Paths to War and Peace*. Oxford: Oxford University Press, 2006.

Meinecke, Friedrich. *Weltbürgertum und Nationalstaat*. 1908. Translated by Robert B. Kimber as *Cosmopolitanism and the National State*. Princeton, N.J.: Princeton University Press, 1970.

Merle, Jean-Christophe. "La réception du *Projet de paix perpétuelle* par Fichte: La critique d'un Kant prisonnier du droit des gens." In *Proceedings of the Eighth International Kant Congress, Memphis, 1995*, edited by Hoke Robinson, 2:893–900. Milwaukee, Wis.: Marquette University Press, 1995.

Mervart, David. "A Closed Country in the Open Seas: Engelbert Kaempfer's Japanese Solution for European Modernity's Predicament." *History of European Ideas* 35, no. 3 (September 2009): 321–29.

Meyer, J. B. *Fichte, Lassalle und der Socialismus*. Berlin, 1879.

Milward, Alan S. *The European Rescue of the Nation-State*. 2nd ed. London: Routledge, 2000.

Moggach, Douglas. "Fichte's Engagement with Machiavelli." *History of Political Thought* 14, no. 4 (1993): 573–89.

———. "Freedom and Perfection: German Debates on the State in the Eighteenth Century." *Canadian Journal of Political Science* 42, no. 4 (2009): 1003–23.
Mosley, Oswald. "Economic Nationalism and World Peace." *Age of Plenty* 2 (April–June 1934): 9–12.
Murphy, Antoin E. "John Law and the Assignats." In *La Pensée Économique pendant La Révolution Française*, edited by Philippe Steiner and Gilbert Faccarello, 431–48. Grenoble: Presses universitaires de Grenoble, 1990.
———. *John Law: Economic Theorist and Policy-Maker*. Oxford: Clarendon Press, 1997.
Muthu, Sankar. *Enlightenment against Empire*. Princeton, N.J.: Princeton University Press, 2003.
Myrdal, Gunnar. *Beyond the Welfare State: Economic Planning and Its International Implications*. London: Duckworth, 1960.
———. *An International Economy: Problems and Prospects*. London: Routledge, 1956.
Nagel, Thomas. "The Problem of Global Justice." *Philosophy and Public Affairs* 33, no. 2 (2005): 113–47.
Neuhouser, Frederick. "Fichte and the Relationship between Right and Morality." In *Fichte: Historical Contexts/Contemporary Controversies*, edited by Daniel Breazeale and Tom Rockmore, 158–80. Atlantic Highlands, N.J: Humanities Press, 1994.
Nippel, Wilfried. "Ancient and Modern Republicanism: 'Mixed Constitution' and 'Ephors.'" In *The Invention of the Modern Republic*, edited by Biancamaria Fontana, 6–26. New York: Cambridge University Press, 1994.
Nomer, Nedim. "Fichte and the Idea of Liberal Socialism." *Journal of Political Philosophy* 13, no. 1 (2005): 53–73.
O'Brien, Karen. *Narratives of Enlightenment: Cosmopolitan History from Voltaire to Gibbon*. Cambridge: Cambridge University Press, 1997.
Pasquino, Pasquale. *Sieyes et l'invention de la constitution en France*. Paris: Jacob, 1998.
Perrot, Jean-Claude. *Une Histoire Intellectuelle de l'économie politique, XVIIe–XVIIIe siècle*. Paris: Éditions de l'École des hautes études en sciences sociales, 1992.
Pesch, Reiner. "Die politische Philosophie Fichtes und ihre Rezeption im Nationalsozialismus." PhD diss., Phillips-Universität Marburg, 1982.
Petzold, Horst. *Die Verhandlungen der 1798 von König Friedrich Wilhelm III: Eingesetzten Finanzkommission*. Göttingen, 1912.
Philonenko, Alexis. *Théorie et praxis dans la pensée morale et politique de Kant et de Fichte en 1793*. Paris: Vrin, 1968.
Pincus, Steven. "The English Debate over Universal Monarchy." In *A Union for Empire: Political Thought and the British Union of 1707*, edited by John Robertson, 37–62. Cambridge: Cambridge University Press, 1995.
Pizer, John. "The German Response to Kant's Essay on Perpetual Peace: Herder contra the Romantics," *Germanic Review* 82, no. 4 (Fall 2007): 343–68.
Pocock, J.G.A. *Barbarism and Religion*. Vol. 2, *Narratives of Civil Government*. Cambridge: Cambridge University Press, 1999.
Pult, Guido. "Le modèle de planification de Fichte." In *L'état commercial fermé*, edited by Daniel Schulthess, 43–56. Lausanne: L'Age d'homme, 1980.
Ragsdale, Hugh. "A Continental System in 1801: Paul I and Bonaparte." *Journal of Modern History* 42, no. 1 (1970): 70–89.
———. "Russia, Prussia and Europe in the Policy of Paul I." *Jahrbücher für Geschichte Osteuropas* 31 (1983): 81–118.

Rawls, John. *A Theory of Justice*. 1971. Rev. ed. Cambridge, Mass.: Harvard University Press, 1999.

Real, Willy. "Die preussischen Staatsfinanzen und die Anbahnung des Sonderfriedens von Basel, 1795." *Forschungen zur brandenburgischen und preussischen Geschichte*, n.s., 1 (1991): 53–100.

Rockmore, Tom. *Fichte, Marx, and the German Philosophical Tradition*. Carbondale: Southern Illinois University Press, 1980.

Rosenblatt, Helena. "Re-evaluating Benjamin Constant's Liberalism: Industrialism, Saint-Simonianism and the Restoration Years." *History of European Ideas* 30 (2004): 23–37.

Rothschild, Emma. "Language and Empire, c. 1800." *Historical Research* 78, no. 200 (May 2005): 208–29.

Ruiz, Alain. "Un admirateur allemand de Sieyès: Karl Friedrich Cramer." *Revue d'Histoire Diplomatique* 88, no. 3 (1974): 259–311.

———. "A l'aube du kantisme en France: Sieyès, Karl Friedrich Reinhard et le traité 'Vers la paix perpétuelle' (hiver 1795–1796)." *Cahiers d'études germaniques* 4 (1980): 147–93.

———. "Neues über Kant und Sieyès: Ein unbekannter Brief des Philosophen an Anton Ludwig Théremin (März 1796)." *Kant-Studien* 68, no. 4 (1977): 446–53.

Russett, Bruce M., and John R. Oneal. *Triangulating Peace: Democracy, Interdependence, and International Organizations*. New York: Norton, 2001.

Saine, Thomas. *Black Bread–White Bread: German Intellectuals and the French Revolution*. Columbia, S.C.: Camden House, 1988.

Schieder, Wolfgang. "Sozialismus." In *Geschichtliche Grundbegriffe: Historisches Lexikon zur politisch-sozialen Sprache in Deutschland*, edited by Otto Brunner, Werner Conze, and Reinhart Koselleck, 5:923–96. Stuttgart: Klett-Cotta, 1984.

Schmoller, Gustav von. "J. G. Fichte: Eine Studie aus dem Gebiete der Ethik und der Nationalökonomie." In *Zur Litteraturgeschichte der Staats- und Sozialwissenschaften*, 28–101. New York: Franklin, 1968.

Schottky, Richard. "Internationale Beziehungen als ethisches und juridisches Problem bei Fichte." In *Der Transzendentale Gedanke: Die gegenwärtige Darstellung der Philosophie Fichtes*, edited by Klaus Hammacher, 250–77. Hamburg: Meiner, 1981.

———. "Das Problem der Gewaltenteilung bei Rousseau und Fichte." *Fichte-Studien-Supplementa* 6 (1995): 343–68.

———. "Staatliche Souveränität und individuelle Freiheit bei Rousseau, Kant und Fichte." *Fichte-Studien* 7 (1995): 119–42.

———. "Untersuchungen zur Geschichte der staatsphilosophischen Vertragstheorie im 17. und 18. Jahrhundert (Hobbes—Locke—Rousseau—Fichte)." PhD diss., Munich, 1962; reprinted in *Fichte-Studien-Supplementa* 6 (1995): 1–319.

Schroeder, Paul W. "Did the Vienna Settlement Rest on a Balance of Power?" *American Historical Review* 97, no. 3 (1992): 683–706.

Schui, Florian. "Prussia's Trans-Oceanic Moment: The Creation of the Prussian Asiatic Trading Company in 1750." *Historical Journal* 49, no. 1 (2006): 143–60.

Schuurmans, Frank. "State, Society, and the Market: Karl Sigmund Altenstein and the Languages of Reform, 1770–1807." PhD diss., University of Wisconsin at Madison, 1995.

Seeley, J. R. *Life and Times of Stein, or, Germany and Prussia in the Napoleonic Age.* 2 vols. Cambridge: Cambridge University Press, 1878.
Shell, Susan. "What Kant and Fichte Can Teach Us about Human Rights." In *The Philosophy of Immanuel Kant,* edited by Richard Kennington, 143–60. Washington, D.C.: Catholic University of America Press, 1985.
Shklar, Judith N. "The Liberalism of Fear." In *Liberalism and the Moral Life,* edited by Nancy L. Rosenblum, 21–38. Cambridge, Mass.: Harvard University Press, 1989.
Simms, Brendan. *The Impact of Napoleon: Prussian High Politics, Foreign Policy and the Crisis of the Executive, 1797–1806.* Cambridge: Cambridge University Press, 1997.
Skidelsky, Robert. *John Maynard Keynes.* 3 vols. London: Macmillan, 1992–2001.
Smith, Helmut Walser. *The Continuities of German History: Nation, Religion, and Race across the Long Nineteenth Century.* Cambridge: Cambridge University Press, 2008.
Sofka, James R. "Metternich's Theory of European Order: A Political Agenda for 'Perpetual Peace.'" *Review of Politics* 60, no. 1 (Winter 1998): 115–49.
Sonenscher, Michael. *Before the Deluge: Public Debt, Inequality, and the Intellectual Origins of the French Revolution.* Princeton, N.J.: Princeton University Press, 2007.
———. "The Nation's Debt and the Birth of the Modern Republic: The French Fiscal Deficit and the Politics of the Revolution of 1789." Pts. 1 and 2. *History of Political Thought* 18, no. 1 (1997): 64–103; no. 2 (1997): 267–325.
———. "Property, Community and Citizenship." In *The Cambridge History of Eighteenth-Century Political Thought,* edited by M. Goldie and R. Wokler, 465–96. Cambridge: Cambridge University Press, 2006.
Spector, Céline. "Le Projet de paix perpétuelle: De Saint-Pierre à Rousseau." In *Principes du droit de la guerre: Ecrits sur le Projet de Paix Perpétuelle de l'Abbé de Saint-Pierre,* ed. B. Bachofen and C. Spector, 229–94. Paris: Vrin, 2008.
Stedman Jones, Gareth. *An End to Poverty? A Historical Debate.* London: Profile, 2004.
———. "Kant, the French Revolution and the Definition of the Republic." In *The Invention of the Modern Republic,* edited by Biancamaria Fontana, 154–72. New York: Cambridge University Press, 1994.
Straubel, Rolf. *Carl August von Struensee: Preussische Wirtschafts- und Finanzpolitik im ministeriellen Kräftespiel (1786–1804/06).* Potsdam: Verlag für Berlin-Brandenburg, 1999.
Strauss, Leo. *Natural Right and History.* Chicago: University of Chicago Press, 1953.
Surber, Jere Paul. *Language and German Idealism: Fichte's Linguistic Philosophy.* Atlantic Highlands, N.J.: Humanities Press, 1996.
Talmon, J. L. *Political Messianism: The Romantic Phase.* New York: Praeger, 1960.
Thiele, Ulrich. *Distributive Gerechtigkeit und demokratischer Staat: Fichtes Rechtslehre von 1796 zwischen vorkantischem und kantischem Naturrecht.* Berlin: Duncker und Humblot, 2002.
Thomas-Fogiel, Isabel. "Sens et statut de la theorie des échanges commerciaux dans le système de Fichte." *Astérion* no. 5 (July 2007): 33–55.
Tooze, Adam. *The Wages of Destruction: The Making and Breaking of the Nazi Economy.* London: Allen Lane, 2006.
Treitschke, Heinrich von. "Fichte und die nationale Idee." 1862. In *Deutsche Lebensbilder,* 34–69. Leipzig: Fikentscher, 1927.
Tribe, Keith. "Cameralism and the Science of Government." *Journal of Modern History* 56, no. 2 (1984): 263–84.

Tribe, Keith. *Governing Economy: The Reformation of German Economic Discourse, 1750–1840*. Cambridge: Cambridge University Press, 1988.

———, ed. *Reading Weber*. London: Routledge, 1989.

Tschirch, Otto. *Geschichte der öffentlichen Meinung in Preussen vom Baseler Frieden bis bum Zusammenbruch des Staates, 1795–1806*. 2 vols. Weimar, 1933.

Tuck, Richard. "Democracy and Terrorism." In *Political Judgement*, edited by Richard Bourke and Raymond Geuss, 313–32. Cambridge: Cambridge University Press, 2009.

———. "The 'Modern' Theory of Natural Law." In *The Languages of Political Theory in Early-Modern Europe*, edited by Anthony Pagden, 99–119. Cambridge: Cambridge University Press, 1987.

———. *Natural Rights Theories: Their Origin and Development*. Cambridge: Cambridge University Press, 1979.

———. *Philosophy and Government, 1572–1651*. Cambridge: Cambridge University Press, 1993.

———. The *Rights of War and Peace: Political Thought and the International Order from Grotius to Kant*. Oxford: Oxford University Press, 1999.

Tully, James. *A Discourse on Property: John Locke and His Adversaries*. Cambridge: Cambridge University Press, 1980.

Van der Linden, Harry. *Kantian Ethics and Socialism*. Indianapolis, Ind.: Hackett, 1988.

Van Deusen, Glyndon. *Sieyes: His Life and His Nationalism*. New York: Columbia University Press, 1932.

Venturi, Franco. *The End of the Old Regime in Europe, 1768–1776: The First Crisis*. Princeton, N.J.: Princeton University Press, 1989.

Verzar, Andreas. *Das autonome Subjekt und der Vernunftstaat: Eine systematisch-historische Untersuchung zu Fichtes "Geschlossenem Handelsstaat" von 1800*. Bonn: Bouvier, 1979.

Vogel, Ursula. "When the Earth Belonged to All: The Land Question in Eighteenth-Century Justifications of Private Property." *Political Studies* 36, no. 1 (March 1988): 102–22.

Waldron, Jeremy. "Kant's Theory of the State." In *Toward Perpetual Peace, and Other Writings on Politics, Peace, and History*, edited by Pauline Kleingeld, translated by David L. Colclasure, 179–200. New Haven, Conn.: Yale University Press, 2006.

Weber, Marianne. *Fichte's Sozialismus und sein Verhältnis zur Marx'schen Doktrin*. Tübingen: Mohr, 1900. Reprinted in Hans Lindau and Marianne Weber, *Schriften zu J. G. Fichtes Sozialphilosophie*, edited by Hans Baumgartner, 1–122. Hildesheim: Olms, 1987.

Whatmore, Richard. "Democrats and Republicans in Restoration France." *European Journal of Political Theory* 3, no. 1 (2004): 37–51.

———. "The Politics of Political Economy from Rousseau to Constant." In *Markets in Historical Contexts: Ideas and Politics in the Modern World*, edited by Mark Bevir and Frank Trentmann, 46–69. Cambridge: Cambridge University Press, 2004.

Wilhelmy, Petra. *Der Berliner Salon im 19. Jahrhundert, 1780–1914*. Berlin: de Gruyter, 1989.

Willms, Bernard. *Die totale Freiheit: Fichtes politische Philosophie*. Cologne: Westdeutscher Verlag, 1967.

Wood, Alan. "Kant and Fichte on Right, Welfare and Economic Redistribution." *Jahrbuch des deutschen Idealismus* 2 (2004): 77–101.

Wood, Gordon. "The American Revolution." In *The Cambridge History of Eighteenth-Century Political Thought*, edited by M. Goldie and R. Wokler, 601–25. Cambridge: Cambridge University Press, 2006.

Wootton, David, ed. *Republicanism, Liberty, and Commercial Society, 1649–1776*. Stanford, Calif.: Stanford University Press, 1994.

Index